The Body Unburdened

ISSUES OF GLOBALIZATION

Case Studies in Contemporary Anthropology

Series Editors: Carla Freeman and Li Zhang

The Cost of Belonging: An Ethnography of Solidarity and Mobility in Beijing's Koreatown
Sharon J. Yoon

Global Nomads: Migration, Insecurity, and Belonging in West Africa
Susanna Fioratta

Indebted: An Ethnography of Despair and Resilience in Greece's Second City
Kathryn A. Kozaitis

Burning at Europe's Borders: An Ethnography on the African Migrant Experience in Morocco
Isabella Alexander-Nathani

Labor and Legality: An Ethnography of a Mexican Immigrant Network, Tenth Anniversary Edition
Ruth Gomberg-Muñoz

Marriage After Migration: An Ethnography of Money, Romance, and Gender in Globalizing Mexico
Nora Haenn

Serious Youth in Sierra Leone: An Ethnography of Performance and Global Connection
Catherine E. Bolten

Low Wage in High Tech: An Ethnography of Service Workers in Global India
Kiran Mirchandani, Sanjukta Mukherjee, and Shruti Tambe

Care for Sale: An Ethnography of Latin American Domestic and Sex Workers in London
Ana P. Gutiérrez Garza

Waste and Wealth: An Ethnography of Labor, Value, and Morality in a Vietnamese Recycling Economy
Minh T. N. Nguyen

Haunted: An Ethnography of the Hollywood and Hong Kong Media Industries
Sylvia J. Martin

The Native World-System: An Ethnography of Bolivian Aymara Traders in the Global Economy
Nico Tassi

Sacred Rice: An Ethnography of Identity, Environment, and Development in Rural West Africa
Joanna Davidson

City of Flowers: An Ethnography of Social and Economic Change in Costa Rica's Central Valley
Susan E. Mannon

Listen, Here Is a Story: Ethnographic Life Narratives from Aka and Ngandu Women of the Congo Basin
Bonnie L. Hewlett

Cuban Color in Tourism and La Lucha: An Ethnography of Racial Meanings
L. Kaifa Roland

Gangsters Without Borders: An Ethnography of a Salvadoran Street Gang
T. W. Ward

The Body Unburdened

Violence, Emotions, and the New Woman in Turkey

ESRA SARIOĞLU

OXFORD
UNIVERSITY PRESS

OXFORD
UNIVERSITY PRESS

Oxford University Press is a department of the University of Oxford.
It furthers the University's objective of excellence in research, scholarship,
and education by publishing worldwide. Oxford is a registered trade mark
of Oxford University Press in the UK and in certain other countries.

Published in the United States of America by Oxford University Press
198 Madison Avenue, New York, NY 10016, United States of America.

© 2023 by Oxford University Press

Library of Congress Cataloging-in-Publication Data

Names: Sarioglu, Esra, author.
Title: The body unburdened : violence, emotions, and the new woman in
   Turkey / Esra Sarioglu.
Description: Cambridge, United Kingdom : Oxford University Press, [2022] |
   Includes bibliographical references and index. | Summary: Introduction
   —The New Woman Feeling Her Way in Turkey—Origins of the New Woman:
   The Cultural Politics of Embarrassment and Its Changing Legal Status in
   Turkey—The New Woman at Work: Global Capitalism and the Gendered
   World of the Service Economy—Tables Turning Against the New Woman:
   The Rise of Moralist Politics—The New Woman in the Gezi Uprising: A
   New Political Actor or a Violable Subject?—The New Woman against the
   Vigilante Man: Violence, Orientations, and—Disorientations—
   Conclusion and Epilogue: The New Woman and Feminism in Uncertain Time.
   Provided by publisher.
Identifiers: LCCN 2022029615 (print) | LCCN 2022029616 (ebook) | ISBN
   9780197667644 (paperback) | ISBN 9780197667651 (epub) | ISBN
   9780197667668 (pdf)
Subjects: LCSH: Feminism—Turkey. | Women—Violence against—Turkey. |
   Women—Social conditions—Turkey.
Classification: LCC HQ1726.7 .S27 2022 (print) | LCC HQ1726.7 (ebook) |
   DDC 305.4209561—dc23/eng/20220728
LC record available at https://lccn.loc.gov/2022029615
LC ebook record available at https://lccn.loc.gov/2022029616

9 8 7 6 5 4 3 2 1

Printed by Integrated Books International, United States of America

CONTENTS

....

List of Illustrations   viii
Acknowledgements   x

Introduction   1

CHAPTER 1   The New Woman Feeling Her Way in Turkey   33

CHAPTER 2   Origins of the New Woman: The Cultural Politics of Embarrassment and Its Changing Legal Status in Turkey   50

CHAPTER 3   The New Woman at Work: Global Capitalism and the Gendered World of the Service Economy   75

CHAPTER 4   Tables Turning against the New Woman: The Rise of Moralist Politics   97

CHAPTER 5   The New Woman in the Gezi Uprising: A New Political Actor or a Violable Subject?   119

CHAPTER 6   The New Woman against the Vigilante Man: Violence, Orientations, and Disorientations   140

CONCLUSION AND EPILOGUE   The New Woman and Feminism in Uncertain Times   163

Glossary of Turkish Terms   173
References   176
Index   191

LIST OF ILLUSTRATIONS

....

Map   Map of Turkey and neighboring countries. p. ix

Picture 1   A woman student undaunted by the attack of a police dog stares unflinchingly into the eyes of police at Cebeci Campus. Ankara, 2017 (Photo by Tamer Arda Erşin). p. 28

Picture 2   Nesrin's living room. Istanbul (Photo by author). p. 34

Picture 3   The author is checking customers out at the cash register at MajorMarket. Istanbul, 2011 (Photo by a colleague). p. 78

Picture 4   The famous picture, popularly known as "the woman in red", was taken at the beginning of the Gezi protest. Istanbul, 2013 (Photo by Osman Orsal). p. 125

Picture 5   Protestors display a placard that reads "If You're Afraid of The Dark at Night, We'll Set This City on Fire" at the Feminist Night Walk. Istanbul, 2022 (Photo by Mehmet Temel-Aktivist Kamera). p. 151

Picture 6   Don't Mess with My Outfit Demonstration. Ankara, 2017 (Photo by author). p. 155

Picture 7   A woman encircled by the police is taken into custody at the Women's Protest in Solidarity with the Chilean Feminist Collective LasTesis. Istanbul, 2019 (Photo by Mehmet Temel-Aktivist Kamera). p. 172

MAP

....

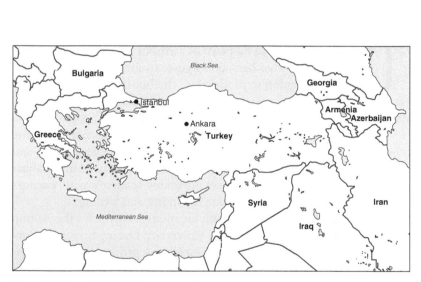

Map of Turkey and neighboring countries.

ACKNOWLEDGEMENTS

....

This book would not be possible without the generous support of my mentors, teachers, colleagues, and friends. At every step, from its inception to production, the book's development benefited greatly from the scholarly guidance, intellectual stimulation, constructive feedback, and emotional comfort a number of people offered.

My heartfelt thanks go to Çağlar Keyder who as a teacher taught me how to think about capitalist globalization and its divergence from and convergence with neoliberalism, which formed the basis of my analysis in this book, and who as a mentor set me on my academic path, encouraging me to venture into independent thinking and writing.

I would like to thank Kati Griffith for sponsoring me for the visiting fellowship at the ILR School, Cornell University. During my stay at Cornell, I was able to develop my ideas into a book proposal with the support of Leslie Gates and Brendan McQuade, who generously welcomed me into their writing group, giving me the much-needed encouragement, constructive feedback, and daily discipline to work through the initial phase of outlining a book project.

My project found a good home at the Center for the History of Emotions at the Max Planck Institute for Human Development in Berlin, where I developed individual chapters and wrote the entire manuscript. I would like to thank the Center's director, Ute Frevert, for her support. Her research on the history of emotions contributed to my analysis of shame and gender politics. At the Center, I had the opportunity to work with and learn from colleagues with whom I share a keen interest in emotions. I especially thank Stephanie Lämmert, Daphne Rozenblatt, Stephen Cummins, and Hannah Malone for their ideas, intellectual exchanges, and more importantly, for their friendship. I was also helped by Karola Rockmann, Anja Berkes, Philipp von Hugo, Susanne Kassung, and Kerstin Singer who offered administrative and technical support while I was working on the manuscript. Daniela Petrosino, our scientific editor, proofread the glossary and acknowledgments. Daniela Regel and Yüksel Durgaç from Max Planck Institute for Human Development library have always been helpful and kind, enabling me to get my hands quickly on the various books and articles needed for my research. Yasemin Tekgürler, my talented research assistant, combed through the entire manuscript and prepared the index. I would also like to offer special thanks to my dear friend, the late Christina Becher, who passed away before I completed the manuscript, for helping me learn the ropes both at Max Planck and in Berlin. I miss her.

Before I took up the research position at the Max Planck Institute for Human Development, I worked in the Gender Studies Division of the Faculty of Political Science at Ankara University. I remain indebted to faculty members Serpil Sancar, Alev Özkazanç, Elif Ekin Akşit Vural, Gülay Toksöz, Emel Memiş, and Funda Cantek for giving me the opportunity to work in a progressive feminist environment with brilliant students and for supporting me as a scholar.

I cannot sufficiently thank Carla Freeman. She influenced my thinking about globalization, gender, and class before I even met her. I feel incredibly lucky that she later became my editor, my mentor, and a cherished friend. I am also grateful to her series co-editor, Li Zhang for her encouragement of the project. At Oxford University Press, I thank Sherith Pankratz for her unwavering support and enthusiasm and Rick Dillenberger for his important contribution to ensuring a smooth production process. The book also greatly benefited from the feedback of the following reviewers and I am very grateful for their thorough engagement with the manuscript:

Kaan Agartan, Framingham State University
Bretton Alvare, Widener University
Aminta Arrington, John Brown University
Deborah Augsburger, University of Wisconsin-Superior
Cynthia Clark, Rutgers University-Camden
Meghan Donnelly, University of San Diego

James Hundley, Rowan University
Matthew Newsom, Southern Utah University
Gül Özyeğin, William & Mary
Tamar Shirinian, University of Tennessee
Raja Swamy, University of Tennessee

I owe thanks to Lynn M. Thomas, Valerie Walkerdine, Zeynep Gönen, and Deniz Yonucu, who gave me invaluable feedback on early drafts of chapters. I am deeply indebted to Gül Özyeğin, one of the manuscript reviewers, who provided substantive feedback and enthusiasm for the book. I also warmly acknowledge the guidance I received from Alev Özkazanç, a feminist intellectual and scholar I admire, who offered me a strong encouragement to make my arguments with confidence since reading the draft of the entire manuscript. Mehmet Temel-Aktivist Kamera, Tamer Arda Erşin, and Osman Orsal were all very kind and contributed enormously to this book by allowing me to use their precious photographs. I am grateful to Charlotte Weber for her careful editing and insightful feedback on the manuscript. '

I was also helped by the dear friends I made during grad school at Binghamton University. I thank Jeff Howison for generously offering his time for proofreading, to Irmak Ertuna Howison for always coming up with the best translations for Turkish terms, to Ayşe Serdar for sharing her own collection of photographs, and to Bülent Batuman for providing the maps. Barış Ünlü read the entire manuscript and made himself available for thoughtful conversations and exciting discussions; for this I will always be thankful.

Thanks are due too to Meram Can Saka and Gamze Özçürümez Bilgili for the steady support they offered. I would additionally like to express my gratitude to Leslie Ihde, whose clear-eyed perspective enabled me to see myself in ways I do not think I would have otherwise understood or appreciated.

Finally, I would like to thank all the women who participated in my research. They shared their experiences with me, let me into their lives, and made my research possible.

On September 12, 2016, having finished her night shift at an Istanbul hospital, Ayşegül Terzi, a twenty-three-year-old nurse, hopped on a bus to return home. It was early in the morning, the first day of the sacrificial Muslim holiday, and Terzi, seated amid the crowd, was checking the **bairam** greetings on her phone while listening to her headphones when a man, out of the blue, kicked her in the face, ominously hollering, "Those who wear shorts must die." Two months later, İpek Atcan, a twenty-two-year-old music writer based in Istanbul, was at the subway station, waiting for the train when a man kicked her in the legs, furiously shouting, "You can't sit here with your legs crossed like this." Six months later, Dilay Özel, twenty, was attacked on the street in Antalya along with her aunt and her mother for their so-called audacious behavior—that is, smoking cigarettes. The two men, upon seeing Dilay walk home in the company of her mother and aunt, who was smoking a cigarette, grew livid and began loudly heckling the women: "Look just how reckless they are. How dare women smoke on the street!" they said, as if talking to each other. When Dilay's aunt confronted them and told them to mind their own business, one man, in just a blink of an eye, punched the aunt and attacked the mother, while the other man took the lit cigarette and extinguished it on Dilay's neck. Speaking about the attack later on national TV Dilay said, "If the men had just angrily catcalled and left us alone, it would not be a problem, because we are accustomed to this kind of treatment in Turkey. However, this is different.

1

Remember the woman wearing shorts? Remember what happened to her? This is the same thing."

Dilay's astute observation captures the unsettling sociopolitical phenomenon this book aims to investigate: the recent ascent of performative violence, specifically, vigilante violence, against women in Turkey, where violence against women is not at all new. Between September 2016 and July 2018, at least nineteen cases of vigilante violence were documented in Turkey, in which male vigilantes meted out violent punishments to women for their alleged moral transgressions in public places. Women, for example, were assaulted for no other reason than wearing shorts, smoking cigarettes, sitting cross-legged in public, engaging in public displays of affection, and exercising in parks. In contrast to domestic violence, which affects women across the board, vigilante violence in contemporary Turkey targets particular groups of women— whom I call New Women—those who ostensibly violate local standards of female modesty. And unlike domestic violence against women, which is often perpetrated in the confines of the home and disguised as a private matter, vigilante violence is deliberately public in plain sight, and committed with the aim of creating a spectacle by male attackers whom the survivors do not know personally. The attacks, by and large, were perpetrated in big cities such as Izmir, Istanbul, Ankara, Bursa, and Antalya. This pattern is particularly puzzling given that norms of feminine dress and comportment have never been strict in those cities and the embodied public presence of women who do not conform to conservative dictates of female propriety has been fairly strong.

The AKP (Justice and Development Party) government's response to vigilantism was markedly tolerant; although government officials denounced the violence, they made a point of lamenting the lack of embarrassment among today's women. In 2016, Binali Yıldırım, then Turkey's prime minister, commenting on Ayşegül Terzi, who had been attacked for wearing shorts, said on national TV, "One can grumble about improperly dressed women, if one doesn't approve it, but one does not attack them." This was not the first time a high-ranking government official denounced violence against women while at the same time condoning the reproach of women for their moral infractions in public. Indeed, in the post-2008 period, the AKP government began to deploy a moralist and alarmist discourse that chastised women whom were judged to have impudent manners, a change that aroused animosity against the New Woman in the country.

The moral vigilantism, at the same time, has been accompanied by a sharp U-turn in gender policies in the country. In the early 2000s, the AKP government introduced one of the most progressive legal reforms in the history of the Turkish Republic with the adoption of a new Civil Code and Penal Code, considerably improving gender equality in the country. By 2010, however, Tayyip Erdoğan, then prime minister, had already become quite outspoken against gender equality, claiming that the principle was alien to Turkish culture. Erdoğan repeatedly declared his faith in the Islamic *fıtrat*, which denotes the idea that there are inherent, God-given differences between men and women. A few years later, the AKP introduced a new paradigm: gender justice. As opposed to the contemporary understanding of gender justice, which seeks to eradicate all forms of gender inequality, the notion of gender justice that the AKP promoted was informed by Qur'anic notions of fair treatment of different genders (Yılmaz 2015; Diner 2018). "Gender justice" strongly echoed the Ottoman imperial notion of justice, an ideology that served to justify and reinforce the fundamental status hierarchies of Muslim/ non-Muslim, ruling elite/common people, and men/women. A prominent aspect of gender justice is fair treatment, which women (along with other groups located in the lower ranks of the social hierarchy) are promised as long as they "know their place" and do not strive for equality. Following the U-turn in the AKP's gender politics, gender equality visibly eroded in the country. In the 2006 Global Gender Gap Report provided by World Economic Forum, Turkey held the 105th position while in 2019, it ranked 130th among 149 countries.

Here it is worth noting that the politics at large also took a sharp turn in Turkey. Over the last few years, it has become ever more evident that New Turkey—a popular term that refers to Turkey under the rule of the AKP, as opposed to Old Turkey characterized by the rule of authoritarian secularist **Kemalist** elite—is lurching towards repressive state rule. In 2002, when the AKP government first came to power and began to work towards dismantling the military tutelage in the country, liberals hoped that Turkey would reconstitute itself as a pluralist democracy where disenfranchised segments of society, including, but not limited to Kurds, Alevis, non-Muslims, LGBTIQ+ communities, and women, would feel included. A few optimists believed that the conservative AKP government, more than the secularists, were committed to democratization and expected Turkey's entry into the European Union. What transpired since then has been far bleaker: the government's launch of a large-scale military operation in Kurdish cities in 2015, a failed coup attempt followed by a state of emergency between 2016 and 2018, an extensive purge of civil servants including left-wing academics and Kurdish office holders, de-facto suspension of the rule of law, the rise of an intensely moralistic vision of politics accompanied by punitive feelings, the complete muzzling of the media and forcible suppression of political opposition despite the trappings of re-transitioning to democracy in 2018, and one-man rule.

One unexpected political development in this dire time was the resurgence of a militant women's movement. Women took to the streets and clashed with police despite the crackdown on protests and public gatherings. Demonstrations they held effectively stopped the AKP government's plans to pass new bills on violence against women, divorce, and marriage that would roll back women's previous gains. The feminist night walks organized on International Women's Day, although dispersed by police with rubber bullets, continued to attract thousands of women at a time when no other collective movement could sustain its street presence. In a period when the AKP government was able to rule by decree, without judicial control or effective opposition, the women's movement has quickly become a prominent grassroots movement opposing the AKP government. The women's resistance movement became the new guardian of democracy and secularism in the eyes of masses who felt besieged by AKP rule, their efforts demonstrating new and more inclusive practices of gender equality. The protesters' embodied presence and acts inform the New Woman, who expresses the new possibilities of being feminine in Turkey.

Drawing on research that combines an ethnography of the New Woman and a study of vigilante violence in today's Turkey, this book offers a novel explanation for the surge of hostility against women in the global era. It turns the spotlight on the New Woman, illuminating her distinct agency while investigating the knotty entanglements between vigilantism, the politics of gender equality, authoritarianism, neoliberal capitalist globalization, and gendered bodies which were marked by performative violence and aggression. The New Woman is a term I employ to describe a new modality of femininity that is given frame and form, to a certain extent, by the politics of gender equality and the complex forces of capitalist globalization. An examination of this new modality of femininity takes the body as its focus, revealing a distinct configuration of emotions, everyday modes of interactions, and embodied orientations, which are no longer tethered to the affective dictates of embarrassment, a contested feminine virtue in Turkey.

The book chronicles the journey of the New Woman from the neoliberal global era to the populist moment in the twenty-first century—that is, from the 1990s to the late 2010s—to show how the New Woman has gone from being a desirable employee in the service economy to a precarious body facing the risk of vigilante violence in the right-wing populist moment. It argues that those emotional and embodied capacities, which made the New Woman attractive to service employers, catapulted her to the center of a highly contentious politics as, simultaneously, both a feminist icon of resistance and the target of violent hostility during the reign of the AKP government. The book not only illuminates the singular agency manifested by the New Woman in the global era, but also explains why her embodied and affective ways of being feminine pose a threat to the AKP government's authoritarian rule. The study of the affective and the corporeal helps disentangle the relationship between the recent ascendance of performative violence and emergent forms of illiberal power, the neoconservative aims of the AKP government, neoliberal global capitalism, affective visions of gender equality, and the New Woman. The book demonstrates that the New Woman's embodied capacities, emotional orientations, and habitual ways of being in the world energizes the global capitalist economy, feminist movements, and authoritarian politics in complex, contradictory, and unexpected ways in today's Turkey. These contradictory forces, in turn, severely affect the New Woman's embodied vulnerability, placing her at increased risk for violence. In this book, phenomenology meets with sociology, emotions with politics, the body with global capitalist structures, and Erving Goffman's insights with gendered organization of the service economy in Turkey; all blend together to render visible the New Woman's distinct agency in a period when globalization is fostering change in the form of discontinuity, uncertainty, disruption, rupture, and backlash.

The New Woman, to be sure, existed prior to globalization in Turkey and beyond. On the cusp of the twentieth century on both sides of the Atlantic, the New Woman was the avatar of change, the harbinger of cultural, social, and political transformations as well as the epitome of the fin de siècle (Cunningham 1978; Frevert 1989; Silverman 1991; Weinbaum et al. 2008). Cultural historians and literary critics studying the New Woman noted her complex affinity with consumerist capitalism, urban life-worlds, feminist activism, the rise of mass culture, and modernist discourses in the late nineteenth and early twentieth centuries (Stansell 2000; Stevens 2003; Rowbotham, 2010). In the early 1930s in Johannesburg, she was a school-educated, young, black woman cutting a cosmopolitan figure, who, at times, competed in beauty pageants, brushing off the older notions that "smiling was an immodest gesture for young women" (Thomas 2008, 103). In the early twentieth century in Europe, unlike other women, who blushed upon being greeted by a man on the street, the New Woman, feeling no shame, engaged in new bodily practices of sports, work, and leisure and "moved easily among men," talking and laughing in public (Frevert 2011, 138). In Turkey, following the establishment of the Turkish Republic in 1923, secular-nationalist political elites eagerly promoted the New Woman,[1] who was a well-educated, professional, middle-class, patriotic woman committed to the ideals of the new republic (Gole 1996; Arat 2000; White 2003). Situated in a historical period of etatism—in which the Turkish state tightly controlled private enterprise and operated state-run enterprises in various industries—the New Woman of the early Republican period was not quite familiar with the cultures of the market economy. It was secularist Turkish nationalism that, to a great extent, fostered, as well as circumscribed, the embodied existence of the New Woman, who was a natural ally of the state feminism promoted by Republican elites through the gender equality reforms of the 1920s and 1930s.

By the turn of the twenty-first century, however, the face of the New Woman in Turkey had changed dramatically. She lost her purely middle-class character, with wider segments of working-class women and women without a college degree coming to embody the New Woman in the global era. Instead of the state, she now relied on the market to sustain herself. In a period when neoliberal global capitalism has taken hold of social life, the New Woman's embodied existence, bodily dispositions, comportment, and practices are no longer uncontested sites of secularist Turkish nationalism or national belonging. The forces that now act on her body are plural: the new urban service economy draws on her interactional and emotional orientations as sources of labor and neoliberal discourses affirm her corporeal ways of being by inventing commodified visions of empowered women. For the AKP government, however, her embodied capacities, in particular sexuality and reproduction, emerge as important sites for neoconservative moralist discourses, while the politics of gender equality push back to help maintain her bodily autonomy. In the era of globalization, the New Woman has become a natural ally of feminist movements in Turkey, which combine intersectional approaches with more inclusive understandings of gender. Meanwhile, the AKP government's attitude toward the New Woman, especially after 2010, when it denounced gender equality, has grown increasingly strained and confrontational, often through violent means. The New Woman's everyday ways of being in the world, her relaxed bodily ways, and her self-confident attitude are profoundly at odds with the gender order the AKP is intent to impose. Things took a turn for the worse for the New Woman when vigilante men started physically assaulting her in public spaces for her alleged moral infractions.

Taking the story of the New Woman into twenty-first century Turkey, I demonstrate that the New Woman's modes of being and living, which suggest new gendered bodily orientations and ways of feeling, evolved out of a transformation of long-valorized feelings of embarrassment and shame over the course of the twentieth century. I consider the two related yet distinct emotions of embarrassment and shame in relation to shame-honor discourse, a disciplinary mechanism used historically to regulate gendered embodiment. Earlier studies on the Mediterranean region have argued that gender binaries subtended emotional ones: culturally dominant notions of masculinity and femininity were often marked and articulated by emotions of honor and shame (Peristiany 1966; Wikan 1984; Delaney 1991; Bourdieu 2001). Scholarly accounts have maintained that these feelings were involved in the production and regulation of self and morality, gendered bodies and their interactions, and bodily capacities such as sexuality and labor, and shaped gendered patterns of violence. As such, men, laying claim to honor, committed acts of violence against women, citing women's moral transgressions. Feminine embodiment, on the other hand, was meshed tightly with shame, which evoked the sexualized ideals of chastity, virginity, and modesty. Upheld as a feminine virtue, the feeling of embarrassment awakened the feminine intention to self-monitor and cultivate modesty. Shaming, on the other hand, was woven into the workings of punishment and was inflicted on women who failed to live up to the norms of feminine modesty and chastity.

I re-engage with the shame-honor paradigm to highlight its return to national politics as an important component of authoritarian rule in Turkey, refurbished as a discourse guiding the AKP's backlash against gender equality and women's autonomy in global era. Feminist scholars of Turkey offer lucid accounts of the contemporary gender backlash in Turkey. Deniz Kandiyoti (2016) has drawn attention to the ongoing operations of masculinist restoration, in which increasing male violence against women is associated with the loss of masculine authority. Alev Özkazanç (2020) has examined different forms of anti-gender discourses proliferating in the right-wing populist moment. And Evren Savcı (2016) has revealed that the ruling party's neoconservative politics drives a backlash against LGBTIQ+ rights. I bring perspectives from the shame-honor paradigm to bear on the emotional politics of the gender backlash led by the AKP government, which disproportionately impacts the New Woman. My departure point, in a sense, is not the analytical productiveness of the shame-honor paradigm to account for today's complex and diverse gender dynamics; what animates this research is, instead, the AKP government's efforts to retool shame-honor as a force for masculinist populism, promoting hostility towards the New Woman. The shame-honor paradigm is inadequately attuned to the gendered moment in Turkey, when the workings of economic, social, and political processes create gender dynamics that are far too diverse and complex to be governed, let alone understood, by the binaries of shame and honor. What the gendered moment in Turkey reveals, among other things, is the eclipse of shame and embarrassment, accompanied by the emergence of new gendered subjectivities. How, in this conjuncture, the AKP government's insistence on reviving shame-honor as a discourse affects and is affected by the New Woman demands a historically-informed understanding of emotions that recognizes the gendered ways shame and embarrassment are embodied and embedded in hierarchies of gender in Turkey.

As a part of my argument, I show how late twentieth century global flows of capital and power, acting on gendered bodies, have reduced the intensity of both the shame and embarrassment that was grounded in predominant understandings of feminine modesty and respectability. The book demonstrates that the salience and authority of the feelings of shame and embarrassment markedly decline with globalization, spawning a new web of corporeal relations in the twenty-first-century urban context. It illustrates in vivid detail how these new corporeal dynamics create new possibilities of feminine bodily existence, using ethnographic observations collected in everyday spaces of work and sociability inhabited by today's New Women—the sales floor, shopping malls, streets, cafes, public transportation, political uprisings, and street demonstrations. It shines a spotlight on the New Woman's embodied presence within quotidian rhythms, as well as her body's response to hostile emotions and male aggression fueled by authoritarian politics, which disrupt her habitual and affective manners of being in the world.

Emotions, especially those that are bound up with self-monitoring (embarrassment) and punishment (shame), are a prime factor in which to study how the separation between the corporeal realm and the political realm has become elided in Turkey's authoritarian revival. By unveiling the New Woman's embodied and affective ways of being feminine, I show that the New Woman in today's Turkey makes political and social demands for equality and autonomy, without resorting to acts or deeds, through her corporeal ways of being in the world. The New Woman's embodied existence—her gaze and gait, poise and touch, feelings and confidence, as well as posture and clothing—all express a new modality of agency that poses a threat to the AKP's authoritarian politics. The AKP government, seeking to tighten its grip on power, has swiftly returned embarrassment and shame into gender politics. Embarrassment as a feminine virtue is fervently re-affirmed and shaming is re-awakened as a form of punishment. I argue that a mode of governing through emotions is vital for the authoritarian regime in Turkey where the social-legal order still fosters gender equality as well as the New Woman's embodied modalities of being, while restraining the AKP's attempts to stabilize its authoritarian rule. The AKP's turn to gendered sources of authority that utilize shaming and embarrassment in the service of authoritarianism aggravates the conflict between the AKP and New Women. My argument draws from an array of theoretical insights inspired by feminist and antiracist scholarship on the phenomenology of the body, the sociology of emotions as well as affect studies, symbolic interactionism, Bourdieusian sociology, and globalization, gender and labor scholarship. I show that the democratic erosion in Turkey drives gender politics into a reactionary masculinist state, while the New Woman, by rising up against such violence, succeeds in confronting the AKP's authoritarianism.

Rethinking Women's Agency

To grasp the sense in which the New Woman's agency poses a threat to the AKP's authoritarian project requires an unconventional understanding of agency, which this study explicitly articulates by focusing on women's embodied orientations, quotidian interactions, and feelings in urban Turkey. In social science literature, conventional indicators of women's agency often encompass women's employment status, disposable income, and participation in decision-making, as well as the collective efforts of women's movements. My approach, which builds on the analysis of agency in feminist thought and phenomenology of the body, offers a fresh slant on conventional understandings of women's agency. The kind of agency I unearth by looking at urban Turkey operates through embodied, affective, and interactional registers.

A saleswoman's interactions, for instance, with customers on the sales floor—her smooth efficiency, her courteous but confident demeanor, her adroitness in getting the conversation flowing, her easy and relaxed attitude when she relates to male coworkers, and her poised comportment, all the minutiae of her embodied work life—reveal this modality of agency that women have acquired in global era. This modality of agency is noteworthy in urban centers, at business offices located in newly built high-rise condos, banks, creative agencies nestled around hip neighborhoods, hotels, restaurants, shopping malls, movie theaters, fast-food chains, cosmetic stores, and supermarkets, all of which have flourished in the urban landscape over the last four decades in Turkey.

Once central to analyses of politics, history, and society, the notion of agency was, to a great extent, sidelined, if not abandoned, after Foucault's enormously influential corpus of work on power and discourse. Foucault's (1980) treatment of power as something simultaneously repressive and productive deconstructed the binaries of freedom/subordination, resistance/power, and structure/agency, transforming profoundly the way scholars think about agency. Wedded to ideas about rationality, autonomy, resistance, and freedom, the notion of agency was widely contested and later reframed by feminist thinkers (Butler 1990) as a product of power relations; that is, an effect of discourse and power, a performative repetition, and a social construct. Poststructuralist and postcolonial scholars, too, drew attention to the limitations of definitions of agency prevalent especially in feminist thinking (Abu-Lughod 1990). Weary of feminist framings of agency as resistance to power, Saba Mahmood (2001), for instance, criticized feminists for their narrow scope, which hinders recognition of a large swathe of modalities of women's agency that escape the binaries of obedience/rebellion, compliance/resistance, and submission/subversion.

More recent years, however, saw a revival of interest in women's agency. Scholars began to explore modes of agency uncharted in feminist thinking, which fall outside the more familiar definition of acts of resistance (Butler 1990; McNay 2000; Coole 2005; Mahmood 2005; Allen 2008; Weiss 2018). While Judith Butler (1990) advocated for a counter-hegemonic understanding of agency that emerges from subversive acts—that is, as resistance to domination—Saba Mahmood (2005) examined how the enactment of norms can create a capacity for action among so-called docile agents (for example, religious women). But what if human agency is not only located in acts or enactments, which demand conscious effort from the self, but also encompasses embodied ways of being and feeling that are often pre-reflective and habitual?

In a novel approach to understanding women's agency, I register those quotidian modalities of women's agency that lie beyond actions and deeds. I follow scholars who have turned to phenomenology with the aim of magnifying corporality beyond physicality as the locus of self (Grosz 1994: Alcoff 2005; Coole 2005; Young 2005). Phenomenology has furnished a post-Foucauldian notion of self by foregrounding bodies rather than focusing purely on language-based and discursive models (Coole 2005; Salamon et al. 2019). A phenomenological approach, which holds that an analysis of the self begins from lived experience, centers the subjective standpoint as well as the first-person point of view. In line with this, phenomenological approaches emphasize the body as the locus of feeling, moving, sensing, and perceiving. From the perspective of phenomenology, the point of focusing on the body, or rather embodiment—the process of inhabiting a body—is to disclose experiential dimensions of the bodily realm and to explore everyday life enacted at the corporeal level.

The primacy afforded to the body in phenomenological thinking dispenses with the body as a discrete entity or substance and, from the outset, emphasizes it's situatedness. Neither a subject nor an object, the phenomenological body is rather "the ground of a style of interacting with the environment" (Dillon 1997, 122). As with Merleau-Ponty's embodied phenomenology, it is the body that becomes "our anchorage in a world" (Merleau-Ponty [1945] 2013, 146) and "our general means of having a world" (147). In this account, the link between the body and the world remains unbroken and relationality is built into the corporeal realm. Not framed in terms of a static-monadic individual existence, embodiment spins a web of relational dynamics with other bodies and the world. It is often the body's receptivity and responsiveness that prompts and maintains this web of relationality. The phenomenological body, as opposed to the Cartesian body, is situated in the world and shaped by social and political forces; it is never merely a passive recipient of those forces. Neither inert nor inactive, the body instead is responsive. It responds to what arises: to others, to the world, and to ideas and emotions in accordance with those energies and capacities it is invested with.

It is often through emotions that the body forms responses at the carnal plane. Anthropologist Michelle Rosaldo (1984) exhorted us to consider emotions as the body's responses to perceptions.[2] The phenomenological approach, similarly, asks us to study shame, honor, fear, love, and disgust as the appraisals and perceptions of the embodied self. Emotions, along with bodily needs and desires, grant the body a particular stance or direction and orient the embodied self in the world. They are not passive states one goes through but can be understood as forces that shape how one responds to and enacts in world (Szanto & Landweer 2020). Such an approach resists considering emotions as corporeal articulations to be parsed along the divisions between passive and active, reason and emotion, the world and the self. Phenomenology instead offers a rich ground for exploring how emotions are ways of attuning to the world and of orienting oneself towards things and others. It brings into relief the complex and dynamic ways emotions, feelings, and pre-reflective—not-yet-consciously formulated—embodied experiences are inextricably related within the flows of everyday life that are all embedded in historical specificities.

The feminist and antiracist strands of phenomenology, in particular, offer a unique perspective to draw out pre-reflective and embodied ways of being in the world, investigating these modes for bodies that are embedded in a complex web of institutions, practices, and discourses that sustain gender (Al-Saji 2010; Dolezal 2015), race (Ahmed 2006; Yancy 2008; Ngo 2017, 2022), and class hierarchies (Sullivan 2014). In *The Physiology of Sexist and Racist Oppression*, philosopher Shannon Sullivan, for instance, singles out embodied habits: "In a world," Sullivan writes, "characterized by sexism and racism, many a person's habits tend to be shaped by and in response to male privilege and white domination, and this shaping often takes place unconsciously" (Sullivan 2015, 10). Such a focus on the body's habitual responses to structural hierarchies primes us to understand the larger phenomenological tradition in feminist thinking, too. Consider Iris Marion Young's groundbreaking "Throwing like a Girl," (1980), in which she argued that feminine bodily comportment in patriarchal societies is characterized by limitations and inhibitions. A woman in a sexist society experiences a profound bodily tension, which is always intensely palpable. She opens up to the world with the aim of accomplishing a task with a sense of agency, but she stiffens simultaneously, holding herself back, feeling heavy with a sense of incapacity. This tension, a bodily effect of a patriarchal social organization, Young argues, underlies woman's bodily hesitancy, timidity, and uncertainty.

Taking my bearings from feminist and antiracist scholarships on phenomenology that reimagine embodiment away from masculinist bias—that offer feminist perspectives on corporeality and the workings of power—I locate women's agency in phenomenological orientations. An imaginative tool developed to further illuminate embodiment, the concept emphasizes the body's receptivity and responsiveness. Orientations refer to an assemblage of embodied and affective configurations that are expressed in attitudes, gestures, beliefs, habits, and temperament that often are manifest in pre-reflective ways of dwelling in the world and everyday ways of approaching others. They follow from the body's settled tendencies or usual manner of being and acting, which can be defined by the term the 'habit body' developed by Merleau-Ponty. Instead of giving priority to actions and deeds that demand conscious efforts from the self, orientation prominently reflects unconscious habits, affective ways of being in the world, and habitual ways of approaching others—of leaning toward or moving away from them, of engaging or shrinking from them. By rethinking agency through a focus on orientations, the analysis I present in this book breaks with the binary of obedience/rebellion, as well as the binary of active/passive that undergirds prevalent conceptions of agency in social science scholarship. In an effort to reconceptualize agency, I posit *disorientation* alongside *orientation*. While the latter enables bodies to dwell in the world in ways that become habitual, disorientation refers to corporeal experiences that disrupt ordinary ways of inhabiting the world (Harbin 2016), evoking "a bodily feeling of losing one's place" (Ahmed 2006, 160).[3]

With the fresh perceptions of agency that the phenomenological approach produces, one can readily observe new modalities of women's agency in urban Turkey. She no longer experiences her body as a burden to be dragged along and vigilantly protected at the same time—the way shame or embarrassment would prescribe. Now, her body is the primary point of contact with the world as well as with others. It expresses a sense of openness, an ability to be present without anxiously guarding itself. The way she walks—her stride not hesitant, her gait sure, her posture erect—becomes her embodied response to the world, a difficult and at times hostile world where she is, nonetheless, capable of carving out a space for herself.

Particularly striking is the working-class woman's embodied presence in the urban landscape. Unlike her mother and grandmother who were not supposed to wander freely on the streets, let alone work outside the home, she now walks the streets heading to work in skinny jeans, Converse sneakers or ballet flats, and her colorful headphones. After work, she visits shopping malls, meets with friends at a café, or takes the bus late at night to return home after a date with her romantic interest. In all these quotidian moments, she carries herself with ease, not feeling constrained in space. Even late at night on the bus, her shoulders do not slump and her arms do not move in front of her body, because she does not feel the need to contract her body to hide her breasts. Neither does she feel the need to lower her head and eyes when exposed to the piercing male gaze. Often, she looks away, pretending that she has not noticed it. Sometimes, though, she returns the gaze, looking back defiantly with an ice-cold expression on her face. There she is: neither timid nor inhibited, but self-assured. The defining feature of women's agency in contemporary Turkey, I argue, is *the absence of embarrassment*. The absence of discomfiture, shame, and uneasiness in women announces that a new mode of embodiment and a new order of social interaction have already emerged in urban Turkey.

The Waning Power of Shame and Embarrassment in Turkey

In 1956, Erving Goffman revisited one of this book's central themes: embarrassment and its social significance. In his article "Embarrassment and Social Organization," Goffman explained that embarrassment is by no means a merely bodily process but has a cultural logic, as well as a history and a social context. Embarrassment, Goffman thought, was so central to the operation of societies that he proposed, "In an empirical study of a particular social system the first object would be to learn what categories of persons become embarrassed in what recurrent situations.

And the second object would be to discover what would happen to the social system and the framework of obligations if embarrassment had not come to be systematically built into it" (Goffman 1956, 270).

In a Goffman-like ethos, I analyze the changes in the political and economic significance of embarrassment in Turkey by looking at how institutions, markets, and political actors have historically invested in embarrassment for their own goals. Why has embarrassment been expected of and even encouraged in women in Turkey? In what ways has embarrassment been systematically built into the gendered organization of society? Which relations of power and domination have embarrassment enabled and generated? How has embarrassment moved gendered bodies into action or oriented them in the world? What specific economic, political, social, and discursive transformations altered the framework of emotional obligations women shouldered over the twentieth century? In which ways did entanglements of emotions, markets, institutions, and gender politics affect women's bodies in Turkey during the global era? In answering these questions, I illustrate how embarrassment and shame—situated at the nexus of gender norms and gender politics—mediate the uneasy relationship between feminine embodiment, women's agency, male violence, and authoritarian politics in Turkey.

Bringing phenomenology's insights into a historically and culturally situated analysis of gendered emotions in Turkey, I discuss shame and embarrassment throughout this book in connection with shame-honor discourse. Central to the functioning of male domination, the shame-honor system, scholars have argued, has long governed gender hierarchies mainly through kinship ties, prescribing codes of conduct and deeds for each gender in Mediterranean societies, including Turkey (Peristiany 1966; Wikan 1984; Delaney 1991). The shame-honor approach, in the last few decades, has been excoriated for its totalizing essentialism (Abu-Lughod 1986) and for its uncritical embrace of modernization theory, which differentiates the so-called premodern, community-based cultures of shame from more modern, individualist cultures of guilt. Recently, scholars from different disciplines have begun to draw on shame-honor without succumbing to essentialism or modernization theory and illustrated that shame and honor—rather than being ahistorical and fixed cultural codes of traditional communities—are emotional modalities of power that have been integral to the operations of modern institutions such as the nation-state

(Parla 2001; Kogacioglu 2004; Sirman 2014), the military (Frevert 2004), sexuality (Ozyegin 2015), the police (Lévy-Aksu 2017), and the judicial system (Tuğ 2017), cutting across the divide of East and West, as well as South and North. I join in these recent critical debates by bringing a historically-informed and phenomenologically-oriented feminist analysis of the articulation of emotions, shame and embarrassment, to the discourse of shame-honor utilized by the AKP government in the current era of authoritarianism.

Throughout the twentieth century, shame and embarrassment were the primary affective forces, each with its own intensity and charge, that granted the feminine body a particular orientation in Turkey. Embarrassment, a self-conscious emotion, operated through the medium of the body, orienting feminized bodies in a particular direction: the direction of feminine modesty. Since the bodily strategies of pious self-regulation are crucial to feminine modesty, women put efforts into cultivating bodily styles, aesthetics, and emotions of modesty (Mahmood 2005; Jones 2010). Shame and shaming, on the other hand, delineated rather painful and aggressive affective modalities, through which one experienced a sense of worthlessness and devaluation. Shame could be self-imposed or, in the case of shaming, utilized by others as a punishment mechanism against women who failed to live up to the norms of feminine modesty. Far from being mere products of one's interiority, both shame and embarrassment have been systematically built into the gendered organization of society, permeating the legal structures and enabling gendered relations of power and discipline. These two emotions imbued the everyday corporeal realm, mostly through the habitual body, in the pre-reflective ways the body moves and extends itself in space and time. They also afforded particular possibilities of feminine self-making and gendered ways of attuning to the world, while at the same time, functioning as a primary means of violence against women in Turkey, making women's bodies vulnerable to attacks and hostility. In other words, shame and embarrassment have acted as generative affective forces that shape not only the embodied modalities of women's agency but also gendered means of violence in society.

By reframing shame-honor as a politically and historically produced discourse,[4] instead of an essential characteristic of a static culture, I also examine how the large-scale societal changes triggered by globalization —such as the expansion of service economy, gender equality reforms, feminist campaigns around women's bodily rights, and the circulation of neoliberal discourses about women's empowerment—altered the complex framework of emotional obligations women shouldered. I show that the political and economic processes prompted by globalization have led to the rearrangement of the corporeal realm, releasing gendered bodies from the regulatory powers of shame-honor discourse. Once a feminine virtue, embarrassment has become an undesired affective habit, a sign of incompetent traits for women workers in service economy. Likewise, practices of shaming—such as enforced virginity tests—were made illegal in the early 2000s following the gender equality reforms, eroding the legal basis of shame-honor discourse. When there is no prospect of shame, women feel free to explore new possibilities of feminine existence, cultivating, often unconsciously, affective habits and embodied manners in response to, and shaped by, emergent principles of autonomy and equality. It is against this context that the book re-genders the politics of right-wing populists, who are making louder and more frequent calls for authoritarian politics with the aim of countering women's agency.

The New Woman and Globalization: A Phenomenological Approach

One prominent feature of globalization in Turkey that has a political bearing on feminine embodiment is Kemalist ideology and its transformation in the post-1980 period. Kemalism (so called after Mustafa Kemal Atatürk) was an official state ideology dominant between 1923 and 1980, in which secularism, statism, and nationalism guided the operations of political, economic, and social institutions. Kemalism was in retreat from the 1990s onward after being unable to meet the political demands of the Kurdish national movement, political Islam, the European Union, and the economic pressures generated by neoliberal capitalist globalization. Scholars of Turkey link this ideological transformation to a broader "shift from state-centered to market-inspired modernity in Turkey" (Özyürek 2006, 18), which reconfigured state-imposed authoritarian secularism and modern nationalist social forms within the context of neoliberal capitalist globalization.

The New Woman provides a unique lens to understand this complex gendered transformation by highlighting emergent femininities in the global era that diverged from the authoritarian Kemalist modernization project. The significance of Kemalism for the New Woman lies in the complex implication it holds as an ideology that joins feminine embodiment and subjectivity with nationalist modernity, which are often defined to be in opposition to Islam and so-called tradition. A focus on the New Woman reveals that Kemalist ideology in the global era, while not entirely powerless, is stripped of familiar top-down ways of governing the terms of gender. It brings the New Woman into a closer engagement with workings of neoliberal global capitalism, the politics of gender equality, and feminism in Turkey. By attending to feminine embodiment, it is possible to identify emerging bodily modes of being feminine in which women are no longer required to project the values and codes associated with the Kemalist state's gender scripts. A study of the New Woman in the global era also brings into focus affective practices that take place in everyday spaces of neoliberal global capitalism, as well as those embodied political interventions into the neoconservative gender order that the AKP government wants to impose. Studying the New Woman offers insights into the new gendered practices of market-driven modernity from below that are shaping up in urban Turkey today.

In the age of globalization, the New Woman resists fixed and static formulations and is actually plural: the almost century-long socio-political transformations in the country, and the last forty years of globalization in particular, enabled not one but many New Women to emerge from different segments of the society and to find their place and position within the hierarchies of the social life. Some New Women are secular women with cultural capital who occupy the higher echelons of the labor market and hold managerial positions in international companies. Others are pious women navigating the politically charged secular/pious division in Turkey, subverting and at times challenging the prevailing cultural frameworks imposed on them. And yet others are New Women who actively confront the gendered status quo through political activism, art, and alternative lifestyles.

The main focus of this book is the New Women from the popular classes who are not sponsored by the nation-state but operate within the framework created by the capitalist market and the larger forces of globalization. Often without a college degree, these young women are likely to find themselves employed in the new service sectors generated by the burgeoning urban capitalist economy. Attuned to a changing world of work, everyday life, and selfhood shaped by global capitalist restructuring—a world marked by changing conventions of feminine respectability and modesty—these women come to develop culturally and historically specific bodily orientations. These globalist features are contrasted against the more guarded, watchful, tense, and cautious modalities that have long characterized women's embodied ways of being in the world in Turkey. My account also reveals how these new corporeal ways of being and feeling, bodily habits, and emotional capacities became politically charged during the turn from neoliberal globalization to populist authoritarianism and were eventually expressed in performative violence incited by right-wing populist politics through vigilante attacks that took place between September 2016 and July 2018.

The embodiment of the New Woman is imbricated with distinct cultural discourses and anchored in this historical moment of globalization. Two remarkable transformations of the late twentieth century are inextricably linked with particularities of the embodiment of the New Woman and the historically specific ways her body attunes to the world: the restructuring of the Turkish legal system, by which gender equality became entrenched in Turkey's legal framework, and the rise of an urban economy dominated by services rather than industrial production, which ushered in a new era of women's paid work. Gender equality reforms facilitated the erosion of the legal basis of shame-honor discourse, while the expansion of the service economy as part of global capitalism created new employment opportunities for New Women, especially for those in the working classes. In interactive service work settings, women, as part of their jobs, immerse themselves in what Goffman (1983) describes as an interaction order. The emotional experiences, moods, affective encounters, bodily habits, and mundane habitual routines that produced a new interaction order at work in the service economy were tangibly connected with new embodied and affective modalities of being feminine that characterize the New Woman. In this era of globalization, there is still a strong relation between politics, government, and the New Woman. The relation, however, is deeply strained—the national government orchestrates heavy pressure from above, with right-wing political parties stirring hostilities against the New Woman.

The line of analysis that I develop in this book revitalizes the scholarship on globalization and gender, suggesting a new direction for the study of "gender and globalization in uncertain times" (Salzinger 2016, 439). The frameworks that inform gender and globalization scholarship have so far been predominantly economic, social, political, and cultural.

And yet, there are other phenomenological, affective, and corporeal processes that are salient to the analyses of globalization. Of particular importance here is the term openness. A buzzword and much-vaunted feature of globalization, openness frequently figures in scholarly accounts and has been neatly equated with trade openness. Although critical accounts of the complex interactions between trade openness and gender have been presented, these accounts tend to shortchange the phenomenological significance of openness. By integrating a phenomenological understanding of corporeal openness, it is possible to offer an analysis that includes more fully embodiment and emotions in accounting for the ways gender takes on political and economic significance in different phases of globalization. I posit that a phenomenological understanding of corporeal openness, which undergirds the notions of body and agency, provides a productive entry point to consider the political-ontological bind that the New Woman grapples with within the global era.

Corporeal openness calls up a perspective that emphasizes contingency, uncertainty, and ambiguity for the body that inescapably dwells in the world (Goffman 1983; Gatens 2003; Butler 2004; Ricoeur 2007; Throop 2018). "The human body," as Moira Gatens argued, "is radically open to its surrounding and can be composed, recomposed and decomposed by other bodies" (Gatens 2003, 110). This vision of corporeal openness pivots not just on the body's capacities but also on its vulnerability and precarity. The body's contradictory status—fostering bodily capacities, on the one hand, and invoking vulnerabilities on the other—affects the self in profound ways. It is by virtue of inhabiting a body that we are simultaneously open to people and places, as well as to violence, attack, and hostility. Embodiment, in this sense, generates a catalogue of possibilities in which the self is open to the other and able to engage with the world, to build relationships and create attachments while simultaneously exposing itself to harm. I present an ethnographic account of the new bodily modalities of being feminine in urban Turkey during the global capitalist restructuring by locating agency in the everydayness of bodily experience. I examine not only the gendered dynamics of embarrassment, but also different facets of corporeal openness that inform the New Woman's affective habits and embodied capacities, as well as the violation and hostility she experiences. This account makes space for the ambivalence, contradiction, and complexity that the forces of globalization generate.

All of these affective and embodied attributes that the New Woman communicates are gathered up in what I call an "orientation towards openness." The openness here denotes a receptivity and a manner of engaging with the world and others—without inhibitions or reserve—that are a hopeful and affirmative mode of living. When a New Woman dissents, threatening the rulings party's desired neoconservative social order, she does so by bringing her distinctive embodied orientations to the resistance, advancing her orientation toward openness in the context of protest and inventing what I call a politics of embodied openness. Yet, at the same time, openness refers to the embodied vulnerability that opens the New Woman to various forms of violence, a process heightened by the shift from the liberal-democratic moment to right-wing authoritarian populism. This highlights the political-ontological bind in which the New Woman struggles in the global era: on the one hand, her new emotional and interactive capacities and orientations allow the New Women to open up to the world in new ways; on the other hand, her bodily modes of being, which are morally devalued by the right-wing populist moment, make her body susceptible to malicious violations.

Right-Wing Populism in the Global Era: The AKP Rule, Emotions, and Male Violence

Scholars have long reckoned with the bodily dimensions of politics and contended that politics often also entails body politics. Described as Merleau-Ponty's "sociological heir" (Bourdieu and Wacquant 1992, 20), Bourdieu taught us to see class politics simultaneously as body politics. His notion of habitus asks us to consider bodily processes, appearance, dress, bodily posture, glance, gait, handshake, and eye contact as embodied dimensions of power relations in class-based societies. These hierarchies of class often, if not always, interact with those of race, ethnicity, and gender. If, by looking at the body, we can understand our place in the social hierarchy, then by the same logic we can trace shifts in class and gender hierarchies by identifying changes in the body. In this context, I pay close attention to the changes in women's embodied capacities—such as emotions, comportment, posture, elocution, values, and interaction patterns—to illuminate a pivotal moment of change in the established hierarchies of gender and class in Turkey, communicated by the everyday bodily ways of being the New Woman in the global era.

Capitalist globalization in Turkey was initiated and managed by the AKP government that came to power in 2002. In its first term, the AKP government—formed by a group of conservative politicians who abandoned the agenda of political Islam—successfully manufactured consent at both the national and international levels for its liberal reform initiatives. The party readily took up the globalization project, strongly advocating for economic liberalism and political liberalism, by enacting a series of democratization reforms to ensure Turkey's accession to the European Union. The AKP government availed itself of the economic opportunities that globalization offered, which made the Sunni bourgeoisie—the main supporter of the AKP—richer and stronger. The democratization reforms, on the other hand, visibly empowered more radical sections of the political opposition, including the Kurdish movement, the left, and feminists, all the while limiting the power of the AKP government. The party's chance to tighten its grip on power emerged with the national elections of 2007. Following its election success that year, which secured the AKP a second term in power, the government maneuvered away from both democracy and secularism and sought ways to circumvent the legal order that limited the use of coercion and violence. As this book demonstrates, inseparable from the AKP's authoritarian project was the reawakening of traditional sources of authority, especially through shame-honor discourse and the gender justice paradigm. These discursive practices enabled the AKP to venture into an ambitious authoritarian project, which exacerbated women's embodied vulnerability. Party officials joined the moral cause, publicly lamenting the loss of feminine modesty on the one hand and adulating the feeling of embarrassment on the other. In 2014, Bülent Arınç, then deputy prime minister, expressed these sentiments in one of his public speeches: "The feeling of shame is important. Shame is beautiful," he said. "It suits ladies more beautifully. Where have all the girls gone? Those girls who were the symbols of modesty and symbols of chastity; those who blushed when [one] looked at their faces, lowering their heads and averting their gaze" (Milliyet 2014).

By looking at feminized bodies from the global era forward to the populist moment, I unveil the one missing piece in scholarly analysis—the link between right-wing politics and gender in the current populist moment. Research in the field of gender and right-wing populism continues to grow, but the studies tend to neglect affective and embodied aspects of gender. By presenting an analysis that brings women's bodies to the fore, I offer a theoretical anchor to uncover the link between gendered embodiment and right-wing politics in the global era. I provide a phenomenological account of the New Women's disorientations by paying close attention to how women's bodies are subjected to physical harm and many other violations. I also delineate women's individual and collective actions—speaking up, wearing certain pieces of clothing, using gender slurs subversively for self-identification, reading books next to police barricades, gazing at men, and lounging at public parks with women, along with street demonstrations and marches. By highlighting the political responses in today's Turkey that women who are not invested in embarrassment attract, I expose the dark underbelly of the cultural politics of embarrassment implicated in the government's moral project of promoting the modest feminine self in a country that is turning away from democracy.

The focus is Turkey, but the findings from this study help shed light on an unexpected political phenomenon that affects global society today: the resurgence of women's struggles across the world. The recent rise of women's political movements seems to have taken all by surprise, even feminists themselves, one of whom has noted: "Of all the opposition movements to have erupted since 2008, the rebirth of a militant feminism is perhaps the most surprising" (Watkins 2018, 5). While women in the United States stand up to "presidential misogyny" (Levine 2017), in Poland they confront the far-right government's push for ever-tighter laws concerning abortion, and in Chile they adamantly fight against rape and sexual assault. By addressing the distinct ways women's bodies and emotions are implicated in politics, posing a challenge to authoritarian political projects, I ultimately show that it is New Women's novel ways of relating to men, to their own bodies, and to the world—more so than their acts of resistance—that expose the failure of populist rule in the global era.

Map of the Book

This book explores Turkey's last decade as it was experienced and in some ways challenged by the New Woman. I follow the New Woman to work, to meetings with friends, and to demonstrations and street marches in order to account for her (changing) relationship to the state, to the market, to men, and to politics in the global era. Since my inquiry is heavily informed by phenomenology, I emphasize the body and emotions as my focal points. The book's narrative also provides an understanding on the one hand of the historical transformations that helped the New Woman thrive and on the other hand of the volatile political landscape that has made her life in Turkey difficult.

Chapter 1, "The New Woman Feeling Her Way in Turkey," presents snapshots from the everyday life of the New Woman: at home on her day off, at work on the sales floor, on a minibus confronting "vigilante man," and at a café chatting about her life plans. By drawing on key studies about shame in feminist phenomenology scholarship, it depicts the New Woman's embodied and affective orientations, which are constitutive of her distinctive agency. It also introduces the cultural politics of embarrassment, which is tied to its traditional mooring in shame-honor discourse, as well as the political debates that the feeling of embarrassment generated about the New Woman in Turkey.

In the second chapter, "Origins of the New Woman: The Cultural Politics of Embarrassment and Its Changing Legal Status in Turkey," I consider the changing influence of shame-honor discourse during the twentieth century. I first show that shame-honor was not only a cultural discourse but one that also made its way into legal structures with the foundation of the Turkish Republic in 1923. I then explore how its legal status was undone following the large-scale processes of urbanization, industrialization, and feminist mobilization, which had multiple effects on women across religious, class, and generational lines.

The third chapter, "The New Woman at Work: Global Capitalism and the Gendered World of the Service Economy," takes readers into the most common workspace of the New Woman, the sales floor. It delves into the minutiae of everyday life on the sales floor to unpack gendered dynamics of the shift from manufacturing to services, from male to female, and from muscle power to affective capacities. It discusses the ways the service economy both sustains and capitalizes on the New Woman's bodily being by focusing on the bodily practices and emotions that inform hiring practices, labor process, workers' bodily modes of being, and immaterial labor—a form of labor that produces an intangible commodity such as communication or information—on the sales floor.

In the fourth chapter, "Tables Turning against the New Woman: The Rise of Moralist Politics," I discuss the growing gendered, moral, and political tensions between the AKP government and the New Woman in the aftermath of the party's election victory in 2007. I examine the moral politics that the AKP government implemented, identifying the differential impact it had on the New Woman and those groups of women that the AKP negotiated with. I illustrate how the revival of shame-honor discourse served as an anchor both for moral politics and the AKP's bid for authoritarian rule.

The fifth chapter, "The New Woman in the Gezi Uprising: A New Political Actor or a Violable Subject?", investigates the escalation of conflict between the New Woman and the AKP government, which was epitomized in the Gezi uprising in 2013. The chapter advances the argument that the New Woman's embodied capacities, bodily gestures, orientations and disorientations, and feelings lent substance to the political demands women made during the uprising. It also highlights how the AKP's moral politics, in response to the Gezi uprising, shifted—a change that set the stage for the resurgence of vigilante violence against women.

In the sixth chapter, "The New Woman against the Vigilante Man: Violence, Orientations, and Disorientations," I focus on vigilante violence incidents that broke out in large cities in Turkey. By locating vigilantism in the larger dynamics of AKP's gender politics, I show that it functions as the latest gendered means of violation against the New Woman in Turkey. I discuss the specific ways women's bodies were subjected to vigilante violence along with the disorienting effects of performative violence on women. I also illustrate how disorientations that feminine bodies experienced became a departure point for women, at both the individual and collective level, to politically mobilize against violence, hostility, and AKP rule.

The conclusion and epilogue, "The New Woman and Feminism in Uncertain Times," offers a summary and reflection on the ways the analysis of the New Woman advances contemporary feminist thinking and politics. It unwraps the vision of a feminist dream embedded in the New Woman's corporeal experiences, her feelings, orientations, embodied modes of being, and modes of acting: a feminist dream of a society in which women are able to fully explore what embodied openness offers to women, without opening their bodies to further harm and violations.

Methodological and Autobiographical Reflections

The book draws on two years of research conducted during two separate fieldworks in Turkey. Let me begin by delineating the outlines of the recent one. In 2017, I began to examine the resurgence of vigilante violence against women and its gendered dynamics. Using data on vigilantism provided by women's organizations, media reports, court cases, and interviews with four feminist activists, three lawyers, and ten New Women, I investigated the legal and political dynamics of vigilantism, connecting them to the everyday embodied experiences of New Women who navigated a social environment in which they were likely to encounter a range of violations. In addition, I participated in demonstrations and public forums in the city of Ankara during the summer of 2017, organized by women's groups against the rise of vigilante violence. I reached out to participants through my personal and professional connections. Initially, I contacted a member of the Human Rights Joint Platform (IHOP) in Ankara, who put me in touch with lawyers with expertise in the area of vigilantism in the Turkish legal framework. I began to discuss my research with young women I met in different contexts, including university students, service workers, and women's rights activists, some of whom later participated in my research. At the time, I was living in Ankara, the capital city, and working at Ankara University as an assistant professor in the Gender Studies Division in the Faculty of Political Science at Cebeci Campus, which enabled me to connect easily with potential participants. My embodied experiences as a feminist researcher and faculty member on campus amid the mounting efforts of the AKP government to suppress campus life have affected the way I interpreted and analyzed that data. In particular, the brutal repression of faculty and students by the political regime at Cebeci Campus that I witnessed informed my approach to thinking and writing about hostility and violence under the AKP government's authoritarian rule.

Historically renowned for its radicalism, Cebeci Campus has been a vibrant setting for both critical thinking and protest. The types of academic freedoms that students and faculty took for granted there were greater and more varied than those enjoyed at most of the other universities in Turkey. It is, for instance, a long-standing campus tradition to criticize the political status quo openly and to teach political subjects that are deemed taboo by the Turkish state. On any given day on campus, one could overhear lively conversations on the Kurdish question or the transformative power of queer feminism in Turkey, as well as excited speeches that exposed the lies of the Turkish state. By contemporary standards of the academy, the campus has also been relatively insulated from the neoliberal metrics of achievement that have become dominant in Turkey's higher education environment over the last decades. The result is a diverse and rich course catalogue involving a wide array of topics—including the Armenian and Kurdish issues, LGBTI+ movements and queer theory, global Black movements, psychoanalysis and feminism, and human rights, that put forth radical critiques of the society—which excite both students and the faculty. The legacy of dissent and the experimentation with critical thinking at Cebeci Campus have also contributed to the liberatory potentials of wider left-wing politics in Turkey.

However, at the time of my research Cebeci Campus was undergoing one of the most turbulent periods in its history. Following the appointment of a pro-government rector in 2012, the pressures on students and professors who were known for their left-wing, feminist, queer, pro-Kurdish sensibilities reached much higher levels than previously experienced. The university administration, colluding with the government, began to open disciplinary investigations against progressive faculty and students. In January 2016, a number of faculty at Cebeci Campus signed a Peace Declaration titled "We Will Not Be Party to This Crime!", which strongly condemned the AKP government's resumption of military operations in Kurdish cities in 2015. It was around this time that pictures of the faculty appeared repeatedly on the front pages of ultra-nationalist pro-government newspapers with epithets such as "enemies of Turkishness and Islam", "sodomy lover", "whore", "Armenian lover", "certified pervert", "terrorist", and "bastard." Finally, between September 2016 and February 2017, approximately seventy academics from Cebeci Campus alone and a total of a hundred academics from Ankara University were permanently laid off from their positions by a series of state of emergency decrees that the AKP government implemented after declaring a state of emergency in the wake of the failed coup attempt in July 2016. Almost all of the faculty dismissed by the state of emergency decrees were those who had signed the Peace Declaration in January 2016.

Between 2015 and 2017, the mundane rhythm of campus life became ruptured by the domineering presence of police cars and riot control vehicles: there were always a few **TOMAs** (Mass Incident Intervention Vehicles) parked by the campus gate, and police officers, as well as riot police units deployed outside the campus became a routine sight. I remember several times when the riot police attacked the campus, occasionally during my teaching hours. I would peek out into the hall and see the building swarming with the riot police in their anti-riot

A woman student undaunted by the attack of a police dog stares unflinchingly into the eyes of police at Cebeci Campus. Ankara, 2017 (Photo by Tamer Arda Erşin).

suits—vests, helmets, gas masks—firing their tear gas guns and chasing down students. Shaken by the screams and shouts, we would remain inside the classroom and wait it out, with windows wide open to mitigate the effects of tear gas hanging in the air.

While Cebeci Campus became a site of police intervention, the larger city was hardly sheltered from violence. In 2015 and 2016 explosions ripped through the urban landscape, with three deadly bombings killing 172 people and leaving several hundred wounded. As for the residents of Ankara, anxiety, fear, discontent, and disorientation were on the rise as the city weathered the unsettling episodes of violence. All of these feelings were part of my life world too, which led me to consider research methods that collapse the distance between historical structures, politics, and personal experiences. The phenomenological method, which is situated in personal experience and places a particular emphasis on embodied and emotional dynamics, seemed a good fit for my research. After all, with the escalation of violence in Ankara, I had an inkling of what it means to be robbed of one's familiar ways of being in the world and the comfort of inhabiting one's own body. I, like many others, lost my sense of personal safety and certainty, not knowing how to move further. Disorientation, more than a mere bodily feeling, evolved into an everyday mode of being in the world.

While I continued my fieldwork—teasing out the social, institutional, and political processes that tie in with vigilantism as well as the moralist discourses that target New Women in today's Turkey—I realized that there were striking similarities between the women who were at increasing risk of becoming victims of moralist vigilantism and the young women employed in the service economy that I had studied between 2009 and 2011 for my doctoral dissertation. Both groups of women were young, mostly in their twenties and thirties, and displayed the same affective and embodied orientations, which delineated the distinguishing characteristics of the New Woman: the absence of embarrassment, and openness to the world and others. I contacted two of my former informants to see if they, too, had been affected by the surge of hostility against women. These interviews confirmed my impression. To better illustrate the New Woman's embodied and emotional modes of being, which served as a pretext for the new vigilante attacks, I decided to draw from my PhD fieldwork that explored the gendered expectations and cultural norms of embodiment in Turkey's expanding service economy during global capitalist restructuring. My PhD fieldwork—fifteen months of field research on saleswomen employed in the new consumption venues between 2009 and 2011—combined in-depth interviews and an ethnographic participant observation study I carried out at a large supermarket in Istanbul. My in-depth interviews with thirty-five saleswomen and four human resource employees offered a range of data about the embodied, affective, and interactional capacities female service workers are expected to possess as well as the gender dynamics of the service economy. And my ethnographic observation study at an Istanbul supermarket where I worked as a cashier between May and August 2011 generated firsthand experience of the working-class New Woman's bodily modes of being and acting in service settings, consumption sites, and the wider urban landscape. During these months, I was not only engaged in the embodied and interactive routines that women workers experienced on the sales floor, but I was also immersed in the everyday life of New Women, learning much about their daily routines, patterns of leisure, romance, and sociability, and their aspirations and life plans. I was able to gain acceptance and fitted in with my female coworkers as we shared similar embodied and affective orientations and were in a similar age group. My coworkers often treated me like a friend, answered my questions without reservations, introduced me to their friends, and invited me to join their social gatherings. On the salesfloor, when I encountered a work-related problem, had difficult interactions with demanding customers, or was scolded by management, there were always coworkers who helped out or gave some word of encouragement that brightened my mood. When I revealed my identity as a PhD student, I think it gave me an added credibility on the salesfloor, as my coworkers valued education highly. Throughout the research and in the book, I used pseudonyms for the participants and the settings to ensure anonymity.

Ethnographic work has a collaborative dimension. "The point of ethnography," writes Anna L. Tsing in describing her own fieldwork, "is to learn how to think about a situation together with one's informants; research categories develop with the research, not before it" (Tsing 2015, ix). Throughout my research I tried to learn how to think about labor, gender, and the body with my informants; for instance, the concept of shame emerged as a pivotal research category during the fieldwork, not prior to it. As my relationship with my key informants from service settings evolved into enriching friendships in the decade after concluding my fieldwork, their everyday lived experiences continued to inform how I think about another important situation that large groups of women in Turkey find themselves in: the vagaries of inhabiting a body in a period when the entangled forces of neoliberal global capitalism and authoritarianism pose unpredictable consequences for feminine embodiment.

Having been born and raised in Turkey, I have extensive familiarity with urban women's bodily movements, stances, manners, dispositions, and postures, which allowed for observations that extended beyond the temporal frameworks of the research projects I carried out. Over the last two decades or so, I have had the opportunity to observe subtle but potent changes in the way women carry themselves in everyday life in urban contexts. In the early 2000s, when I became interested in the topics of gender, body, and work as a young feminist graduate student, it was hard to miss the new bodily orientations, particularly visible in the ways younger women inhabited the urban space. It remained a question for me, however, whether these new bodily movements, stances, and manners were only available to middle-class women with cultural capital. In 2006, when I conducted a research project on the global informal economy that focused on women industrial homeworkers in Istanbul, I observed that young working-class women were not exceptions but part of a younger generation of women who had new corporeal ways of being and feeling—their bodily habits, emotions, and corporeal tendencies displaying the emergent dimensions of the embodied life in Turkey under globalization. I saw these subtle but significant changes in feminine embodiment also in connection with feminism, which rapidly expanded its influence in Turkey within the same time span of some twenty years. When I started out as a college student in the second half of the 1990s and become loosely involved in feminist circles in Istanbul, feminism was having its moment of institutionalization in Turkey (Bora and Günal 2002). The vibrant street activism that feminist groups created in the1980s receded, but some ideas espoused by feminists at that time made their way into mainstream institutions in the 1990s. Feminism picked up momentum from the 2000s onward, ever more actively shaping the political landscape, as well as the workings of institutions in Turkey. It reoriented the class, ethnic, and gender politics of various groups, which I explain in more detail in the following chapters. Along the way, feminism too has changed: it may now seem almost intuitive to consider feminism in Turkey in terms of feminism(s) and varied feminist agendas instead of a homogenous feminist movement.

In the chapters that follow, I focus on the New Woman, seeking to understand how her affective encounters, bodily habits, and mundane habitual routines have assumed a new phenomenological and political significance under global capitalist restructuring. Focusing on these moments, we get an understanding of how the New Woman's desires for financial autonomy and bodily autonomy are inseparable and that AKP's authoritarian politics accommodates neither: the New Woman opens up to the world, discovering new employment opportunities and forming new habits of sociability and spending along with new everyday bodily orientations, all the while facing new precarity and violability aroused by the politics of right-wing masculinist populism.

Endnotes

1. The presence of and the discussions around the New Woman is by no means limited to the history of the Turkish Republic. The image of the New Woman can be traced back to the *Tanzimat* (Reorganization) Era (1839–1876) in the Ottoman Empire. For a discussion of the link between political reforms during *Tanzimat* and the promotion of the principle of equality and the New Woman, see Elaman-Garner (2013) and Cakir (2018). The works of Lerna Ekmekçioglu (2016) and Victoria Rowe (2003) provide detailed accounts of

how the idea of the New Woman relates to Armenian womanhood in the late Ottoman Empire and early Republican period.

2. An emphasis on evaluative dimensions of emotions opened up new vistas in anthropological thinking, setting the agenda for what we now know as the anthropology of emotions. For instance, in her seminal *Unnatural Emotions*, Catherine Lutz (1998) gestured toward the link between orientations and emotions, arguing that emotions hold "value as a way of orienting us toward things that matter rather than things that simply make sense" (Lutz 1998, 5). Lutz did not provide an analysis of orientations but rather emphasized the capacity of emotions to grant a sense of directedness to the self. Emotions, for Lutz, are not something that individuals have. Rather, they are "culturally defined, socially enacted, and personally articulated" (5) and intermediate the self, meaning-making, and collective social forms. They matter not for what they are but for the fact that they are always of something or about something, that is, involving an element of intentionality. Lutz's work wrested emotions out of the dominant psychological frameworks of the day, which separated thoughts and appraisals from emotions. However, her account does not necessarily center on the embodied understanding of emotions.

3. A phenomenological understanding of orientations also entails a non-reified approach to feminine modesty, a notion that has long been fraught with questions of normativity. By recasting feminine modesty in terms of orientations, I contribute to the recent theoretical efforts to de-center the normative understandings of feminine modesty. Feminist and antiracist phenomenology reveal the complex links among corporality, culture, power, and history—resituating feminine modesty in wider, critical debates about embodiment, affect, bodily modes of being, attitudes, gestures, and habits. Such an approach not only deflects normative assertions embedded in the prevailing accounts of feminine modesty, but also challenges the deeply entrenched assumptions that undergird thinking about women's agency, power, and social hierarchies.

4. Ayse Parla (2020) also advocates an understanding of honor as a discursive formation that relates to social experiences and institutional discourses in Turkey.

CHAPTER 1

The New Woman Feeling Her Way in Turkey

On a hot, humid August night in 2017, Nesrin and I were idly lying on couches in her living room chit-chatting, our conversation interspersed with occasional snorts of laughter and sleepy yawns. We had been chatting on and off since late morning, when I stepped into her tiny apartment on the ground floor of a newly constructed building located on the periphery of Istanbul. It took me two hours to get there from Taksim, the heart of the city. Because it had been a few years since we last saw each other, we had a lot of catching up to do. We talked in the kitchen as she prepared a big breakfast, something she liked to do on her days off, and continued talking in the sunlit living room, zapping through TV channels late into the afternoon. When she went back to the kitchen that evening to make a chocolate cake for us, I tagged along for more chatting. Early that night, her sister, who recently married her second husband, dropped by. While nibbling on sunflower seeds she brought along, the three of us talked about her life, her husband, the baby she was expecting, and the problems she was having at work, which included very long hours and difficult tasks. By midnight, however, quiet had descended on the city, not even a passing car could be heard from the street, and it was just me and Nesrin at home, each of us lazily lounging on two matching sofas that faced each other across a cream-colored rug. We were feeling exhausted by the stifling heat and all the talking but, just when we were about to phase-out, she said something about her boyfriend, and we were in a serious conversation again. "We are very different, you know," she mused. "I'm a high school dropout, got my diploma later on from a distance learning high school program, while he went to college instead of getting a job, because he came from a well-off family. And never before in his life had it occurred to him to get a passport and go abroad! If I were him, if I had the money and time he had, I would travel all over the world." If it had not been for Nesrin's encouragement, her boyfriend would not have applied for a passport and traveled to Germany with Nesrin. "Left on his own," she continued, "he would hang out with his male gang, drive around the city and fritter the day away at cafes. Now, he likes telling his friends that I have changed his life." She shrugged slightly; a movement barely detectable in her broad shoulders. I eyed her and asked, "Some of your close friends feel the same way about their boyfriends, right?" She nodded and continued, "Take Dila. Her fiancé is a nice guy, but all he does is keep up with her. Dila is the one who wants to travel, who wants to go to movies or visit museums and explore new things. "It is nice that he plays along with her wishes"—she paused for a moment to

Nesrin's living room. Istanbul (Photo by author).

sit up on the sofa— "but it is not in him. He is not genuinely interested in these things; he just adapts to her. In fact, all he wants is to go home and lie down on the sofa. Do you know why he is always up for going to movies?" she asked, casting a mischievous glance my way, smiling wryly. "Because he can sleep there!" A pensive look settled on her face. "I make an effort to understand him. He is under a lot of stress at work and feels tired at the end of the day, but Dila works hard, too. It is just that they are different."

The divergence between women and men was something I had talked about with Nesrin several times before. When I first met her in 2011 during my PhD fieldwork on saleswomen in Istanbul, she told me almost the same thing: "Women are way ahead of men, Esra, especially when it comes to open-mindedness." Back then, she was married and working as a saleswoman at a big supermarket, all the while feeling weighed down by her parents-in-law, who watched her closely. Now she was divorced, feeling a lot freer, still employed— this time at a big international clothing store as a saleswoman—with a boyfriend and an apartment of her own. A hard-working woman who had first started working as a child at textile workshops during summer breaks, Nesrin made her way into sales work after earning a high school diploma. Now in her early thirties, she was toiling to pay the mortgage on her apartment and had just enrolled in a secretarial and office management program at a university in Istanbul. Her aspirations, curiosity, and diligence were not matched by any of the men around her.

Nesrin, the central character in this book, is the quintessential working-class New Woman, whose embodied orientations and affective habits this chapter fleshes out by examining the quotidian life of work, intimacy, friendship, and hostility that Nesrin, along with other New Women I myself have met, and routinely experienced during my research. Drawing on insights offered by feminist phenomenology, the chapter presents a portrayal of the contemporary New Woman, a gendered figure who emerges at the intersection of overlapping and, at times, opposing forces: forces of embarrassment, forces of the body, forces of openness, and forces of labor. All these forces—which are generated and conveyed by bodies—mediate the emergence of new practices of femininity and new modes of gendered interactions, destabilizing the predominant configurations of power constituted by class, gender, and sexuality.

Forces of Embarrassment

A self-conscious emotion closely related to one's self-image, embarrassment describes an affective scenario in which a person feels flustered and cannot make herself feel comfortable or relaxed around others. Within the framework of shame-honor, embarrassment holds an elevated status, indicating the moral status of the woman, who is encouraged to display feelings of embarrassment and shyness instead of concealing them. Embarrassment has, since before the founding of the Turkish Republic, wielded great power: it was the enunciative site for enacting modest femininity. Its medium has always been the body—a woman's gaze and glance, gait and posture, touch and handshake, smile and voice—all have been vastly significant for the maintenance of feminine modesty. The sway of embarrassment, moreover, reached well beyond the everyday bodily modes of being feminine. When gender equality became the hallmark of the newly founded Turkish Republic in 1923, it was the feeling of embarrassment (or lack thereof) that fanned the flames of discontent among conservatives who opposed the modernization project the Republican elites had embarked upon. The extensive gender equality reforms introduced by the Republicans drew a harsh reaction from Islamists, conservative nationalist thinkers, and politicians alike, who framed the Republican project of "women's emancipation" as "the prostitution-ization of women" (Bora 2005, 252). For nationalist conservatives who harkened back to an imaginary golden age, embarrassment conjured up a particular vision of gender. Osman Yüksel Serdengeçti (1949), a prominent thinker of the nationalist-religious right, delineated this gender order mainly by drawing on embarrassment:

> I long for a world, though not for the kind in which women get a rosy hint of blush on the cheeks from outside, by applying make-up on. In the world I long for, women blush from inside when looked at, a blushing stirred by a beautiful, humble shame, which defines girlhood and real womanhood. Women would not hang out on the streets shamelessly, would not mess with men. In the world I long for, woman, whom so-called revolutionaries saved from behind the bars in order to display in a cage on the street, would not be pressured to be an instrument of pleasures, whereby people satisfy their animalistic lust, the cheapest commodity copiously available on the market. (. . .) Woman would not leave the orbit of her home. (Serdengeçti [1949] 1992, 147)

In the ideal society envisaged by the nationalist conservatives, embarrassment is systematically built into the gendered organization of that society. This vision has also drawn a lot of strength from religion in Turkey, where the majority are Sunni Muslims. Islam attaches great value to shyness or embarrassment, with pious women enacting these emotions through facial expressions, bodily comportment, and patterns of interaction, speech, and dress codes. The demure comportment, the sexual propriety, limited and controlled interactions between unrelated men and women in public, a dressing style that conceals body curves, hair, and sometimes the face; all announce women's modesty (Abu-Lughod 2005; Mahmood 2005). Accordingly, great care has been taken in Turkey to inculcate norms and codes of modest demeanor in girls from a young age. Families and the community often watch the way girls dress, their bodily comportment, and interactions with others. This watchfulness over women's modesty, however, is not just a sign of religious observance, but also a requirement of the cultural politics of embarrassment, which is firmly rooted in shame-honor discourse. Religious and nonreligious mores and norms folded together in this discourse, designating a set of emotional and embodied obligations women should adhere to in Turkey.

A discourse that emphasizes the centrality of sexual desire to all human contact and feeling, shame-honor functions as an affective instrument of discipline. It regulates bodies and touch, face-to-face interactions and glances between men and women, and modes of self-fashioning primarily through self-conscious emotions. These two heavily gendered emotions also denote a system of gender stratification, with honor linked to men's status and shame to women's status in the web of social hierarchy. Shame and honor, moreover, serve as affective sources of self-worth for both genders: man's quest for self-worth is attached to honor while woman's is to shame. Man accumulates self-worth through his honorable deeds and actions in the world, whereas woman maintains her self-worth by avoiding shame and shameful situations and by remaining sexually chaste. In order not to slip down in the social hierarchy, she avoids shame at all costs. Shame also delivers the punishment for a woman who commits moral transgression, shattering her self-worth. Shame and honor are also relational in that a man derives honor via the reputation of women in his family (his daughter and wife), so if the woman falls out of line, her transgression imperils the honor of the man.

When taken as constitutive emotions of shame-honor discourse, both embarrassment and shame entail more than transitory affective states. Instead, they are primary feelings, from which the feminine experience of body and of the world issue. To use an example from Sandra Bartky's (1990) phenomenology, feminine shame, like the atmosphere surrounding the world, envelopes women's embodied existence. It is an affective force that women are attuned to, "not a discrete occurrence, but a perpetual attunement, the pervasive affective taste of a life" (Bartky 97). Barkty, together with Iris Marion Young (1980), opens a direction for thinking about a phenomenology of shame-honor discourse. In a male-dominated world, for instance, the woman's body, encumbered by the task of modesty, becomes a medium of embarrassment, while masculine ways of being in the world, even the most quotidian bodily practices such as "manspreading" (men sitting in places with legs wide apart) are deeply bound with the honor men have been bestowed with. How does a feminized body governed by shame take up space in the world? How exactly does the world appear to her?

For a woman whose body is governed by shame-honor discourse, the world does not appear like a place she can settle into effortlessly. Nor does she feel comfortable and confident in it. Instead, it seems like a place lurking with dangers, threatening her self-worth and bodily inviolability. There she could find herself in situations of moral transgression, for instance, inappropriately dressed or exposed in public. Her purity, the most valued and sacred feature of her femininity, is precarious and tenuous, and cannot be reinstated when tainted or insulted, so it must be watched vigilantly. With the prospect of punishment looming large over her, she is leery of the world and of others, and takes pains to steer clear of potential sources of moral transgression. In this environment, her body is not something that enables her access to the world; instead, it is a violable thing she needs to guard. In response to her body's socially constituted violability, she cultivates particular modes of being feminine. She grows reserved and reticent. Her orientation is guarded, tense, cautious, and diffident, reflecting a heightened self-consciousness.

It is this world of shame that the New Woman departs from. She forms new emotional habits away from shame. This does not mean that the New Woman never experiences feelings of shyness, embarrassment, or shame. Rather, it means that shame is not the primary force that governs her embodied existence, shaping her bodily comportment, economies of attention, bodily engagement with things, and interactions with people, as well as her self-image. Shame, for the New Woman, is an emotion with its force on the wane, too weak to dictate her sense of being. Now she feels comfortable in the world. She feels at ease.

Ease, according to Pierre Bourdieu, is indeed the opposite of embarrassment. It reveals itself in "a sort of indifference to the objectifying gaze of others which neutralizes its powers, presupposes the self-assurance which comes from the certainty of being able to objectify that objectification, appropriate that appropriation, of being capable of imposing the norms of apperception of one's own body" (Bourdieu 1984, 207–208). Ease is the feeling of those who navigate the world feeling comfortable in it. It is a feeling enjoyed by those who do not have to watch themselves closely to make sure their actions are in line with prescribed norms and codes.

In contrast, embarrassment—the bodily experience of unease and timidity—suggests a generic alienation and is constitutive of body-for-others. It is "the experience par excellence of the 'alienated body'" (Bourdieu 1984, 207), and ties in closely with class hierarchies. Of all the classes, embarrassment, Bourdieu thought, belongs most to the petit-bourgeoisie, characterizing the petit-bourgeoisie mode of being in the world:

> Although it is not a petit-bourgeois monopoly, the petit-bourgeois experience of the world starts out from timidity, the embarrassment of someone who is uneasy in his body and his language and who, instead of being 'as one with them' observes them from outside, through other people's eyes, watching, checking, correcting himself, and who, by this desperate attempts to reappropriate an alienated being-for-others exposes himself to appropriation, giving himself away as much by hyper-correction as by clumsiness. The timidity which, despite itself, realized the objectified body, which lets itself be trapped in the destiny proposed by collective perception and statement (nicknames etc.), is betrayed a body that is subject to the representation of others even in its passive unconscious reactions (one feels oneself blushing). (Bourdieu 1984, 207)

The New Woman in today's Turkey, irrespective of her class background, is comfortable in her body. She is not checking, watching, and correcting herself. This is not to suggest that the New Woman now has the world at her feet. Rather, the world appears to her as a place characterized by antagonism and threat along with opportunity and possibility.

The world is still filled with danger and hostility, but encountering these takes on a new meaning now. In the world the New Woman finds herself in, she might endure defeats, alienation, or indignities that lead to the experience of shame. No longer a permanent affective experience, however, shame becomes a discrete occurrence, a fleeting emotional state, something she is now allowed pass through like every man.

Forces of the Body

Discrete shame is a remarkable change that affects the New Woman's bodily forces. Now that the New Woman is disinvested in shame, her body regains strength that was previously not available to her. She can access the powers of her body and acquires a sense of "I can." She can, for instance, find inventive ways to counter the male gaze.[1] Selda, a twenty-one-year-old waitress working at a café in downtown Ankara, told me about one of the strategies she developed when tackling the intrusive gaze of male customers at the workplace:

> These four men sit together at a table. Every time I walk past the table, they stare at me and make it obvious. What is the reason? Why are you disturbing me? When I have to deal with men like these, I take their orders, treat them formally, and in the end inflate the table's bill. If they order tea, I serve them the most expensive tea. If they order two cups of tea, I serve them five cups. When they notice that I have given them the wrong order, I say, 'Oops, sorry, my bad,' like I'm not aware of it. Then they don't return the order because I act kindly. They pay the inflated bill, too. I couldn't care less what happens to these men. They cannot treat me this way. They deserve way worse than what I give them.

For the New Woman, the meaning attached to the male gaze has become obsolete. Once there was rather an uncomplicated relationship between the male gaze and feminine embarrassment (women blush and lower their gaze when looked at). When a woman lowered her eyes in response to the male gaze, it announced that she, as a woman, recognized her place in the gender hierarchy and acknowledged the authority of men.[2] Now, the male gaze no longer commands authority over the New Woman. She instead finds it aggressive, intrusive, and harassing. The male gaze might be menacing and hostile but in no way has legitimate authority over women that they acknowledge, let alone obey. Lale, a twenty-six-year-old saleswoman working at a cosmetic store in

Ankara, told me about the different types of male gaze, those evoking discomfort, she dealt with at the store:

> Men stare at us when we are inside the store working. It is easy to block out the gazes. Sometimes, however, their gazes become fairly creepy. It is before the New Year. A man who looks older than my father walks in and extends his hand after saying hello. I greet him. He looks at me, his glance is so disturbing. 'I want to get a present for my girlfriend,' he says, 'any suggestions?' I keep my distance from him and show him the products. He keeps moving close to me. I keep moving away from him. That was truly unpleasant.

The New Woman is nevertheless less willing to endure male hostility. Silence, after all, is not a survival strategy for her. At times, when feeling scared, she might retreat into silence, although it is possible for her to fight back as well. This was what Asena Melisa Sağlam, a university student, did when an Istanbul man, Ercan Kızılateş, assaulted her for an alleged moral transgression. The man admonished Asena for wearing shorts on a minibus during the month of Ramadan in 2017, and reprimanded her, "it is not proper for you to dress up like this on a public vehicle. There are manners and modesty you should follow," he said. When Asena told him to not to look at her if he felt uncomfortable, the man promptly rose to his feet and slapped her. Then, something happened, something that totally appalled him: Asena fought back with full force. The attacker described, in his court statement, what Asena did as well as how he felt in that moment: "She came to her feet and started yelling at me 'Who are you to shove me?' she shouted. She pushed me. I thought, at that moment, she must be an athlete because she attacked me with great courage and fierceness" (Kızılateş vs. Sağlam 2017).

The man's shock at Asena's power to defend herself—his distress over Asena's command over her body—says something about the male attacker who encounters the New Woman's bodily forces. The man was startled most likely because he underestimated the bodily forces a woman could summon up. He was confounded by the strength the New Woman unleashed, pushing and shoving him around, squeezing his arm, or twisting it with force. He was taken aback by what the New Woman embodied, a woman bringing her whole body to a jarring physical task with spontaneity, without being timid or diffident. He was vexed, because the New Woman did not treat her own body as the repository of men's honor, and did not tolerate male surveillance. Instead of investing her psychic and bodily energies in watching herself, she marshaled them to fight the man who attacked her.

This brings us to probably the most pernicious aspect of shame-honor discourse; the foundational role it has played in the constitution of women as violable subjects. As gendered beings whose bodies are exclusively burdened with the task of avoiding shame, women are vulnerable to aggression from men if they transgress moral codes. It is in this sense that shame-honor discourse has long functioned as a gendered means of violation in Turkey, exacerbating women's embodied openness to violence and hostility, and turning women into violable subjects. The feeling of shame has a place in this context, too, eroding women's self-worth and marking their existence violable. A woman who commits a moral transgression is easily singled out as deserving of violence, violation, shaming, and humiliation.

Forces of Openness

Violability, on the other hand, is not just about violence but also about fractured embodied capacities, stunting the body's capacity to be open in particular. Once a woman's violability is kindled, her embodied capacity to be open to the world and to others—a precondition for communication, relationship, and transactions with the world—is severely thwarted. Shame as a feeling reinforces this fractured mode of being, since it, as Silvan Tomkins taught us, is often a limiting feeling. "Shame is the affect of indignity, of defeat, of transgression, and of alienation," writes Silvan Tomkins in his *Affect Imagery Consciousness III* (1991, 111). Not only does it inhibit interest and joy, but its affective power also stifles the ability to be open to the world in which one explores new possibilities for the self. When there is no prospect of shame to face, in contrast, one feels free to embrace one's openness and take chances.

In a world where woman's violability is mitigated, the New Woman can thrive, willing to explore what her openness entails without having to face the prospect of violation, and she can venture onward. Inasmuch as she feels on an equal footing with (male) others in the world, her gaze now meets the other, claiming mutuality, contact, and communication. She might look for passionate attachments, or else friends, exploring new forms of identification and forms of being feminine. This generates an everyday sensibility that is orientated toward interest, enjoyment, communication, and contact with others. As these transformations relate to global capitalist restructuring, everyday sensibilities also make the New Woman available for labor and market exchanges and engagements that have economic as well as cultural implications. If a husband, father, or boyfriend blocks her efforts, she does not yield easily. When the masculine desire to control women's lives and bodies takes more subtle and insidious forms, the New Woman still persists. Instructive in this regard is the way the New Woman responds to male jealousy. Instead of taking jealousy as an expression of men's love and attention, the New Woman often regards male jealousy as an illegitimate claim to control women.

Lale, for instance, when asked about men's jealousy, shook her head vehemently as if to announce that she found the attitude itself unacceptable. "First of all," she said to me, "this is not about jealousy. It is about a man's insecurity. He is not self-confident, and because of that, he wants to stop woman from working or doing other stuff she wants to do. Men can't accept that one day she might work at a better place than him; she might earn more than him. Men can't accept this." In a similar way, Özge, a twenty-six-year-old married saleswoman, had a fight with her husband after he asked her to delete her Facebook account. "He wants me to delete my account because there are men in my friend list," she said to me one morning as she hurried toward the checkout counter with the cash register box in her arms. "The guys on my Facebook list are my coworkers," she continued, "I have worked with them. Facebook is the only fun thing in my life right now and my husband is trying to take it away from me."

Her openness, at times, enables the New Woman to venture beyond the heteronormative dictates of intimate life, belonging, and care. Feeling entitled to explore the uncharted possibilities that intimate attachments and engagements offer, she does not follow well-trodden paths but rather charts her own, despite the hostile response from her immediate family. One such woman was Ferda, twenty-three, who worked at a café in downtown Ankara while living with her parents and trying to earn a college degree. In October 2018, I met with her at a fast-food restaurant at lunchtime, where she told me the story of how her sister found out that she was gay. A few years earlier, when she was seventeen, she lied to her parents one day to attend an LGBTIQ+ party. Oblivious to the fact that she was followed by one of her older sisters, she made her way into the night club. Upon receiving a call from her sister, who asked Ferda to come outside and meet her by the gate, she immediately walked out to prevent her sister making a scene at the club in front of her friends.

> My sister started questioning me, 'Ferda what are you doing here? Why are you even here?' she asked. I countered her by saying I was gay. She became all dramatic and started crying. Do you know the first sentence she uttered to me upon hearing that her sister was gay? 'Ferda,' she said to me, 'you will never be a public employee.' And I gave a chuckle in response. 'You are making fun of me,' she said. I thought to myself 'who cares about being a public employee, I am in a different place. All I want is to be with women.'

Ferda's sister, alarmed about Ferda's career prospects as a public servant, was alluding to the Civil Servants Law No. 657 regulating the legal status and rights of civil servants in Turkey. The law, indeed, cites convictions for so-called shameful offenses—those that literally turn one's face red—as grounds for barring one from employment in the public sector. The list of offenses categorized under this rubric, however, is circumscribed and includes acts like embezzlement, forgery, theft, and bribery, with no mention of sexual orientation. That said, people have been and are openly discriminated against in the labor market because of their sexual orientation, and military penal laws specify homosexuality as grounds for banning men from the army.

It would, however, be a mistake to think that the New Woman is able to embrace her openness wholeheartedly. For one thing, class hierarchies severely circumscribe the possibilities and opportunities available to her. Her access to education and employment, the main venues through which she can carve out a space for herself in the world, heavily depends on her class position. Besides, gender hierarchies, more so than class hierarchies, endanger her bodily existence, heightening her violability. For instance, it remains a dream for her to wander the empty city streets alone at midnight, getting lost in her thoughts and wishes, without regard for the outside world and the imminent threat it poses. Nevertheless, the New Woman's willingness to explore remains.

Forces of Labor

In a 1949 essay entitled "Why Don't They Get Married," Osman Yüksel Serdengeçti, the previously mentioned right-wing writer, reviled the New Woman—a product of the Turkish Republic—for working outside the home:

It is said the woman who is the product of the street and the cinema brings no auspiciousness. (. . .) Too much human contact, too much touching, too many people walking on a single way street, all these drag women into the society, who is indeed supposed to take care of the children. (. . .) Once women start working to make a living, they become forgetful of their girlhood, womanhood. They evolve into strange creatures, in between male and female. Their existence taints the seriousness of workplaces and bureaus: these women do not get married. Even if they want to, no one wants to elope with them. There are especially many of them in Ankara, the center of the political government. Public managers are surrounded with these short-haired, long-nailed women. (Serdengeçti [1949] 1992, 216)

Five decades later, in the 2000s, when the New Woman put her emotions, interactional capacities, and embodied orientations in the service of capital accumulation, a significant social and political change was unfolding that affected women's being in a profound way: globalization. The New Woman was no longer enclosed within the framework of the nation-state; instead, global capitalism largely shaped her life opportunities. With Turkey's integration into global markets, she found herself in a favorable position to obtain jobs in service settings, which seemed to accommodate new gender norms and feminine sensibilities. The discursive voices that once put her on the spot in ways that made her vulnerable seemed to have been muffled, partly by the increasing salience of gender equality and, in part, by the new discourses drawing her increasingly into the capitalist market. And more importantly, a new global discourse that glamorized the young woman was proliferating all around the world: so-called girl power.

The girl power discourse that began to hold sway in the 1990s articulated a neoliberal vision of young women (Harris 2004; Mc Robbie 2008). The discourse spotlighted young women mainly due to their capacities to earn money and pursue consumption-based lifestyles. Touted for her confidence, resilience, and autonomy, the young woman was represented as capable of attaining freedom within the premises of the neoliberal market. This commodified understanding of freedom, which the market was supposed to deliver to young women, bred new gender hierarchies on the one hand and opened up new bodily possibilities for gendered existence on the other (Walkerdine et al. 2001). In Turkey, for instance, the trope of the Free Girl that came into vogue in the early 2000s pushed the boundaries of acceptable femininity in the society. Widely circulated in the consumerist culture, the trope promoted the young woman as the harbinger of gendered social change.

Perhaps no woman represented the Free Girl trope in Turkey more than Nil Karaibrahimgil, a pop singer and songwriter who achieved immense popularity in the early 2000s when she appeared in TV commercials for a leading mobile phone operator, Turkcell, promoting a free-spirited, daring girl, hitchhiking across the country alone. Featuring Nil Karaibrahimgil as a young hitchhiker wearing her backpack and singing, "I am independent, not because I am special, not because I walked off, but because I am free," the commercial became an instant TV hit in 2000. When Sony Music offered Nil Karaibrahimgil the chance to make an album, she sang her own lyrics that put her feminine sensibilities on full display. Her lyrics—like "Mom, I gotta run, I don't want to cook rice. You also ask for a grandkid, I don't want to take care of a baby"—illuminated more about the free-spirited young woman, for whom being single was now marker of independence, not of undesirability.

The Free Girl's defining features, her much-desired mobility, independence, and confidence, did not make any reference to feminism but were predicated on class privilege, high purchasing power, and atomistic individuality. While neoliberal discourses insist that the unfettered operations of the capitalist market create opportunities for *any* young woman who is ready to seize the moment, the promise has never been powerful enough to lure the working-class New Woman entirely into the neoliberal project. The New Woman's relation to the Free Girl trope is rather complex.

To begin with, working-class New Women, far from being hapless consumers, are keenly aware of the pitfalls of the consumer lifestyle. Born in the world of consumer capitalism, they are all too familiar with how one can easily get carried away by the illusion of consumerism: with a credit card. They also know very well that this illusion will last only until the arrival of the credit card bill at the end of the month, bursting the bubble. In a sense, they have not fallen prey to the neoliberal market discourse that banks on young women's aspirations for independence and autonomy. Being the frontline workers of consumer capitalism, New Women were already disillusioned with commodity fetishism, too, as most of the commodities they sold no longer possessed much allure for them. They were also acutely aware that the capitalist market would not deliver and, that without enough cultural capital, they would be stuck in low-paying and dead-end jobs.

Education was a game-changer and many of the New Women looked for ways to improve their educational credentials. Nesrin, for instance, had enrolled in a distance learning high school program in order to enhance her prospects in the labor market, even though her husband and family were not supportive of her endeavor. When I first met her in 2011, she recounted how her immediate family had responded to her plans to get a high school diploma:

> I started out working at garment workshops from primary school onwards. At first, I was only working over the summer, but then I dropped out of the school and switched to working full-time. Just before I got married, I quit working. Neither my husband nor my parents-in-law wanted me to work. But I was already used to working and making my own money. When I decided to go back to school and signed up for distance learning at the general high school level, my husband and parents-in-law started making fun of my efforts. To suggest the uselessness of my effort, my husband one day asked me jokingly, "What will you do with a high school diploma? Are you going to hang it on the wall and show it off to our neighbors?" When I applied for a cashier position at MajorMarket, they hired me almost automatically thanks to my high school diploma. At first, my husband and parents-in-law discouraged me from working, but then they saw that it was decent work for a married woman. Later on, my mother-in-law asked me if I could help my sister-in-law, who was also a high school dropout, to get a job at MajorMarket. I told her it was not possible because MajorMarket requires workers to have a high school diploma.

Nesrin's effort to earn a high school diploma was met with sarcastic remarks. When she contemplated pursuing higher education, her husband explicitly opposed the idea: "He thinks if I go to college, the cultural gap between us is going to increase. My parents-in-law agree with him. They want me to have a child and be a mother instead," she said. A few years later, however, Nesrin decided to divorce her husband and steer a new path.

To invest in education is not easy, however. New Women from the ranks of the working class lack the financial resources to pursue a college education. Their families tend to focus on their urgent economic needs and forsake women's higher education. Selda, for instance, took up a job, for the first time in her life, during her last year in high school: "That year I was supposed to study for the university exam and take the exam at the end of the year. Suddenly, my father ended up in debt and I with my sibling started working so that we could help them financially. Then I kept on working." Some women, after getting a job in the service sector, enroll in university programs that offer distance education to get a college degree or sign up for courses that will teach them extra skills such as Photoshop or a new language. Many, however, have to let go of their educational aspirations due to the high demands of work and family life. It is under these conditions of precarity and difficulty that the working-class New Woman starts out as an adult in life in today's Turkey.

. . .

The contemporary New Woman in Turkey is at once animated by, and draws on, forces of labor, the body, openness, and embarrassment. She has her own emotional styles, codes, and habits that this chapter has sketched out in broad strokes. All of these emotional and embodied practices, far from being merely the product of individual self-cultivation, arise from larger social and political processes that relate to gender and sexuality. They are fashioned, to certain extent, by institutions such as the family, law, religion, the market, and the state, but these emotional practices have also been, at the same time, historically open to change. The next chapter examines the historical forces behind the New Woman's emotional styles and habits in Turkey. It explores a whole set of sociopolitical and economic changes that destabilized the framework of emotional obligations which women shouldered over the course of the twentieth century, allowing for new ways of inhabiting the urban space and new embodied practices of femininity.

Endnotes

1. Social anthropologist Sertaç Sehlikoglu (2015), whose work focuses on pious women's subjectivity in contemporary Turkey, demonstrates that new bodily modalities of headscarf-wearing women in urban contexts disrupt both the invasive male gaze and the secularist gaze that aim to discipline pious feminine subjects. Focused on headscarf-wearing young women modeling for fashion magazines, Sehlikoglu links pious women's new bodily modalities to changing sexuality culture in Turkey.

2. A literary rendition of power dynamics embedded in gendered glances has been offered by novelist Elena Ferrante (2013) in her Neopolitan series, in which she recounts the engrossing story of a complicated friendship between two working-class women growing up in the Napoli region of Italy, a region where shame-honor discourse has been historically influential in shaping women's embodied ways of being. In *The Story of a New Name*, the narrator, Elena, relays their outings in the city in which male gaze was omnipresent and woman's act of returning the male gaze was a sign of defiance: "On the street the men looked at all of us, pretty, less pretty, ugly, and not so much the youths as the grown men. It was like that in the neighborhood and outside of it, and Ada, Carmela, I myself—especially after the incident with Solaras—had learned instinctively to lower our eyes, pretend not to hear the obscenities they directed at us, and keep going. Lila, no. To go out with her on Sunday became a permanent point of tension. If someone looked at her, she returned the look" (Ferrante 2013, 156).

CHAPTER 2

Origins of the New Woman

*The Cultural Politics of Embarrassment and Its
Changing Legal Status in Turkey*

“ We are all prostitutes,” wrote Stella Ovadia, a Turkish Jewish feminist,
in a piece published in 1990 in *Feminist*, a consciousness-raising
journal promoting women's liberation in Turkey. This was a peak
moment in the feminist campaign against the inauspicious Article 438
of Turkey's penal code, which reduced prison sentences for rapists if
the victim was a sex worker. In her piece, Stella Ovadia advocated a
materialist and radical feminist agenda,[1] which espoused reasons why
all women should oppose the law. Article 438 was not merely about
sex workers but concerned all women, Ovadia noted; not a single
woman was exempt from this value system. Differential treatment
of women and female sex workers in rape law had roots in the normative understanding of femininity, which promoted a vicious hierarchy
among women with the virgin and chaste woman at the top and the
prostitute at the bottom. Indeed, a woman's worth in society was entirely dependent on her chastity. Article 438 was one brutal regulation
among many that shored up this value system, which not only denied
certain groups of women legal rights but also held all women in place
by the structures of male domination. As Ovadia reasoned, there was
only one way out of the chaste woman/prostitute binary foisted on
women: *all* women should mobilize under the banner of prostitutes,

identify themselves as such, and subvert the moral binaries that the construct of feminine modesty bred.

"We are all prostitutes" became the subversive slogan of the period and women's groups systematically worked toward shredding the norms of shame-honor in the country. Soon, feminist activists organized a gathering in Istanbul's Zürafa Sokak, a street that historically housed sex workers, to protest Article 438. During the demonstration, women chanted the slogan "We don't want to be virtuous women" and distributed handouts to sex workers that read, "We, women, are actually not that different from each other; men who are our husbands are the same men who come here to be your clients" (Düzkan 1990, 23). The eradication of moralized and sexualized hierarchies among women was at the core of the feminist agenda in the late 1980s and early 1990s. Feminists' vision of gender equality reflected the joint commitment to achieving equality between men and women, as well as among women themselves. The counterpart to this vision of gender equality would be the unmaking of feminine shame in Turkey.

This chapter focuses on the key shifts that transformed the legal basis of the cultural politics of embarrassment during the twentieth century. The cultural politics of embarrassment have long shaped the norms and meanings of femininity—sexuality, the feminine body, sexualized behavior and comportment—and gendered interactions that pervaded social, economic, and legal structures and institutions, fostering gender inequalities in Turkey. The chapter shows how shame-honor discourse—the traditional anchor of the cultural politics of embarrassment—acquired a legal status with the formation of the Turkish Republic in 1923 and then lost it in the early 2000s following reforms in the penal code and civil code brought on by the feminist movement. It also charts the major changes in the cultural politics of embarrassment and the effects these changes have had on women's existence across religious, class, and generational lines —reviewing the impact of large-scale processes like urbanization and industrialization, the institutionalization of the welfare system, and the changes in women's education in Turkey.

Shame-Honor Discourse Legalized

With the founding of the Turkish Republic in 1923, the idea of gender equality emerged as one of the stated core principles of the new secular state. In Turkey, where the population was and still is predominantly

Muslim and Turkish,[2] the new Republican elite represented by the CHP (Republican People's Party) broke with the Ottoman Empire and its Islamic legacy by condemning Ottoman Sunni patriarchy, especially the practices of polygyny and seclusion of women (Gole 1996; Kandiyoti 1997). Although the new Turkish Republic outwardly championed women's civil and political rights, women's emancipation, nonetheless, was carried out strictly at the behest of the state, with zero tolerance for an independent women's movement (Zihnioğlu 2003).[3] A new, secular civil code replaced the Ottoman Islamic legal code in 1926, which recognized the formal equality of man and woman. The new civil code abolished polygamy, granted equal access to divorce to men and women, and permitted child custody rights to be given to both parents rather than just the father. Women's enfranchisement took place in two steps, with women first being granted the vote in local elections in 1930 and at the national level in 1934.

Notwithstanding the sweeping legal reforms in the early Republican period that furnished women with civil and political rights, other reforms, at the same time and to a certain extent, transformed cultural shame-honor norms into legal norms. Turkey adopted the civil code from Switzerland but when it came to introducing a penal code, Republican elites turned to the Italian penal code when drafting it in 1926 (Yalçın 2019). This choice comes as no surprise considering the Italian code's preoccupation with precepts of shame and honor. The new code in Turkey, like its Italian counterpart, wrote the normative precepts of shame and honor into law and approved the family's, and the public's, authority, to monitor woman's bodily capacities.

The notion of male honor heavily informed the definition of sexual crimes, the scaling of penalties, and the indefatigability of punishment and reduction of sentences. To begin with, the penal code of 1926 codified sexual offenses against women's bodies—including rape, abduction, adultery, and sexual abuse—under the section entitled crimes against public morality and family order (*Adab-ı Umumiye* and *Nizam-ı Aile*) instead of under the section of crimes against the individual, which included punishments for crimes such as murder, assault, and battery. The code recognized the inviolability of women's bodies, but it did so only on the basis of male honor, which granted men the de facto right to "watch women's purity" and "protect women's chastity." With the introduction of the penal code, the task of protecting women's purity was taken over partly by the new nation-state (Parla 2001).

Perhaps the starkest expression of male honor embedded in the penal code was found in the articles that regulated rape. Even the words and terms used in code were heavily slanted toward an understanding of a woman's body as the repository of male honor. In Turkish, the word for rape is *tecavüz*, whereas the code described rape with another Turkish term, *ırza geçmek*, a phrasal verb that literally means violating one's honor. The harm caused by the act of rape was assessed in reference to the moral notion of *ırz*, an Ottoman-Turkish word that can be translated as honor and purity. Once protected exclusively by men, the normative notion of *ırz* was now recognized as something to be protected by the new nation-state.

The legal protection the new nation-state offered to redress injury brought about by rape entailed measures such as marrying one's rapist, because marriage for women, even if it is to her own rapist, was morally superior to remaining without a man. This was actually the case with the infamous Article 434 of the penal code of 1926, which stipulated that the rape charges against a man who abducted and raped a woman would be dropped if he subsequently married the victim. The same article also specified that when a female under fifteen was raped by a group of men, all of the men would escape prosecution if one of them afterward married the victim. The permanent stigma attached to the rape survivor as "unmarriageable" was regarded as the real damage to the victim, and the law, in compensation for the loss of chastity women suffered, made rapists marry their victims—the "unmarriageable women"—as punishment for their deeds.

Article 434 that granted impunity to rapists was one among many legal clauses in the penal code that exacerbated women's exposure to violence and violation. The code, for instance, prioritized the sanctity of family honor, granting leniency to crimes committed in the name of honor such as honor-based murders. For honor killings, which refer to the murder of a family member or a relative—often a woman—who is believed to have stained the honor of the family, perpetrators received reduced sentences if the (female) victim was caught in the act of committing adultery or so-called illegitimate sexual relations. Women were also made vulnerable to sexual violence within the contract of marriage. The code, indeed, neither recognized nor penalized marital rape, because sexual practices within marriage were not regarded as violations of women's chastity or of husbands' or families' honor.

Woman's violability, however, varied with her position within the moral order, intensifying the risk of assault and injury for unchaste women. Courts, for instance, handed down shorter sentences to rapists if the victims were considered unchaste and immoral. Article 438 of the penal code lowered the sentence for rape by one-third if the victim was a sex worker. The code, on the other hand, acknowledged virginity as a value, and men who engaged in sexual intercourse with a virgin on a false promise of marriage were given six months to two years prison time. The sentence was suspended if the perpetrator agreed to marry the woman.

Beside honor, notions of *hayâ* and *ar*—which refer to shame and its force to motivate one to avoid or escape the situation that creates feelings of shame—played a considerable role in determining sexual offenses that warranted punishment. In everyday parlance, a person without *hayâ* or *ar* is automatically considered an immoral person, especially with regard to matters of chastity and sexuality. Article 419 delineated a category of **hayâsızca hareketler** (shameless behavior) that mandated prison time ranging from fifteen days to two months. What constituted shameless behavior was, however, not articulated, which gave broad latitude to law enforcement agencies and courts. Historically, the article was used to criminalize LGBTIQ+ populations, sex workers, and a variety of practices ranging from wearing inappropriate outfit styles to the act of drinking alcohol in public which were considered transgressions of public morality, although homosexuality was not penalized by the law (İlkkaracan 2007). The same article also mandated up to a one-year prison term for those who had sexual intercourse in a shameless manner, again not specifying what a "shameless manner" was. Article 426 introduced the concept of public morality (**genel ahlak**) and criminalized the distribution of publications, books, journals, music, movies, et cetera, which went against public morality, offended the public's feelings of shame—*hayâ* and *ar*—or provoked sexual desire.

Shame-honor discourse made its way into the civil code, too. The law, which codified male honor, recognized the husband as the head of the marriage union and granted him the final say over the choice of domicile, as well as matters regarding children. Women's economic freedom was hemmed in by restrictive legislation. Article 159 required women to obtain formal authorization from their husbands to take employment outside the home. Other regulations required the wife to take her husband's last name, granting men the symbolic power to define the family unit by branding family members with his surname. The majority of these laws remained effective until the adoption of a new civil code in 2002 and penal code in 2005. Nevertheless, in the early 1980s, the ascendance of a militant and devoted feminist movement set the stage for important changes to the law. Tenacious feminist activism resulted in the repeal of some portions of both the civil and penal codes as early as the 1990s.

The Virginity Test as a Gendered Means of Violence

In Turkey, virginity has functioned as a significant cultural mechanism regulating women's violability. Women, on the basis of virginity, were classified into two categories: **kadın** and **kız**, a distinction that is also reflected in colloquial Turkish (Ozyegin 2009). While the word *kız* (girl) denotes virginity, the word *kadın* (woman) refers often to married women. Both categories signal the expression of virginity norms, with the notion of *kız* implying sexual purity and female chastity within the institution of marriage. However, "a non-virgin unmarried woman has no place in the societal classification" (Ozyegin 2015, 47). Such women, in the eyes of society, violate the virginity norms, putting them at risk for not only hostility but also state violence.

The modern state, by definition, has a legitimate monopoly over the means of violence. The newly founded Turkish state exercised its monopoly over violence not in a gender-neutral way but through mechanisms of violence that were gendered and sexist. One such violent practice was so-called virginity tests. "A particularly modern form of institutionalized violence" (Parla 2001, 66), enforced virginity tests were vaginal examinations performed on women by doctors. Although virginity tests were not prescribed by law in Turkey, the fact that a woman's status as virgin or nonvirgin factored into the penalties of the penal code set the stage for this violent practice (Yalçın 2019). In other words, with shame-honor discourse acquiring a legal status, distinctly gendered means of violence such as virginity tests got underway in the Turkish Republic. Conducted upon request by the police, gendarmerie, or high school principals, the practice of virginity testing subjected especially young women in hospitals, orphanages, state-run dormitories, prisons, and high schools to institutional violence (Parla 2001).

Partly due to this practice, the new Turkish Republic's vision of a heterosocial public culture was restricted to the educated middle and upper classes. Elite women were encouraged to venture into social life as men's peers. Cafes, restaurants, banquet halls, and city streets emerged as prominent places where new gender performances were carried out; where new masculinities and femininities were achieved through mixed-gender interaction and performative acts of conversing, dancing, and celebrating (Gole 1996). That said, the precepts of shame-honor infiltrated the lives of elite Republican women, too, who, after abandoning the veil, put a lot of effort into demonstrating their chastity. They sought to distance themselves from their Western counterparts (flappers) who were deemed rather decadent (Sirman 1989). To do so, they first distanced themselves from the trappings of individualism—with its emphasis on autonomy from the community—that did not fit with the Republican nation-building project. Following the introduction of mandatory mass schooling—a state-sponsored education system—and legal reforms advancing women's rights, a small group of elite women became educated, active professionally, and visible in public space. The women strongly communicated the idea that they were serving the nation-building project as chaste actors, not to fulfill personal ambitions and career aspirations. Professional women also embraced their primary status as honorable wives, dutiful daughters, mothers, and caretakers of the home, although they were able to enjoy higher status than the traditional housewife (Gole 1996; White 2003). Finally, elite Republican women, having abandoned the veil, adopted a nonrevealing modern clothing style, wearing boxy suits and long skirts so as not to draw attention to their bodies.

The everyday lives of women from popular classes, however, remained within the orbit of prospective shame. If an underprivileged young woman from a regular neighborhood engaged in similar gender performances in public spaces, for instance by casually chatting with an unrelated man at a park, she might end up paying a huge price for her behavior. For one thing, it was perfectly possible (and legal) for a police officer to approach a woman, accuse her of immoral conduct, and detain her on the grounds of indecent behavior, a charge that might quickly become blown out of proportion and devolve into allegations of illegal prostitution. Or, she might be sent to hospital for a virginity examination. The police duty law authorized police officers to detain individuals whose conduct violated public morality and norms of decency, both of which were ambiguously defined to give officers wide latitude to determine what constituted a moral infringement.

So intense was the shame and humiliation associated with the virginity tests that it sometimes claimed women's lives, even decades after the Republic's founding. Two harrowing incidents in the early 1990s alerted the public's attention to the violence of the practice after high school girls committed suicide following their virginity examinations. In the spring of 1992, four young female students who attended the religious *İmam Hatip* high school in Ula, a small town in the western part of the country, went on a picnic with some boys in the town. Upon spotting the group, a forest protection officer contacted the school principal and complained about the girls' conduct. The school principal, in return, accused the four girls of impropriety and sent them to the local hospital for virginity examinations. Unable to endure the shame, two of them attempted to commit suicide. One was saved in the hospital, but the other girl passed away (Cumhuriyet 1992). Weeks later, another high school student committed suicide to protest her virginity examination. The fifteen-year-old girl had overheard a conversation at the school between her father and the school principal, who informed him that his daughter had been hanging out with boys and might not be a virgin. The principal suggested that the father take his daughter to undergo a virginity test. Upon hearing this conversation, the young girl fled the school and jumped off a cliff to her death.

These incidents became the impetus for vibrant feminist activism in the early 1990s, galvanizing women against legal practices that intensified women's violability. Despite the advocacy and the broadened public awareness of virginity tests, however, the Turkish state failed to enact legislation against virginity examinations. Instead, in 1995, the Ministry of Education issued a Statute of Awards and Discipline in the High School Education Institutions, which granted disciplinary committees at high schools the authority to expel female students from the formal education system on the grounds of unchastity, proven by virginity examinations (Yalçın 2019). Forced virginity tests in Turkey were finally banned in 2002 (Lasco 2002).

The Iron Hand of the Neighborhood

While the Turkish state had a monopoly over the (gendered) means of violence, it de facto bequeathed to the local community the unlicensed use of private violence over women's bodies under certain conditions. Community-based violent interventions concerning women's bodies were encouraged by shame-honor discourse; the neighborhood was historically allowed to exact punishments on women who acted in ways to bring shame upon themselves, allegedly tainting the "neighborhood's honor" *(mahallenin namusu)*.

The *mahalle* (neighborhood) had been central to urban life since the early sixteenth century (Behar 2003). Culturally, it has always represented more than merely a location. The *mahalle* was a cohesive community formed by and organized around male honor. In the closed and homogenous circle of the neighborhood—where residents were similar in terms of family, ethnic, or sectarian religious identity—male honor guided the invention of gendered surveillance mechanisms, many specifically designed to monitor "public morality." There were, for instance, self-appointed groups of male youths acting as vigilantes to defend the *mahalle's* honor from threats outside the neighborhood, as well as from illicit and immoral behaviors by neighborhood residents such as alcohol consumption, gambling, and nonmarital sex.

Monitoring public morality, however, often meant watching women's embodied existence within the *mahalle*. Indeed, the *mahalle* as a moral community had enormous power to brand a woman as chaste or immoral (Boyar 2016). Once a woman was marked, she was vulnerable to attack by the state, as well as by the neighborhood. Any member of the *mahalle* was vested with authority to monitor unseemly feminine behavior, and when deemed proper, *mahalle* inhabitants could exact punishments over women who transgressed moral norms. Of all the punishment mechanisms the neighborhood deployed, the raid was the most violent and humiliating (Boyar 2016). A public shaming mechanism used to punish women with loose morals up until the late nineteenth century, raids were launched against their houses by the community under the leadership of the *imam* who was informally responsible for his neighborhood's morality.

All of the punishment mechanisms available to the neighborhood, ranging from raids to gossip, were corporeal and hence affective. They all pivoted on humiliation and shame. Incited by the perceived loss of feminine modesty, the punishments exposed women to hostile gazes, to intrusive touches, and to attacks, often in the form of spectacular violence exercised by men. Shame-honor norms, in other words, routinely put women in danger of assault and injury. These forceful means took on a political significance—not just because they justified violence against women on moralistic grounds—but perhaps, more importantly, because they came to represent the politics of imposing shame and embarrassment as a necessary, naturalized part of every woman's being and a politics in which a woman's body became a vessel for violence and violation.

Traditional *mahalle* life was one of the legacies of the Ottoman Empire that carried over into Republican life, allowing for the traditional practice of neighborhood surveillance of women, particularly young women. In the neighborhood, the presence of young women in outdoor space, particularly on the streets, for socializing and entertainment was considered a sign of sexual availability that merited punishment, although the raid was no longer a punishment in the Republican period. Men continued to position themselves as an informal force that guarded the honor of the neighborhood, which meant they felt entitled to patrol women's embodied existence by restricting their mobility and interaction with unrelated men, as well as ensuring that their dress conformed to the dictates of feminine modesty. Within the parameters of shame-honor discourse, even sexual attacks and assaults were taken as signs of carelessness by a woman, incriminating her. The ensuing shame would stick to her permanently, defiling her purity, ruining her prospects for marriage, and drastically reducing her chances of getting an education and finding employment.

The pressure that neighborhoods exerted on women often pushed them to cultivate particular attitudes. A woman's embodied orientation assumed an alert manner, with her gaze and gait pronouncedly conveying a sense of haste, as if she knew that she had no business being outside her house. Hurrying down the streets of the neighborhood, she would avoid eye contact with the young men gathered around the corner of coffeehouse, shift her gaze downward, and walk briskly, her strides short and quick and her entire body displaying a strong sense of direction. She would head home without wandering and without enjoying her surroundings, social exchange or even just the pleasure of a beautiful day.

Working Outside the Home: A Source of Shame or Honor?

That paid employment could be a source of shame for certain groups of women in capitalist societies is not a new insight. In her study on the working classes in England, feminist sociologist Beverley Skeggs noted that "the label working class when applied to women has been used to signify all that is dangerous, dirty, and without value" (Skeggs 1997, 74). In the Turkish case, just as women's embodied existence was mired in the problem of public morality, so too was their work outside the home, making women all the more entangled with the affective force of shame. This was especially the case for women with few educational credentials who occupied the lower echelons of society and were qualified only for low-skill jobs such as factory or domestic work. As a cultural discourse, shame-honor largely set the norms for underprivileged women with respect to joining the workforce, seeking education, and socializing with men— whether they could and under what conditions.

During the early Republican period, workplaces that employed women—such as factories— were often regarded as "dirty," although the dirt there had strong moral undertones, with allegations of prostitution frequently leveled at them. That perception was prevalent when the Ottoman Empire was incorporated into the capitalist world economy beginning in the nineteenth century. Muslim women in Anatolia were integrated into commodity production in the wake of industrialization, and yet they were less likely to work outside the home compared to non-Muslim women in the Ottoman Empire, including Armenians and Greeks (Quataert 2002). For both Muslim and non-Muslim women, however, working outside the home was an act that compromised their moral standing. For instance, in the last quarter of the nineteenth century, a silk factory operating in the area that is now called Lebanon—at which non-Muslim women made up a significant portion of its workers—was disparagingly called a brothel by locals because men and women worked together. After receiving a warning from state officers, factory management refashioned the workplace, designating gender-segregated areas.[4] Factory owners also resorted to the religious authority of the archbishop, who attested to the moral appropriateness of factory work for women after examining the factory space. It was only after the archbishop's sanction that local men permitted their daughters to work for the silk factory again (Yıldırım 2013).

Chastity during this period shaped women's chances in the labor market, too. Muslim women's integration into the workforce in the late Ottoman Empire hinged on their so-called moral status rather than their marketable skills. At times, they were even asked by employers to provide a certificate of chastity. For instance, the Society for the Employment of Ottoman Muslim Women (Kadınları Çalıştırma Cemiyet-i

İslâmiyesi)—a foundation created in 1916 to expand employment opportunities for Muslim Ottoman women who were in economic need—specified chastity as a condition for women's eligibility for work. The Society stated its requirements as follows: "Chastity and modesty. Each candidate should submit a certificate of chastity, prepared by the neighborhood authority, *mukhtar* and approved by the municipal police" (Karakışla 2015, 144).

The issue of underprivileged women working outside the home remained attached to chastity in the Republican period, too, with workplaces regarded as morally shady spaces for women to work. The suspicion was that privately-owned workshops and factories could easily succumb to moral disease and allow activities like illegal prostitution to fester. Even when there were no allusions to prostitution, women's workplaces were deemed morally dubious. After all, there was always the risk of sexual harassment and, once a woman was harassed, it would defile her purity and family honor. This perception influenced official strategies too, molding the ways law enforcement addressed sexual harassment at workplaces like factories. In 1928, following an incident at an Istanbul tobacco workshop in which a group of women workers had been allegedly sexually assaulted by men, the state authorities mapped out a plan for law enforcement responding to such incidents in the future. The police, according to the new plan, would arrest the perpetrators and send them to court, and the assaulted women would be held in detention. The women would be observed for signs of indecent conduct and, if any behavior in offense against public morality was detected, they would be sent to a brothel (Toprak 2017). In the aftermath of the public release of the new plan, Sabiha Sertel—one of the first female journalists in Turkey—penned a piece in the left-wing magazine *Resimli Ay*, accusing the state of punishing women who worked to earn a living. Even under circumstances where women had committed so-called moral sins, Sabiha Sertal demanded that the convicts be reformed and reintegrated into society, not senselessly punished by placing them in brothels (Toprak 2017).

Not all underprivileged women who worked outside the home, however, were charged with sexual immorality in the early Republican period. The public, at times, granted clemency to women who had clearly taken employment out of helplessness and poverty. Poor young single women in dire need of money for a dowry, or widowed women lacking male support, were seen as chaste and considered hard-working, living from hand-to-mouth. In the eyes of the public, they were not morally fallen; they just found themselves in unfortunate circumstances, lived an upright life, and were earning an honest penny without compromising their chastity (*namusuyla yaşamak*).

One important change in the gendered industrial workforce was introduced by the establishment of State Economic Enterprises, which, starting in the 1930s, became emblems of the Republic's project of industrialization. These state-run enterprises, especially Sümerbank and Etibank, recruited both men and women for their factories, offices, and stores. Both the wages and work-related benefits—such as accommodations, meals, maternity leave, and recreational facilities—offered at these factories were above standard. But more importantly, working in these factories did not put women's modesty at risk—or for that matter the honor of her husband and family—simply because these factories were owned and run by the state. The state was the institution which, unlike the market, would be the ultimate protector of women's chastity. The number of these factories, however, was small, which severely limited employment opportunities. For instance, the number of women workers employed in Sümerbank enterprises in the entire country was only six thousand by 1943 (Makal 2010).

Indeed, between 1923 and the early 1960s, Turkey's economy was mainly rural, with a majority of the population living in the country where industrialization hardly had any effect.[5] As noted by Buğra and Özkan (2012, 94), "The urban population constituted about 24 percent of the total population in 1927, and it reached 25 percent only by 1950." This began to change in the early 1950s, following the onset of industrialization and the mechanization of agriculture, which spawned a massive exodus of people from the countryside into the cities. The post-World War II era with the twin dynamics of urbanization and industrialization prompted a significant shift in patterns of women's work, bringing in declining rates of women's labor force participation.

The decline in women's labor force participation rates in early phases of urbanization is an almost universal phenomenon, not specific to Turkey. Capitalist development often generates a U-curve shape for women's labor force patterns.[6] When agriculture is the dominant economic sector, women are, to a great extent, present in the labor force, typically working as unpaid family workers in household businesses or on family farms. With the expansion of market forces, the mechanization of agriculture, and the advance of industrialization, however, women gradually eschew employment, and female labor force participation rates begin to decline. Women's labor force participation rates begin to increase again following the rise of the service economy, as well as women's increasing educational credentials (Boserup 1970; Goldin 1995; Inglehart and Norris 2003).

Changes in development policies in Turkey during the 1960s, such as the adoption of import-substitution—an industrialization model that aimed to reduce the country's foreign dependency through increasing domestic industrial production—resulted in an influx of rural migrants to cities. Until the 1980s, Turkey's industrial sector grew under state protection, expanding employment opportunities for men rather than women. Men's integration into the urban labor force operated in accordance with male honor, with men moving into the newly emerging blue-collar jobs as the breadwinners of their families. Women, meanwhile, were expected to stay at home to undertake domestic chores and care for their children. This nuclear family household built on a male breadwinner and female caregiver model became embodied in Turkey's formal institutions and laws during the second half of the twentieth century. The social security system established in the 1940s institutionalized the male breadwinner/female caregiver model (Buğra and Özkan 2012). Within this familialist system, women were considered dependents of their male relatives and gained access to gender-differentiated benefits, such as health, old age, and survival benefits, primarily as wives and daughters (Kılıç 2008; Buğra and Yakut-Çakar 2010).

Familialism gained a renewed ideological emphasis between 1945 and 1965, so much so, that domesticity, above all, was endorsed as the locus of femininity (Sancar 2012).[7] The feminine ideal of domesticity stood opposed to work and labor, spawning a binary and a hierarchy among women, which installed the housewife and mother as explicitly superior to the working woman and the family as the keystone of society. The valorization of familialism in general and feminine domesticity, in particular, was situated in the broader historical and political context of the nascent Cold War and Turkey's transition to a multiparty system that framed gender politics in new ways. The 1950 national elections ushered in a new era of the multiparty system, marking the end of the rule of the Republican secular elites, who handed the power over to the Democrat Party, the center-right political party. The era of the Democrat Party saw the revival of Islamic discourses along with Turkey's pro-American stance (Sarıtaş and Şahin 2015). It was partly through the elevation of domestic femininities that Turkey's pro-American and thus anti-communist stance was announced, which set out to counter the communist regime's ideal of women workers (Emen-Gökatalay 2021).

The low levels of female education, both in terms of literacy rates and schooling levels, further reduced women's chances in the urban labor market. By 1965, for instance, the female illiteracy rate was about 67 percent, while the female secondary school enrollment rate was 9 percent (Buğra and Özkan 2012). Between 1965 and 1985, female secondary school enrollment went up from 9 percent to 28 percent, while female enrollment for tertiary education increased from 4 percent to 9 percent (Buğra and Özkan 2012). Despite mass schooling and the state-sponsored education system, 32 percent of women were still illiterate in 1985.

Gecekondu, Women, and the City

The arrival of rural migrants to cities in the 1950s altered urban life significantly, with new neighborhoods mushrooming in urban spaces and new codes of mixed-gender interactions becoming popular among the new residents. Perhaps no one word encapsulates the migrants' urban life better than *gecekondu,* a compound word which literally translates as "built overnight." *Gecekondu* refers to the informal housing system new migrants invented in the city, because affordable housing was not available to them. Migrants built their own houses without delay by occupying state-owned lands. Soon, as more and more people migrated from their villages, the urban space became dotted with *gecekondu* neighborhoods. Relatively diverse in terms of the inhabitants' religious denominations and place of origin, some neighborhoods were comprised of different Islamic sects (Alevi and Sunni), while some others that followed a process of chain migration were homogenous.

In *gecekondu* neighborhoods, it was not common for women to work outside the home, although they were engaged in a lot of work, including the building of houses. The men took up jobs in the proliferating industrial sector or worked in informal jobs, for instance as street vendors, whereas women stayed in the neighborhood and became housewives, an identity which was regarded as more prestigious for women. Women's work outside the home had a warping effect on their husbands' reputations as honorable men, as they were seen to be failed breadwinners (White 2004; Gündüz-Hoşgör and Smits 2008; Beşpınar 2010).[8]

The gender dynamics of city life created a host of new challenges and conflicts for migrants as urban structures continued to evolve. Urban life, beginning from the 1950s, assumed a more mixed-gender character compared to the previous period, and heterosocial interactions—which were no longer limited to a small section of society—expanded to include the lower-middle classes and working classes, who were also able to participate in cultural activities and attractions in the city (Tuncer 2018). More women used public transportation, engaging in new activities of leisure and entertainment and visiting new consumption spaces. Parks, outdoor dining spaces, and casual dining establishments like ice cream parlors and pudding shops (*muhallebici*) were in widespread use by the wider public and functioned as locations where young individuals could socialize. (Tuncer 2018). The cinemas, theaters, and concert venues dotting the urban landscape also offered a rich cultural life. Although this urban sociability accommodated mixed-gender interactions, women were rarely alone and were almost always accompanied, preferably by a relative, in mixed-gender public places.

Now that gender mixing was the norm in their city life, new migrants had to find a way to maintain mixed-gender interactions in public without upsetting the shame-honor discourse or, for that matter, the norms of Sunni Islam. Prior to their arrival to the city, migrants lived in villages, in small and relatively homogenous communities, and kinship ties set the terms of social relationships. In the cities, they reimagined fictive kinship ties and began to use the ground rules and norms of kinship to guide social interactions in public. By making use of familial forms of address, such as "sister" and "brother," women and men concocted an ingenious way to desexualize their interactions and navigate around sexual taboos. It was now perfectly acceptable for a woman to approach a random man on the street and ask for directions, and for him to help her, as long as the two addressed each other through familial terms such as "daughter" and "uncle," or "sister" and "brother." Fictive kinship, on the other hand, was often wrought with gender imbalances in power, automatically locating women in the lower rung of gender hierarchy. Take the term *bacı*, the most common term used to address women, which can be translated as sister, denoting a low-status kin position. The term *bacı* evokes a paternalistic disposition toward women, placing them automatically in an inferior position vis-à-vis man, reinforcing the gendered familial asymmetry between men and women. Furthermore, fictive kinship reinforces men's surveillance over women's lives, since, within the framework of shame-honor, a woman's body is considered to be the repository of man's honor. In short, it is through fictive kinship ties that women were able to inhabit spaces in public and were, at the same time, pigeonholed into a subordinate status.

It would, however, be a mistake to think that the use of family evocation was limited to the new migrants or lower classes. In fact, the use of family evocation in everyday life became quite widespread, infiltrating various segments of the society during the 1960s and 1970s. The ascendant left-wing grassroots movement, for instance, enthusiastically embraced fictive kinship ties as a strategy to cultivate stronger political ties with the masses. Women who were active in unions and political organizations, as well as in *gecekondu* neighborhoods, were strongly encouraged by their male comrades to self-identify as *bacı* and to cast their relationships in familial terms with males and the masses who lived by conservative or religious values. Interestingly, the political Islamist movement, which was diametrically opposed to leftist ideology, had been using the same strategy all along. Islamist women within the movement were stripped of their sexuality and become "sisters" to men (Aktaş 2005).

The expansion of political freedoms beginning in the 1960s opened a space for women to undermine the prevailing norms concerning feminine chastity. For instance, with the growing presence of grassroots movements in the public sphere, the use and meaning of those spaces began to change. Once spaces of family sociability, streets and parks became locations for demonstrations and political meetings (Tuncer 2018). Moreover, the expansion of political freedoms enabled women intellectuals to tell women's own stories and speak openly about their sexuality. Adalet Ağaoğlu, a prominent novelist, published a trilogy, entitled *Dar Zamanlar* (Dire Times),[9] that recounted the compelling story of urban, educated leftist women in the 1970s. Trapped in a society fractured by a military coup, one that exacerbated the politically pragmatic and philistine tendencies of the old and new bourgeois classes, the women in *Dar Zamanlar* continued their efforts to cultivate a life of the mind, as well as to experiment with sexual freedom. Despite the oppressive atmosphere, they discovered the complexity of their own sexual desires, intimate attachments, and inner conflicts.

The 1970s also saw the intensification of public discussion about birth control and abortion. Organizations such as the Turkish Medical Association, the Turkish Society of Gynecology, and the Turkish Family

Planning Association sought to legalize abortion and increase awareness about birth control by publishing reports and carrying out lobbying activities (Karaomerlioğlu 2012; Atay 2017). Their efforts helped shift the discussion of women's sexuality away from shame-honor to medical-scientific discourse.

Women Shattering the Shame-Honor Discourse

None of these efforts in the 1970s, however, were targeted directly at shame-honor discourse. The change came with the feminist movement that took the stage in the early 1980s. Indeed, the strenuous struggle of feminism in that period against the dictates of feminine modesty was unprecedented in the history of Turkey, and as such it severely undermined the national hegemony of the cultural politics of embarrassment. Feminists began to organize at a particularly difficult moment—during the bloody aftermath of the 1980 military coup in which fifty people were executed, some five hundred thousand were arrested, many more disappeared, and torture in prisons was widespread (TBMM 2012). Intimidation was rampant and the military junta clamped down on left-wing movements, both Turkish and Kurdish, by shutting down the unions and political parties and organizations, heavily curtailing civil and political rights in the country, and imprisoning political activists.

As a part of its strategy to suppress grassroots movements, the military junta elevated the "Turkish-Islamic Synthesis"—an ideology that blends Sunni faith with Turkish nationalism—to the level of a de facto state ideology. Sunni Islam became a hallmark of right-wing politics, positioned against the left-wing and Kurdish liberation movements. Concurrent with the Turkish-Islamic Synthesis, compulsory religious education for all primary and secondary schools was introduced in 1982 (Pak 2004). Religious *İmam Hatip* high schools grew from 72 in 1970 to 382 in 1988 (Baran 2010). It was a period during which shame-honor discourse regained strength through the enforcement of Sunni codes in public life.

In this context, secular and educated women in feminist groups began to organize, first through informal meetings at homes and cafes and then through marches and protests on the streets (Sirman 1989; Arat 2000). What sparked the street gatherings was a 1987 court decision on domestic violence. In Çankırı, a city in central Anatolia, a woman's bid to obtain a divorce on the grounds of domestic violence was refused by a male judge. In announcing the court's refusal to grant the woman a divorce, the judge cited a common Turkish expression, "never leave a woman's back without a stick and her belly without a baby," as justification (Marshall 2013, 67). Infuriated by the court's effort to legitimize domestic violence, women organized a gathering in Yoğurtçu Park in Istanbul, which was in later months followed by street demonstrations against domestic violence (Ekal 2011).

Two years later, in 1989, feminists launched the "Purple Needle" campaign and women activists handed out needles with purple ribbons to women on the streets and in public transportation (Tekeli 1992). In distributing needles that women could use to poke men who harassed them on the street, feminists encouraged women to fight back not only against male attackers but against women's historically constituted violability. In an effort to reclaim urban spaces, women activists regularly paid visits to male-dominated coffeehouses, spent time in parks, and encouraged all women to attend male-dominated events, like soccer games or coffeehouse card games. Throughout 1989, feminists in both Istanbul and Ankara ratcheted up the struggle against shame-honor discourse through effective campaigns such as "Our Body Is Ours," "Against Sexual Harassment," and "No to Article 438," which garnered a lot of attention.

Islamist women, during the same period, were also working on the gender front and their efforts helped revamp the public presence of pious Sunni women. Islamist women were part of a larger, politically oriented mixed-gender Islamist movement that grew in the 1980s. Educated women, who had developed a renewed interest in practicing Islam, demanded corporeal visibility in public life for their Muslim identity by adopting a pious lifestyle (Esim and Cindoglu 1999; Arat 2005). By redefining the codes of conduct for religious women, they expanded the normative parameters of Sunni Islam to the point where women's political activism and work outside of the house become acceptable under the rubric of serving the community (Marshall 2005). To be sure, this rhetoric did not encourage lower-class women to serve the community by working but targeted their middle-class counterparts.

Another challenge to shame-honor discourse came from the Kurdish liberation movement, which emerged as a socialist, anti-colonial, and secular political movement in the late 1970s, and from its women's faction. Their political activism exposed, among other things, the multilayered and complex modalities of power and hierarchy that the precepts of shame and honor assumed in Turkish and Kurdish political contexts. For instance, the Kurdistan Workers' Party (PKK) gradually placed more political emphasis on women's oppression, advocating, as a part of individual and national liberation, women's liberation (Göksel 2019). An important dimension of this struggle was to overturn the masculinist power over women's bodies and sexuality. Abdullah Öcalan, the leader of the PKK, in an effort to delink masculine honor from the control of women's bodies and sexuality, reframed honor in terms of protecting and defending the Kurdish homeland (Çağlayan 2019). The Kurdish liberation movement also pushed back against the Turkish state's discursive politics around honor killings that framed the Kurdish population as "culturally backward." In the meantime, the Kurdish women's movement, which initially emerged from the liberation movement but nevertheless developed into an autonomous movement over time, vigorously waged "a double struggle" (Al-Ali and Tas 2018, 459) against, on the one hand, state-perpetrated and ethnically motivated (sexual) violence, and on the other hand, patriarchal practices in Kurdistan. Today, the Kurdish women's movement, one of the most powerful feminist movements in the world, is globally recognized and known for its revolutionary potential to radically challenge the oppressive structures of both state and male domination, as well as for its capacity to empower women of Kurdistan both individually and collectively.[10]

Shame-Honor Discourse Legally Dismantled

Various forms of activism by women throughout the 1980s eventually forced the state to take some preliminary steps toward reforming Turkey's gender system. As early as 1983, abortion was legalized with a decree on population planning (Yalçın 2019). In 1990, an amendment to Article 159 of the civil code abolished the requirement that a married woman obtain her husband's permission to work outside the home (Çarkoğlu, Kafesçioğlu, and Akdaş-Mitrani 2012). In the same year, the Prime Ministry established the General Directorate on the Status and Problems of Women (KSSGM), a special division responsible for improving the rights and status of women in Turkey. And finally, in 1990, the infamous Article 438, which granted a sentence reduction to rapists if the victim was a sex worker, was repealed by the Grand National Assembly (Yalçın 2019). By 1998, the law on domestic violence (Protection of Family Law) was finally adopted.

Women's advocacy in Turkey during this decade was buoyed by international awareness of gender equality that worked in favor of the activists' cause. Beginning in the mid-1980s, the Turkish state became signatory to the chief international conventions and treaties on the elimination of discrimination against women, such as the Beijing Declaration, the Platform for Action, and the Convention on the Elimination of All Forms of Discrimination against Women (CEDAW) (Diner and Toktaş 2010; Acar and Altunok 2012).

From the mid-1990s onward, larger structural changes regarding gender began to take hold in society. Female enrollment rates from primary to tertiary education increased considerably. In particular, with the educational reforms of 1997, the government extended the period of compulsory education from five to eight years—covering middle school—and thus educational opportunities for women expanded. The result of this change became tangible in a decade. By 2010, adult illiteracy rates for females decreased to 9.9 percent. According to TURKSTAT data, the net schooling ratio for females in primary education increased from 78 percent in 1997 to 98 percent in 2011, while the net schooling ratio for females in secondary education rose from 34 percent to 63 percent. Female enrollment in tertiary education increased from 9 percent in 1997 to 32.6 percent in 2011. In the meantime, throughout the 1990s, centers for women's and gender studies were established at a dozen universities, which became beacons of feminist knowledge production, as well as agents of social change.

In the early 2000s, gender equality, which was an important feature of globalization, became a more pressing issue for Turkey. Gender equality reforms adopted by the rather conservative AKP, which came to power in 2002, introduced a new civil code and penal code. Initially, gender equality reforms were carried out to ensure Turkey's candidacy to the European Union, in particular to meet the Copenhagen Criteria. The AKP government was not really invested in the project of deepening gender equality in the country, however. Nevertheless, feminist activists, who had been working on drafting a new penal code and civil code for decades, seized this moment and exerted mounting pressure on the AKP government through lobbying and activism. Between 2002 and 2004, women's organizations and LGBTIQ+ groups together carried out a successful campaign to change the law. Thanks to the movement, what started as a minimal legal change that took no account of women's demands grew into far-reaching legislation furthering gender equality in the country.

The scale of legal changes during this period was unprecedented. Deniz Kandiyoti, weighing in on the gender reforms, wrote that they were "arguably the most progressive legislation for women since the Kemalist reforms of the 1920s and the 1930s" (Kandiyoti 2010, 174). The new civil code ended the supremacy of men in marriage, putting in place full equality of men and women in the family. Specifically, spouses were granted equal rights over family decisions, including equal property rights for properties acquired during the marriage. The new law also gave equal authority to marital partners in issues of legal representation and transactions, work, travel, and place of residence decisions.

Perhaps no legal amendment demonstrates the dismantling of shame-honor discourse more strikingly than the reform of the Turkish penal code. Introduced in 2005, the new penal code included thirty-five amendments that women and LGBTIQ+ organizations had pushed for that recognized women's legal entitlement to sexual and bodily autonomy and rights, despite strong opposition from the AKP government (İlkkaracan 2007). Sexual offenses were no longer categorized under the rubric of offenses against public morality and the family but were classified as violations of individual rights. Concepts deriving from shame-honor discourse such as morality, honor, virginity, and chastity (*ırz*, *ar*, and *haya*) were all eliminated from the code completely. In the scaling of punishment for sexual offenses, the new law removed any distinctions between married and unmarried women, or virgins and nonvirgins. Likewise, honor killings—for which the previous penal code granted leniency—were, for the first time, acknowledged as aggravated homicides under the new law. Moreover, the law outlawed genital virginity examinations carried out without the consent of the woman, recognized marital rape as a criminal act to be punished, and acknowledged and outlawed sexual harassment along with workplace sexual harassment (Süral and Kiliçoğlu 2011). With the comprehensive legal reforms of the early 2000s, not only did the shame-honor discourse lose its legal status, but women's violability was also significantly diminished. Previously, women had been granted bodily inviolability on the basis of their ties to men; now they were entitled to bodily inviolability without male mediation.

The economic changes prompted by globalization were advanced in the favorable climate of gender equality. Against the

political background of the gender equality movement, which mitigated women's violability, a significant shift took place in employment
opportunities away from manufacturing to services, away from muscle
power to cultural capital, and away from male to female. The expansion of the service economy entailed more than a sector-based shift in
employment and encompassed a larger shift in gender relations. The
old world of industrial production was, to a certain extent, enabled,
shaped, fueled, and stabilized by shame-honor discourse. As moral
approval of shame-honor disappeared in the global era, the old world
of industrial production—characterized by a predominantly male
labor force—also began to dissipate. The processes of the service economy are imbued with meanings and norms about gender, but shame-
honor discourse is not central to them. The service economy rather
relies on, and is fostered by, a gendered labor force, whose feminine
working subjects are *not* governed by the shame-honor discourse. But
in what specific ways does Turkey's transition to a service economy
relate to the New Woman? Does the thriving service economy just
offer women expanded employment opportunities and disposable
income or there is a stronger link between its gendered dynamics and
the New Woman? In which manner does the service economy draw
on the New Woman's embodied and interactional capacities? How
does the service economy, with its changing skill requirements and
workplace culture, appeal to the New Woman and her sensibilities?
The next chapter provides answers to these questions by carefully
examining the gendered world of the service economy in Turkey.

Endnotes

1. Based on information from email correspondence with Stella Ovadia, March
   2020. She emphasized that it was the materialist and radical feminist theory
   that informed her activism.
2. The religious and ethnic homogenization of the population in Turkey was
   engineered by the political elite through a series of violent political strategies
   during the period of 1912–1923. For more, see (Ünlü 2018).
3. For instance, the Women's People Party, founded in 1923 by feminist
   intellectual Nezihe Muhiddin with the aim of advancing women's political
   rights, was not recognized by the government, and its operations were shut
   down (Zihnioğlu 2003).
4. The moral critiques of women entering the labor market, and control
   measures used on them, are widely documented in the literature. Studies

show how factory managers, religious leaders, or family members in different countries including Malaysia (Ong 1987), the United States (Peiss 1986), and Mexico (Fernández-Kelly 1984; Salzinger 2003) were involved in feminine bodily comportment by utilizing morality and moral precepts.

5. In the countryside, peasants were the dominant group, and the classical patriarchy associated with the reproduction of the small peasantry was the main force shaping women's lives, as well as patterns of female economic activity (Kandiyoti 1988). The classical patriarchal system that has functioned for many centuries in the rural areas of Middle Eastern countries, including Turkey, is characterized by extended households where the senior male has exclusive power over the family's social and material resources, while property, residence and descent all pass through the male line (Caldwell 1978; Kandiyoti 1988; Moghadam 2004). Women were primarily valued for their birth-giving and unpaid labor. Given the high fertility and low educational levels of women and their restriction to the home, girls are given in marriage at a young age before entering the husband's household as dispossessed individuals to be subordinated to all the men, as well as the senior women in the household, especially the mother-in-law. The bride can only establish her place in the family by giving birth to sons, gaining access to power and security in old age through her married sons. Hence, the major task of the bride is producing offspring, while the major task of the man, on the other hand, is to provide income and security for the family. Women's domestic tasks encompassed home production, household chores, and caring for the children. In addition, they were required to provide unconditional services to their extended kin. Norms of shame-honor demanded that women be kept hidden because they could evoke men's sexual desires. Engaging in conversation or even receiving glances from unrelated men defiled her.

6. Among scholars of Turkey, there seems to be a consensus that women's labor force participation in Turkey follows a U-shaped curve (Gündüz-Hoşgör and Smits 2008). Recently some scholars have argued that that women's labor force participation in Turkey follows an L-shaped pattern (Erinc 2017).

7. In her *Türk Modernleşmesinin Cinsiyeti: Erkekler Devlet, Kadınlar Aile Kurar* (Turkish Modernization's Gender: Men Make the State, Women the Family) Serpil Sancar (2012) argues that between 1945 and 1965 in Turkey the gendered character of modernity reinforced domestic feminine positions by encouraging women to take up the identity of a modern homemaker.

8. It may be plausible to argue that this was the case for both Muslim and non-Muslim women in that period. Speaking of the same period, Stella Ovadia noted that in the Turkish Jewish community women only worked if they were widowed and in need of money (Ovadia 2019).

9. Adalet Ağaoglu's *Dar Zamanlar* trilogy comprises "*Ölmeye Yatmak*" (Lying Down to Die) (1973), "*Bir Düğün Gecesi*" (A Wedding Night) (1979), and "*Hayır*" (No) (1987).

10. There is now a substantial and ever-growing body of scholarly work on Kurdish feminism and the Kurdish women's movement in Turkey. For some of these studies, see Karaman (2016), Çağlayan (2019), Üstündağ (2019), Göksel (2019) and Goral (2021).

CHAPTER 3

The New Woman at Work

*Global Capitalism and the Gendered World
of the Service Economy*

During the summer of 2006, while I was carrying out a research project on women industrial homeworkers in Istanbul,[1] I had a chance encounter with a young woman that opened my eyes to the unmistakable presence of the New Woman in Turkey. One August evening, after conducting interviews with homeworker women in working-class neighborhoods on the periphery of the city, I walked down to the Yenikapı ferry dock in Bakırköy to take the sea bus back home. It was one of those hot, muggy days when everyone felt dazed and tired under the glaring August sun. I was waiting on the crowded pier when a young girl a few steps ahead of me caught my eye. A carefree girl in her late teens, she was probably a college student, I thought to myself. She was wearing a plain t-shirt, leggings, a cotton tote bag, and high-top Converse sneakers, all black except for her colorful headphones. Looking self-assured and at ease, she threw glances at the sea to see if the sea bus was getting nearer. The scene, however, changed swiftly. After only a minute, she suddenly collapsed in front of me. The crowd instantly surged forward to help her. Luckily, she recovered fairly quickly. I accompanied her to the sea bus, and we sat together by the window on our way to Bostancı. During the approximately twenty-minute trip, she regained her energy after drinking the **ayran** and nibbling on the cheese sandwich I bought for her, and we began chatting. Apparently, she had neither eaten nor drunk enough that day and became overheated under the blazing sun. When she told me she spent summers working at a garment workshop while finishing high school, my curiosity was piqued. I was pleasantly surprised and impressed to hear that she was not what I thought her to be, a middle-class college student with a certain amount of cultural capital. Contrary to my assumptions, she came from an underprivileged background and was working at a garment workshop in one of the global subcontracting chains I was examining. Delighted to have met a strong, independent young woman, I explained my research and asked her some more questions. Before we parted ways, I inquired what she would like to do instead of working at a garment workshop, and she answered without hesitation: "I'd rather prefer working as a waitress at a café or as a salesperson at a shopping mall." Surprised, I asked her why and she responded quickly: "Oh, these places are not like garment ateliers; both the environment and the people are nice in cafes and you have a chance to meet many people. Also, you work in the heart of the city."

Long after this encounter, I found myself thinking about this young woman. There was something different about her. The way she carried herself, her manners and aspirations, did not match the image of working-class women I was familiar with and studying. Many of the women I met during my research in 2006 were housewives and mothers who had taken up industrial home-based work while living mostly within the bounds of their neighborhoods. Or else they were dispossessed Kurdish women who had recently migrated to the city to escape the civil war between the Kurdish movement and the Turkish state and were engaging in home-based work to scratch out a living.[2] Reflecting on the encounter later, I realized what it was that had struck me about the young woman: it was her distinct orientation, the particular embodied manner in which she inhabited the urban environment. Her posture was neither uptight nor self-conscious, but relaxed and self-possessed; her comportment was not burdened by class and gender hierarchies. She seemed buoyant, light-footed, and unafraid of the world. This encounter proved to be my first glimpse of a New Woman from the working classes in Turkey. It was also the first time I got a sense that service jobs had a specific appeal for New Women.

The New Woman was commonly employed in the service economy. A host of scholarly studies have shown that she often worked as a saleswoman or had an office job, usually performing secretarial tasks.[3] A product of modernity, the New Woman had complex affinities for consumer capitalism, through which she was incorporated into the urban economy as both a producer and consumer (Weinbaum et al. 2008; Freedman, Miller, and Yano 2013). While toiling in the shop or office, she, at the same time, enjoyed her newfound autonomy in participating in new consumption venues, frequenting the movie theaters, restaurants, bars, cafes, dance halls, and amusement parks that arose rapidly in China, South Africa, and India, as well as Europe and the United States in the late nineteenth and early twentieth centuries (Benson 1986; Dong 2008; Peiss 1986; Ramamurthy 2008; Stansell 1986; Thomas 2008). Through consumption of dime novels, fashionable clothing, and cosmetics, she enjoyed the freedom to experiment and created a new identity for herself that transgressed older, community-based norms of morality and religion (Frevert 1989; Enstad 1999).

In this chapter, I look closely into gendered dynamics of the service economy in urban Turkey, which has grown at the intersection of neoliberal global capitalism and gender equality reforms, to flesh out the ways it sustains as well as capitalizes on the New Woman's embodied orientations. By exploring the minutiae of everyday life on the sales floor, I highlight how bodies and emotions—especially embarrassment or its absence—inform hiring practices, training stages, and the labor process on the sales floor. I first explore the gendered dimensions of hiring practices in certain service occupations to better account for employers' tendency to hire New Women for interactive service jobs. I then move to the sales floor to investigate (a la Goffman) the affective and gendered dimensions of interaction order that service settings promote.

"Shy Women Cannot Do It"

On the first day of my stint at the MajorMarket (a pseudonym I use for the large supermarket in Istanbul where I conducted my fieldwork), I was sitting along with other new hires in a large conference room listening to our trainer. "Do not ever forget to make eye contact with the customers!" she said, a fair-haired woman in her mid-forties, whose tired-looking face, rapid and expert speaking, and lackluster attitude gave away the long years she spent as an employee at MajorMarket. Unlike her, almost all the new hires in the conference room seemed young and enthusiastic, lounging causally on a row of black plastic chairs, listening attentively to the instructions our trainer jotted down on the white board, occasionally taking notes. The training program for new hires was short; it lasted two days and featured sessions including a two-hour lecture about the company's history and its corporate culture, a brief training about the administrative procedures used in the store, and a session on the standards of behavior for customer-worker interactions on the sales floor.

During this session, our trainer gave short instructions regarding how to greet customers, thank them, and handle difficult situations. We were required to exhibit what she called "positive emotions" for the customers to perceive us as polite, cheerful, and helpful. "Eye contact is a delicate matter," said our trainer and warned us against sending mixed signals to customers. "When you make eye contact with the customer," she said, looking at us steadily, "make sure that it is neither too short nor too long. If it is too short, the customer will think that you do not respect him. If it is too long, the customer might assume that you are flirting with him. And if you are handling a couple, do not forget to make

The author is checking customers out at the cash register at MajorMarket. Istanbul, 2011 (Photo by a colleague).

eye contact with both of them. We are living in Turkey; you should be careful about family norms."

Our trainer was preparing us for the routine service transactions that we were going to execute every day when catering to the needs of our customers. We were not serving clientele from diverse socioeconomic backgrounds; our customers were secular and predominantly middle and upper-middle class. Before neoliberal globalization gained a foothold in Turkey, they used to shop at the *bakkal* (corner store), *kasap* (butcher), *manav* (grocery), and *pazar* (outdoor fresh market) in their neighborhoods. When the heavily capitalized, and increasingly corporate, service industries of the global era killed off family-owned stores—especially in large cities such as Istanbul, Ankara, Izmir, and Konya—the middle classes began to frequent shopping malls, branded outlets, shopping centers, hypermarkets, supermarkets, warehouse clubs, giant discount chains, and specialty stores. The number of shopping malls in Turkey was 53 in 2001 but just a decade later had reached 308, with the majority in Istanbul (Erinc 2017). Likewise, the number of hypermarkets and supermarkets increased from 2,979 to 6,474 between 2000 and 2006 (Ersun and Arslan 2008). These venues came to symbolize consumerist ideology, the crushing power of corporations over small business, and the unquenchable demand created by neoliberal capitalism; yet the implications for gendered change were far less straightforward. These venues contributed to the rise in the feminization of service labor in Turkey, although many occupations in the service sector were low-wage jobs with long hours and very few career prospects.

As factories with smoking chimneys receded to the periphery of urban life and then disappeared completely from the built environment, low-wage service jobs have quickly flourished. To be more precise, when the erstwhile urban manufacturing zones of the "Third World," including Istanbul, became connected to global networks and markets—functioning as central points of services (Sassen 1998; Keyder 2005)—women began to take up new employment opportunities in the expanding service economies. In fact, women's labor force participation in urban Turkey has followed a steady upward trend from the early 1990s until today. While the female labor force participation rate in urban Turkey was 17.7 percent in 1988, it reached 24.8 percent in 2011 (TURKSAT). In 2013, the majority of urban women in the labor force were employed in service and sales jobs, which accounted for 22.5 percent of women's employment, followed by professionals at

19.8 percent (Aile ve Sosyal Politikalar Bakanlığı 2014). However, not every woman was suited for work in the new service economy. A human resources manager of a major corporate retail company explained to me the desired characteristics of the saleswomen they like to employ:

> Our workers encounter a lot of different people at the store. We have a lot of people coming into the stores. For instance, seven thousand people visit our stores during weekdays and this number reaches up to twenty thousand at weekends. Only 35 percent of these people are shopping. But our workers should handle all of these people in a friendly and professional way. We want our workers to be presentable, open-minded, and sociable. We cannot work with shy people. Our customers are coming from very different cultural backgrounds. You know, some people are touchy, some talk a lot. Besides, we are located in Istanbul, which is a cosmopolitan city. Tourists and people from different religions are also shopping here. No matter what kind of customers our workers deal with, they should treat customers in a genial and courteous way. This requires emotional stamina as well as physical effort. We want our workers to maintain the same positive attitude during their work shifts.

Companies that offer consumer services, as the manager told me, did not want to hire shy people. Embarrassment, or shyness for that matter, denotes an affective tension that interrupts the interaction between the self and another. If an individual, for one reason or another, grows self-conscious and feels embarrassed in the immediate presence of another, the connection between them is compromised, if not interrupted. This was what Silvan Tomkins (1963) suggested when he wrote that shame "is both an interruption and a further impediment to communication" (Tomkins 1963, 136). If feelings of shame and embarrassment thwart communication, as Tomkins suggested, these feelings should be banished from the sales floor, where the flow of communication is of utmost importance. This was the case in the new consumption venues, where service encounters were managed carefully, with principles of equality and courtesy underlying the transactions. We sales workers were expected to pay quick and respectful attention to customers, deliver the services they requested with our words, gestures, and manners, and display both deference and enjoyment through our interactions. Paying equal regard to customers, making eye contact with them, being friendly, courteous, extraverted, and sociable on the sales floor—all were essential parts of our job. The sales floor, in other words, rendered embarrassment and its bodily expressions—such as avoiding eye contact or a downcast gaze—useless. Once a primary emotion that announced woman's modesty, embarrassment became an undesired affective habit that immediately indicated a malfunction on the sales floor, signaling the incompetency of the saleswoman and proving her unfit for the occupation.

Besides embarrassment (or rather the absence thereof), there were a range of affective and interactive capacities, emotions, moods, and bodily orientations saleswomen were expected to possess as part of their requisite skills. These skill requirements, which gave the New Woman a lot of leverage in getting hired, could hardly be met by the modest female for whom shame-honor discourse had caused a subject position. The New Woman, thanks to her embodied orientations, could effortlessly execute smooth interactions with a variety of individuals on the sales floor, carrying out face-to-face interactions with ease and no sign of discomfort—blushing or breaking voice—detectable in her approach. Service companies like MajorMarket—which targeted the urban, educated middle and upper-middle classes that had secular and Western lifestyles—disproportionately hired New Women precisely because their embodied mode of being was not governed by feminine shame. The New Woman, with her emotional orientations and specific interactional modes of being, had the skill set that the service economy increasingly demanded.

This often meant that those service companies did not hire women wearing headscarves for frontline jobs such as cashier and sales positions.[4] From the corporate retailers' point of view, such women did not convey the appropriate image to the affluent, modern, westernized consumers they targeted. To be sure, this practice cannot be easily divorced from the highly contentious politics of secularism in Turkey, and it caters to the psychic needs of the secularly oriented urban upper and middle classes, who felt increasingly besieged with the ascendance of the AKP and its political attacks on secularism.[5]

For service economy employers, the easiest way to find New Women was to tap into a particular segment of the labor pool: urban, high school graduates, often from a working-class or lower-middle-class family background. Such women were more likely to possess the desired interpersonal skills of sociability, open-mindedness, and extraversion, and were, thus, considered well suited for work in retail stores.

One human resource employee explained why high school-educated women were hired for sales work:

> The high school graduate girl is different from the less educated girl. She is different because she is already urbanized and has achieved a level of education. She does not work purely out of necessity. Of course, she needs money, but she also wants to stand on her own feet. Besides, girls with a high school education are better at communicating with people. They know how to talk to customers and maintain a friendly demeanor.

Ela, a thirty-three-year-old MajorMarket worker, elaborated on the importance of interpersonal capacities and habits for landing a position on the sales floor:

> I think employers hire people who can handle the type of social interactions taking place in a store. Generally, people who are tolerant and open-minded about interactions with the opposite sex get hired. And high school graduates are more suitable for working here because at school, girls and boys sit next to each other in the classroom. If a girl is a high school graduate, she thinks it is normal that girls and boys are close friends, because interacting with boys is a part of her upbringing and education. She probably has had a couple of romantic relationships, too. But if a girl has only a primary school diploma, it means that, later in her life, she lives in seclusion. She would find it strange that girls and boys are close friends, working all day and sometimes at night together. She would not get used to the environment here and would feel out of place. Just as the guys [her coworkers] here feel uneasy when they talk with a gay person, the girl with a primary school diploma would feel uneasy interacting with men, customers and coworkers alike.

Although shyness and guarded modes of being are undesirable on the sales floor, this is not to suggest that feminine modesty is rendered completely irrelevant. A certain modicum of sexual modesty is incorporated into the job requirements. For instance, one personnel director I interviewed recalled rejecting one applicant because she thought her demeanor was too coquettish. As she told me in all seriousness, "I did not hire her because these kinds of women want to work here only to flirt with customers." Sexual modesty is reflected through eye contact, as well as in dress codes. A dress code was strictly enforced at Major-Market, with workers being required to wear standardized uniforms:

company-issued polo shirts and loose-fitting pants for women and men alike which downplayed the workers' sexual identities in favor of a masculine look.

Young workers on the sales floor were nevertheless allowed to be playful within certain limits. They would wear ripped jeans on some days, or sport cool hairdos and flashy nail polish. Early in my stint, when I was still uncertain about the dress code on the sales floor, I wore a cardigan on a hot day to hide a small tattoo on my arm. Upon observing this, the supervisor approached me and, smiling, said, "You don't have to hide your tattoos here, our company is okay with this, don't worry." Her reassurance was yet another indicator of the larger shift in sexual mores taking place in working-class work environments. In the commercialized service environment, saleswomen's bodies and bodily conduct, including hairstyles and outfits, did not have the moral value that they had in the shame-honor discourse. In such an environment, traits of extraversion and open-mindedness constitute working-class women's labor market value. This shift was also demonstrated by a gendered interaction order on the sales floor, which entailed a greater sense of freedom for New Women at work.

The Gendered Interaction Order on the Sales Floor

In interactive service work settings, women, as part of their jobs, immerse themselves in what Goffman (1983) describes as an interaction order, where "emotion, mood, cognition, bodily orientation, and muscular effort are intrinsically involved" and "ease and uneasiness, unselfconsciousness and wariness are central" (Goffman 1983, 3). The interaction order, according to Goffman, cannot be divorced from social structures; after all, face-to-face interactions are far from free-floating, but are tacitly guided by cultural assumptions and norms. Taking my bearings from Goffman's analysis, I examined the gendered interaction order on the sales floor and found that the sexual mores and norms informing it—from the vocabulary saleswomen used to their emotions and bodily gestures, including facial expressions, visual regard for others, and the degree of their involvement in conversation—further weakened the shame-honor discourse.

Gender performances in new consumption spaces like the shopping mall are not anchored in conventional, strict gender norms, as labor scholars in Turkey have noted (Ozbay 2015). These new commercial spaces, Gul Ozyegin observes, have "granted them [young workers] more freedom in self-expression, youth sociability, sexual communication and neoliberal self-making" (Ozyegin 2009, 108). Equally important in the context of global capitalist restructuring is the transformation of traditional spaces, accompanied by the emergence of new consumption spaces. One such change took place in the *mahalle* (neighborhood). The boom in the construction industry, for instance, gave a new silhouette to the cities and to the *mahalle*, catalyzing a renewal of residential arrangements, with new apartments, gated communities, mass housing projects, and gentrified apartment buildings spreading across the urban space. In the course of this urban transformation, which was steered by the AKP government, the *mahalle*—with its close-knit structure and relatively homogenous community—was replaced by larger, heterogeneous residential areas that brought together people from similar economic classes. However, no sense of community existed in them, thus fostering a sense of anonymity as opposed to the familial space of *mahalle*.

This was a complex change, both in terms of its origins and repercussions,[6] a shift that the New Woman seemed to embrace largely because of the gendered changes it entailed. The unmaking of neighborhood surveillance mechanisms—such as gossip and the presence of neighborhood men who assumed the role of protecting the *mahalle*'s honor—sat very well with the New Woman. Talking about her neighborhood, which had grown considerably over the last decade after construction of the subway, a twenty-three-year-old saleswoman, Pelin, explained why she preferred living in a large neighborhood rather than in a *mahalle*:

> It makes me feel comfortable. I have no problems wearing sleeveless shirts here. Neither do I feel bothered when I go home late at night. We don't have neighborhood men harassing women. Our neighborhood is big and people do not watch each other. Years ago, when the neighborhood was small, there were some restrictions, my mother told me. But now it is big and crowded.

However outdated those groups of neighborhood men patrolling women were in Pelin's eyes, they still pervaded urban life. Many women I met from smaller neighborhoods observed that these men still instilled a disturbing sense of intrusion in their lives. The new type of neighborhood, however, where anonymity was the norm of social relations, offered a desired alternative to the traditional *mahalle* structure. Nesrin, who at the time had not yet bought her own home, was living in a relatively smaller neighborhood with a more traditional social structure. She told me why living in a neighborhood with high-rise building complexes appealed to her:

> Since I dyed my hair orange, people in my neighborhood have been staring at me. It is annoying. If I took my boyfriend to the neighborhood, people would start gossiping immediately. I feel like I have to watch myself here. I want to move to one of these neighborhoods where they have new building complexes. Life is so easy over there. Nobody knows each other. A woman, for instance, can live with her boyfriend in these building complexes, but in our neighborhood this type of arrangement wouldn't be tolerated.

It goes without saying that the transformation of the *mahalle* generated a gender crisis for those men invested in male honor, which had sanctioned their claims over women's bodies. Now New Women wanted a life away from these men and found male surveillance over their bodies illegitimate, calling them out for what they saw as male aggression and intrusiveness. However, for the Sunni intellectual establishment, the weakening of male honor was yet another indicator of the encroachment of global modernity on local gender values. In 2003, Nazife Şişman, a female writer who reflected on the everyday Muslim experience under the changing dynamics of modernity, decried this change with a sense of vehemence:

> The modern paradigm shifted not only the understanding of what it means to be a woman but also a man. The men who, back in the day, were in charge of the honor of the neighborhood, those men who protected us, watched over us are today being lumped into the category of machos, if they attempt to continue acting in the same way. On the other hand, there is a grave shift away from the protective masculine type, towards a man with feminine qualities. We are experiencing a period when genders converge; gender in its classical meaning has completely changed its function. (Şişman 2003, 12)

Nazife Şişman adopted an alarmist tone about the gendered changes in Turkey, which severed the ties between male honor and control over women's bodies in the global era. Perhaps even more alarming was the entrenchment of women's rights and gender equality in the law and the increasing traction social-constructionist understandings of gender gained even in popular culture. The media enthusiastically disseminated the trope of the Free Girl, with magazines, television programs, and newspapers all featuring affirmative images of autonomous women pursuing their own dreams as well as relationships with a new kind of man, gentler than the tough men of the *mahalle*. And the New Woman emerging from the ranks of the working class was making headway under this era of "gender convergence" that accommodated her presence in urban society.

"No *Bacı* Talk Here; It Makes Me Feel Free"

I came to realize what the sales floor represented to New Women only after many of them expressed relief at not being called *bacı* at work. "Nobody treats me like a *bacı* (sister) on the sales floor" was an expression I heard frequently from saleswomen when they described the appeal of sales work. In response to my inquiries about why they preferred working at sales jobs, women cited the nonfamilial vocabulary as a positive aspect. Esma, for instance, said, "I like working here because there is no '*bacı* talk' here. We call each other by our names; it is not like the factory."

In addition to the *bacı* theme, the differences between factory workers and saleswomen—as well as the contrasts between the shop floor and sales floor—came up repeatedly throughout my research, even though my questions did not make any reference to industrial workplaces or workers. Initially, I did not see the connection between industrial workplaces and the moral universe of shame-honor that the word *bacı* suggested. Instead, I thought saleswomen concocted these comparisons to negotiate class hierarchies and, through these comparisons, they distanced themselves from stigmatized femininities, warding off class shame.[7]

Class-based approaches, however, although immensely valuable in showing how class structures operate at the level of the individual psyche—shaping one's embodied comportment, feelings, taste, and aspirations—might easily lead to overlooking how class is complicated by the dynamics of gender, ethnicity, or race. In my case, it only gradually occurred to me that class might not be the only dynamic at work in saleswomen's discomfort with the term *bacı*. In fact, it was the term's history that alerted me to the operation of male honor in women's lives across the class spectrum.

The use of *bacı*, as illustrated in the previous chapter, has never been restricted to the working classes. Widely used in urban life by millions of adults when addressing each other in everyday encounters, this family evocative was even employed by progressive, secular left-wing activists throughout the 1970s and 1980s. Originally devised to circumvent the restrictions posed by shame-honor norms, or for that matter Sunni mores on mixed-gender interactions, *bacı* has begun to create uneasiness over the decades, even among those who at first enthusiastically adopted the strategic use of fictive kinship ties in everyday interactions. In a study on pious Sunni professional women's experiences at middle-class mixed-gender workplaces, women engineers, architects, and doctors who all wore headscarves reported feeling undermined when their male colleagues addressed them as *bacı*. As one of them explained, "When they see you, a head-scarved woman, they identify you with their moms or grandmoms. You can't quite be the Engineer Mrs. So and So. You're the 'sister,' period," (Cindoglu 2011, 48). Although the term once functioned to create space for mixed-gender interactions without upsetting shame-honor norms, it now comes across as dismissive of women's professional status and equality with men.

More importantly, the term *bacı* alludes to a world in which women's bodies were tied to male honor, which enabled men to control women's embodied existence in myriad ways. Women acutely felt demeaned when their professional identity was conflated with a subordinate position within the kinship hierarchy, when their autonomy was eclipsed by a term that emphasized men's gendered authority over them. The term *bacı* pervaded, and was reinforced, in the workplace through gendered interactions and codes of behavior where men expressed paternalistic attitudes to assert superiority and authority vis-à-vis women by characterizing female colleagues as daughters or sisters (White 2004; Arslan 2020). In short, *bacı* was an essential part of the fictive kinship hierarchy that men utilized to advance claims to authority and control over women.

Women's changing feelings about the term *bacı* over the last few decades, from an unhesitant embrace to downright discomfort, reveals the extent to which the moral universe of shame-honor has become unacceptable for women across classes. A workplace divorced from the moral universe of shame and honor would make the job far more appealing to women. At least this was the case for Ela. In discussing the pros and cons of her position at MajorMarket, she compared the sales floor favorably to the shop floor, which, according to her, foreclosed interactional opportunities for women, bringing them under suspicion of immoral conduct:

> I have a distant relative living in Zeytinburnu district. It is a squatter settlement area, full of garment workshops. I don't think workers in those workshops can be close friends with each other. I mean women and men. If they become friends, like regular friends, people around them would immediately start gossiping about them.... Here, we can be close friends with our male coworkers without worrying about accusations or gossip. Nobody here would think that I am being promiscuous because I am close friends with the male coworkers. They do not misinterpret things here. But in an environment like a garment workshop, people think that if a man talks to a woman it means that there's something sexual going on between them. She would be considered as an immoral woman. In our environment, friendship between men and women is normal. We don't even think about it; we take it for granted.

Body Armoring at Work

From a phenomenological perspective, Ela's account of women working in the garment workshop alluded to the ways in which gendered interaction, undergirded by the norms of shame-honor, worked directly upon the body.[8] The woman's body inhabiting the space of the garment workshop was never solely a worker's body expending labor power but was, at the same time, a feminized body treated by others as the repository of male honor, and depending on the circumstances, seen as morally flawed. Because her body was subject to the logic of capital accumulation and the norms of feminine propriety at the same time, the labor process on the shop floor was, thus, integrally bound up with the moral universe of shame and honor. Under this scenario, the feminized body, in addition to toiling for long hours for six days a week, has to bear the burden of constantly adjusting her gestures, postures, and expressions to fend off gendered meanings—including moralized accusations about her bodily conduct—that get continuously projected onto her. Burdened with anxiety and tension, the feminized body, in an effort to defend against harassment or gossip that could easily warp her reputation, would be wary of even lapsing into a casual conversation with male coworkers.

Like Ela, Sena was one of those women who had worked at a textile workshop before coming to MajorMarket. One day she described in more detail how a gendered interaction order inside the garment workshop demanded from women particular embodied attitudes like guardedness, defensiveness, and vigilance:

> I felt relieved after I started working here. While I was working at the factory, people would have considered us immoral when we talked to guys working in the factory. There are strong taboos against close interactions between men and women in the factory. According to people over there, men and women cannot be friends. Men and women might get married and have sex, but cannot be friends. And it is impossible to change their ideas. Especially, middle-aged factory workers are so strict. They would say, "Why would you be friends with men? Aren't girlfriends enough for you?" It was such a domineering environment. I had to watch myself all the time. Even though it is perfectly normal for me to be friends with men, I couldn't dare hang out with the guys working in the factory because I did not want people to gossip about me. I kept my distance from the guys.

Nesrin had also worked in textile workshops. During one of our afternoon breaks when I probed her work experience there, she commented, "Oh! That's hard." She was sitting across the table from me in the staff canteen. She leaned back in her chair and held up her hand, bringing her fingers into a tight fist. "Look," she said, showing her fist to me. "As a woman you have to be like this all the time." When I told her I did not understand the meaning of the hand gesture, she explained: "You have to be tough, you see? Be firm and stern so you can keep people away from you or you'll be regarded as loose." Her hand gesture in a way replicated how a feminized body grew rigid under the pressure of the normative demands placed on her at work. The medium of the body reflects this pressure immediately: muscles tighten, the body stiffens, and habitual postures close down. In an environment where any signs of informality or casualness in a woman's manner are taken as signs of sexual licentiousness, she has to forfeit her bodily capacity to be relaxed. As opposed to a body with a sense of openness and possibility—which is able to take on a smooth and fluid demeanor in performing tasks—the body Nesrin described was like a suit of armor, a bodily armor the feminine subject unconsciously assumed in an effort to make herself unapproachable and, thus, inviolable when confronted with moral accusations or sexual harassment inside the workplace.

For the New Woman, to be able to dwell in spaces where she could drop her bodily armor, or where the need for it had vanished, created a sense of comfort and freedom. Indeed, many of the saleswomen told me that they could earn more money as factory workers because their wages were comparable to, and at times higher than, those working in textile production. However, all argued that they would not prefer working there because they found the work environment restrictive.[9] Women liked that sales work promoted face-to-face interactions between genders as a part of the labor process. They liked casting relationships with their coworkers and managers in nonfamilial terms, calling each other by their names and addressing each other with "Mr." and "Mrs." or "Ms." in the presence of customers. These interactions not only relieved women of the need for bodily armoring but also furnished them with a sense of egalitarianism. For instance, for some saleswomen, sociability was the biggest perk of the service floor, apart from the wages. They found that working together with college students especially, many of whom took up a sales job as part-time employment, imparted a peer-group culture to the interaction order, flattening, at least temporarily, the class hierarchies between sales workers and college students. When asked about friendship ties on the sales floor, Zehra said with excitement, "The staff canteen sometimes feels like a university canteen. Young people like me come together and talk about different things, like fun places to go, books, movies and even inter-rail. I have come to meet a lot of college students here."

The ethos of sociability on the sales floor, however, was a double-edged sword. On the one hand, it enhanced saleswomen's employment experiences; on the other hand, it functioned as one of the key instruments of supervisory control. By fostering sociability and ensuring the formation of a work team that resembled a wide circle of friends, management was better able to guarantee young workers' commitment to their employers. Supervisors also skillfully utilized sociability to blur the lines between work and leisure time. In doing so, they were able to coax workers into long hours of work and to manage their stress. Creating a friendly environment allowed the supervisors to expect greater cooperation from the women in response to requests for overtime and to demand, in general, high-quality work, as well as small favors like making tea and picking up a take-away lunch during a break.

The problems on the sales floor were not limited to sociability. While women enjoyed a sense of openness and freedom there, they also found the work demanding and poorly compensated. Women often worked six days a week, with the pace of work being quite stressful. Workers' desire for more regulation and shorter working hours were not only dismissed by managers, but also explicitly rejected by Recep Tayyip Erdoğan, then prime minister. In 2010, when small business owners, confronted with the sweeping dominance of large-scale service retailers, demanded that shopping malls and large supermarkets shorten their working hours and close on Sundays, Recep Tayyip Erdoğan brushed off the appeals. He curtly responded: "We cannot accept the demands regarding the shortening of working hours at shopping malls and super-markets. We can't let go of Sunday openings either. My citizen spends his leisure time in shopping malls. Family members come together at weekends and visit different malls. I have to listen to people's demands" (Hürriyet 2010).

For saleswomen, in addition to long working hours, it was hard to manage their jobs' interactional requirements, especially with custom-ers. Throughout my research, a reoccuring theme was the customers' disrespectful attitudes toward workers. Customers' bullying actions—such as loud, angry outbursts or micro-aggressions—were part and parcel of the daily sales floor. Everyday problems with working con-ditions were compounded by the limited career prospects in the sales industry. Possibilities for promotion were few, with no chance to ascend the corporate career ladder without a college degree. Frustrated by working conditions, pay rates and career limitations, women often tried to find alternative career options available to them, but mostly without success.

Saleswomen's complicated relationship with the sales floor—which fluctuated between appreciation and disaffection—was perhaps ampli-fied for the single saleswomen, who were more invested in the sales floor, compared to their married co-workers. Single saleswomen found the sales floor welcoming, offering a greater acceptance of being single without facing social disapproval. Ela was thirty-three years old and single. Speaking about the shop floor, she told me, "Over there, you are regarded as a spinster on the day you turn twenty-five." Ela's description of the approach her coworkers adopted when talking about her single status made clear why she did not have a strong need for emotional armoring on the sales floor:

> People working here don't think that way. When I talk to my coworkers about marriage, the comments they make uplift me. They say that I couldn't find someone because I am very selective or have high standards. They make me feel good. They don't make me feel like I am not eligible or it's my fault that I am still single.

That said, saleswomen often responded to the idea of being single with a troubled sense of possibility, a sense of general angst. These feelings, to be sure, reflect the pressure exerted by the hegemonic power of the institution of marriage in Turkey, which pressures one to inhabit the heteronormative life trajectory where they are expected to marry, have children, and rely on family for care and love. In Turkey, the majority of women of childbearing age (age 15–49) are married (68 percent), nearly one-third (28 percent) have never married, and the remaining 4 percent are either divorced, separated or widowed (TDHS 2014). By 2020, the mean age for women at their first marriage was 25.1, compared to 18 in 1950 (TURKSTAT 2021; Jelnov 2019).[10] Moreover, the dearth and obscurity of single adults in Turkey, which leaves single women without any guidance or role models, contributes to women's angst. These feelings often came up in my interactions with other saleswomen during my stint as a saleswoman at MajorMarket. Especially before I revealed my identity as a graduate student, it was puzzling for saleswomen to find out that I was happily unmarried at the age of thirty-two and sharing an apartment with a man other than my boyfriend. One day, when I was chatting before our shift, Ufuk, a single saleswoman, remarked, "I wish I could live like you do, it would be nice to be living on my own, without my parents." Another time, Şule, a saleswoman working at the deli section, called out to me, "Hey, Free Girl, you are perfect," smiling and giving me an approving thumbs up. Later that day, I asked her why she thought I was a "Free Girl." She laughed and replied, "It is obvious that you have your freedom, holding it tightly in your own hands. And you are different from us." She went on to describe our difference: "Sometimes when you tell me something I feel like I am looking at an alien and sometimes when I talk, you look at me as if I am an alien."

The Free Girl trope, which had become hugely popular in Turkey in the 2000s, was one that appeared to fit me better than Şule, as she was quick to glean from my lifestyle, demeanor, and attitude. It seemed that I had somehow won the battle for independence and had come to embody the global neoliberal icon that gained huge popularity in Turkey in the early 2000s. My life, like that of the Free Girl, was characterized less by regulation and control than by liberty and self-sufficiency. For Şule, who was well aware of the limitations a meager wage and low educational attainment posed for achieving full autonomy, I was a puzzle. Once I revealed my identity as a graduate student, however, it became clear that it was through higher education and professional employment that I was able to inhabit the Free Girl status. After all, it was perfectly acceptable for an educated woman to live alone and remain single, which was not the case for working-class women who typically lived with their parents until they get married.

Single saleswomen, nevertheless, broke free from family surveillance, with employment enabling them to have considerable control over their free time. Nihal explained how her relationship to her parents had evolved after she began working: "Now, I spend less time with my family. I use the house like a hotel. I go there after work and sleep. On my day off, I spend at most two or three hours at home." Pelin's experience was similar: "For me, home is a place where I go only to sleep and take a shower," she told me.

Working-class New Women were, however, acutely aware of the limits of their own freedom, which they still felt not to be fully within their reach. The trope of Free Girl, to be sure, was attractive to those who aspired to be independent from patriarchal control. Nevertheless, the trope of the Free Girl offered almost no guidance to working-class New Women for achieving an independent livelihood, social mobility, and access to full female autonomy. Moreover, although a window of opportunity had been opened owing to the structural changes in the service economy accompanied by gender equality reforms, it would soon begin to narrow. Indeed, a strong backlash spearheaded by the AKP government was already in the making as the New Woman sought to forge a new path in the city.

Endnotes

1. For more information on this research project about industrial homeworkers and the research findings, please see (Sarıoğlu 2013).

2. In the late 1980 and early 1990s, the civil war took a new turn when the Turkish state started to burn down Kurdish villages as a part of a new military strategy. This spawned a forced exodus of Kurdish migrants to the big cities. Upon their arrival, migrants were often completely dispossessed and could barely speak Turkish. They comprised a cheap, as well as precarious, source of labor for the labor-intensive export-oriented industries developing in the 1990s in Turkey (Keyder 2005).

3. The link between the expansion of the service economy and gendered social change has been well studied. As early as 1968, Victor Fuchs drew attention to the transformation of the United States into a service economy that "provided tens of millions of new job opportunities for women" (Fuchs 1968, 46). In his book *The Service Economy* (1968), Fuchs argued that, since service jobs do not make special demands on physical strength, women are able to enter the labor force more easily than they could previously and with more employment opportunities. Since then, interest in and literature on women and service employment has grown almost exponentially alongside the expansion in service employment itself. Scholars from a wide range of disciplines have documented emerging employment trajectories for women (Esping-Andersen 1999; Korpi 2000; England 2005; Thistle 2006; Orloff 2006), offered explanations for why the service workforce has become feminized (Goldin 1995; Ehrenreich and Hochschild 2003; Inglehart and Norris 2003), and explored the gendered implications of the feminization of service employment (Ehrenreich and Hochschild 2003; Inglehart and Norris 2003; England 2005). For scholars adopting the postindustrial society approach, a sector-based shift in employment signaled a broader shift in the gendered organization of the society: the growth of a new type of economy and social order, named the postindustrial society and/or service economy. In postindustrial societies, changes in household organization, the expansion of higher education, and the transformation of gender mores has allowed women to become rapidly integrated into the workforce (Esping-Andersen 1990, 197).

4. All human resources employees that I interviewed stated that there was no written rule about wearing headscarves, but admitted that the retail companies that target secular middle and upper-middle classes did not hire women with headscarves for cashier and sales positions. According to my interviewees, corporate employers placed a particular emphasis on appearance, seeking out workers who already knew the company

brand's cultural meanings and matched the lifestyle associated with the brand image. Corporate retail employers did not think that excluding women who wore headscarves from work on the sales floor amounted to employment discrimination. Their rationale was that they looked for workers whose appearance matched the brand, so they saw this selection policy as a legitimate business practice that resonated with customers' preferences. Scholars, however, note that the evaluation of such "soft skills" is very subjective. For instance, researchers argue that the demand for soft skills tends to be associated with employer discrimination against African Americans in the United States (Zamudio and Lichter 2008). The term "aesthetic labor" refers to soft skills related to personality, manner, and appearance that are required for employment in service sector occupations. Employers select workers with the required aesthetics who express their dispositions and habits through work. As Warhurst, Thompson and Nickson (2009, 104) explain, "with many front-line service workers now expected to embody the company image or required service, it is the commodification of workers' corporeality, not just their feelings that is becoming the analytical focus." In this study, I did not employ the term "aesthetic labor"—which approaches the body only as a site of labor— because I focus on bodily orientations and embodied capacities.

5. For a study that discusses the links between politics of secular modernity and the skill requirements in the interactive service industries in Turkey, see (Sarıoğlu 2014).

6. To learn more about the complicated transformation urban renewal instigated, see Ünsal and Kuyucu 2010; Borsuk and Eroglu 2020.

7. See "New Imaginaries of Gender in Turkey's Service Economy: Women Workers and Identity Making on the Sales Floor" (Sarıoğlu 2016) for an elaboration of this argument.

8. The term body armor or muscular armor was coined by famous psychoanalyst Willhelm Reich (1945) to describe the way bodies store traumatic experiences, as well as psychic conflicts. Certain emotional patterns or muscular tensions displayed unreflectively or habitually, according to Reich, make up the body armor. In my reliance on Reich's concept of body armor, I adopt descriptive aspects of armoring, in which the habits of the body are shaped in relation to psychological tensions, but I do not subscribe to the psychoanalytical explanation for its source, or to the method of treatment Reich advocated for dissolving body armor.

9. Women's valuation of the service industry's symbolic capital and physical appeal is a phenomenon that goes beyond the case of Turkey. For instance, Carla Freeman (2000) found that in Barbados women in the data entry

and informatics industry openly acknowledge that they could earn more money in the cane field but they strongly preferred the open office for its appearance of white-collar service work, and the freedom to dress and be feminine actors in ways they highly valued (48).

10. In the United States, the mean age at first marriage for women was 26.5 in 2011, while in 1950 it was 20.4. With respect to the ratio of married people to total population, in 1960, 72 percent of all adults ages 18 and older were married in the United States; by 2011 this number dropped to 51 percent (Cohn, Dvera, et al. 2011; Jelnov 2019).

CHAPTER 4

Tables Turning against the New Woman

The Rise of Moralist Politics

One June morning in 2011, before heading to work at MajorMarket, I was browsing through my Facebook feed when the news about the abolition of the Ministry for Women and Family popped up. Recep Tayyip Erdoğan, then prime minister, announced that the ministry would be replaced by a Ministry of Family and Social Policies. The Ministry for Women and Family was founded in the early 1990s when the Turkish state revamped its institutions to promote gender equality in response to feminist campaigns and the ratification of CEDAW (The Convention on the Elimination of All Forms of Discrimination against Women). The new ministry not only omitted the term women from its name, but its focus was curiously broadened to include issues related to children, the elderly, the disabled, and the families of soldiers who died during active service. Women, comprising almost half of the population, now seemed to have been lumped into the category of dependent population. Under the framework introduced by the new ministry, women were de facto designated as a nonworking population who depended on the institution of the family or the welfare state for the goods and services they consumed. In defense of the government's decision to abolish the Ministry for Women and Family, Erdoğan stated that the AKP was a conservative-democratic party and the institution of the family was important to the ruling party (Birgün 2011).

The term conservative democracy gained popularity after the AKP government came to power in 2002 (Yılmaz 2015). Having distanced itself from the preceding Islamist political parties that denounced the twin evils of westernization and capitalism, the AKP from day one declared itself as a conservative-democratic political party, supported Turkey's accession to European Union, and steered the globalization project in Turkey. It was not until 2008 that the AKP government embarked fully upon what it officially coined as the project of strengthening the family, advocating aggressively for the retrenchment of Islamic values that promoted the conventional gendered division of labor in everyday life, which meant women's withdrawal from the labor force to stay home and raise children. Indeed, the year 2008 was a turning point for gender politics in Turkey. The neoconservative gender ideology, often framed by moderate Islamism, became much more pronounced, while gender equality was sidelined as a political concern (Acar and Altunok 2013; Koyuncu and Özman 2019).

The AKP government's new sensibility became gradually more palpable. For instance, on International Women's Day in 2008, Erdoğan still endorsed the principle of gender equality and stated, "We don't want women to be exploited in garment workshops, we want them to have employment insurance and be eligible for retirement. We support equal pay for equal work so that more women can join the workforce" (IHA 2008). In the following years, however, he began to preach more frequently about how women should live, advising them to have at least three, preferably five children, advice he later reiterated on several occasions. In public meetings he condemned working women who chose not to become mothers and who did not take care of household chores: "A woman who rejects motherhood," he said, "a woman who does not run the household is deficient and an incomplete woman no matter how successful she is at work" (BBC 2016).

For feminists, the replacement of the Ministry of Women and Family by the Ministry of Family and Social Policies was yet another step toward pushing women back to the domain of the family. The AKP government's decision was promptly met with reaction by women's organizations that had been actively fighting for gender equality and who, at times since the 1990s, had formed loose alliances with the Ministry for Women and Family. Feminists raised their voices against the closure of the Ministry for Women and Family on various media platforms, organized protests and street demonstrations, and submitted a petition with three thousand signatures to the Prime Ministry a few days prior to the announcement (Bianet 2011a). The closure, according to women's organizations, was a menacing political move that placed gender equality in Turkey in jeopardy. Hülya Gülbahar, a prominent lawyer-activist from the Platform for Equality Mechanism, stated to the press that "at least five women are killed in Turkey every day. Nevertheless, the Women's Ministry is being lifted. This heralds the end of state policies related to gender equality" (Bianet 2011b).

On the day of the announcement, it was almost midnight when I finished my shift at MajorMarket and returned to Kadıköy, a secular, liberal, middle-class stronghold on the Anatolian side of the Bosporus. The neighborhood was alive and buzzing; the winding streets were filled with activity, the bars, eateries, and restaurants packed with locals. Wide-eyed tourists wandered around the fresh market, and the sidewalks were occupied by carefree young women and men sipping cans of beer, their bodies relaxed, their faces glowing with summer joy. Phenomenologically speaking, everyone's mood was uplifted: people seemed to enjoy the life of the city. Neither on guard nor apprehensive, they occupied the urban space with buoyancy, moving around fluidly and self-assuredly without expecting to encounter any threat or hostility.

This was how Turkey looked when I was wrapping up my ethnographic research on service industries in Istanbul in 2011. The forces of globalization that have operated for the last three decades in Turkey seemed to have produced a new social reality for women: with the growth of new types of service industries and the expansion of educational opportunities, more women had begun to work outside the home. They postponed marriage and were having fewer children, an expected consequence of accelerated urbanization that reduced fertility rates to a level of two children per woman by 2008, which was expected to drop to 1.69 by 2050 (Koç 2014a, 189). The nuclear family had become the dominant household form, comprising 70 percent of all households, with new familial structures such as dispersed families and single-person households becoming more acceptable while the older form of the patriarchal extended family was increasingly dissolving (Koç 2014b). The government allocated more money to higher education and there were around four million college students in the country (Keyder 2013). All of these structural changes, accompanied by progressive legal reforms advancing gender equality, transformed what seemed possible for women, enabling them to chart new ways of being in the world. Women acquired new embodied orientations that affected the scope of their actions and choices. For instance, my unmarried co-workers at MajorMarket, and even the married ones, were making vacation plans exclusively with "the girls" for the summer. Some fancied the idea of sharing an apartment with other women. After-work gatherings at cafes offered opportunities for them to reflect upon and talk about their lives, romantic relationships, divorce, and educational opportunities. In one of these gatherings, Nesrin resolutely expressed her own aspirations:

> I am not the type of person who dedicates herself to her husband, takes care of the kids and cooks all day. I've had the chance to realize this fact during the time I have worked at MajorMarket. Now I know that another life is possible. I can't get along very well with the conventional married women working here. Instead, I get along with college students who work as part-timers. Now, I want to go to college and in ten years be a woman who can stand on her own feet. I don't want to work at MajorMarket till I die.

Still, the New Woman's life was characterized by long hours of work, six days a week. Moreover, she felt apprehensive about the political turn, sensing the tightening grip of government. Sometimes she complained of the bully-like attitude of Erdoğan, yet she was often reminded by a male co-worker that it was thanks to the credit opportunities provided by the government that she was able to spend money and even help the family with house payments. She responded, "Of course I'm grateful for that but. . .," and would not complete her sentence, a tone of exasperation detectable in her voice. The majority of male sales workers at MajorMarket were by no means AKP supporters. Younger generations of men, at least some of them, considered themselves Republican People's Party (CHP) voters but respected the AKP government for its effective economic policies, whereas relatively older male workers were openly anti-AKP, condemning Erdoğan loudly during lunch breaks.

The rifts that the AKP created among people at MajorMarket resonated on a wider social level, too. There were complex and contradictory forces at work shaping society. For instance, the structural transformations that drew more women into the workforce and enabled them to attain higher educational levels seemed to be at odds with the AKP government's conservative stance on gender matters. The capitalist markets and the government were both invested in women's bodies, albeit in different and contradictory ways. The question of how gender relations in

Turkey would be shaped in the course of economic and political transformations brought by globalization did not have an easy answer. In the meantime, I spotted New Women from different backgrounds everywhere in the city, and I watched the Pride Walk, International Women's Day, and International Day for the Elimination of Violence against Women attract larger and more confident crowds each year. As a left-wing feminist woman, I was feeling safe and hopeful about the future direction of the country.

It was during this period that the AKP's moralist politics quickly picked up pace. This chapter discusses how shame-honor discourse, which was worn away in the context of global restructuring, made a fast comeback in politics in the post–2008 period. It examines the moralist politics advanced by the AKP government to tease out how the executive branch—in an effort to acquire unconstrained and indefinite capacities for establishing authoritarianism—resuscitated shame-honor discourse. The AKP government's bid for authoritarianism augmented traditional sources of authority and utilized shame-honor discourse in several ways. First, the government imagined a moral-political community with each member of the community having the de facto right to impose the norms of shame-honor, a move that emboldened males to involve themselves into women's bodily comportment. The practice of utilizing feminine modesty to assert male entitlement to bodily control rapidly grew in the period. Second, the government increasingly used terms of male honor, including masculine honor codes, in politics, as well as its policies. Third, it reactivated the affective intensities of public embarrassment and shaming, which allowed the government to separate women who were seen as deserving of paternalist protection from those who were not. While these political moves had some relatively benign effects like the implementation of social policies aiding underprivileged women with the AKP restructuring the social welfare system, it had mostly vicious consequences. Male honor that animated the AKP's moral politics stirred moral intolerance and hostility toward the New Woman, rendering her embodied existence precarious. Particularly important were Erdoğan's masculinist public performances against the New Woman. By drawing frequently, if not exclusively, on the strategy of shaming, Erdoğan concentrated his efforts to label and stigmatize New Women. Nevertheless, as this chapter demonstrates, new modes of being feminine could not be contained within the shame-honor discourse that the AKP government brought back into politics.

Making Globalization Familial:
The AKP's Social Policies

The impact of globalization, as welfare regime scholars like Gøsta Esping-Andersen (1999) suggest, is not uniform across countries but is filtered through welfare regimes—the complex configurations of the welfare state, labor market, and household structures in a given country. The AKP government's comprehensive reforms introduced in the first decade of the 2000s—with the exception of few areas such as health insurance and employment benefits where gender-differentiated entitlements were neutralized—went resolutely in the direction of familialism, where the social policies encourage women to depend on the institution of family for survival (Kılıç 2010; Yazici 2012; Toksöz 2016; Akkan 2018). In contrast to legal reforms in the civil and penal codes in the early twentieth century that set out to ensure the entrenchment of gender equality, the restructuring of the welfare state was modeled on the logic of male honor, in which social policies were planned with reference to a family form with a male breadwinner and a female dependent. In this frame, women with few educational credentials who were not supported by male breadwinners, or who lived with so-called failed male breadwinners, gained access to social welfare benefits. For instance, the conditional cash transfers implemented following the economic crisis in 2001 provided social assistance for the poorest 12 percent of the population, but were available only to mothers (Şener 2016). The government also implemented a state-run assistance program for low-income widows, extending the safety net through monthly allowances to those women no longer supported by male breadwinners.

Institutionalized after World War II, the Turkish welfare regime had already featured the family as the central institution of welfare (Buğra and Keyder 2006). In this system, men as the breadwinners gained social rights to pensions, unemployment insurance, and other benefits on the basis of their status in the labor market, whereas women as caregivers gained access to benefits through their ties to men. Household maintenance and care work for children, the elderly, the sick, and the disabled were carried out exclusively by women. During the AKP period, the newly implemented policies did not shift the provision of care services from family to the state or to the market. Instead, new policies sharpened the gendered polarity between breadwinning and caregiving, strengthening the AKP's familialism. The AKP's neoconservative gender agenda, however, differed from the early familialist policies such that the AKP government now acknowledged a particular form of women's care work in the family as a form of labor to be compensated through payment. Perhaps nothing illustrates the AKP's familialist strategy better than the Regulation on the Determination of Disabled Persons in Need of Care and the Basis of Care Services. Introduced in 2006, the legislation granted a payment close to minimum wage to family members who were caregivers for severely disabled persons in low-income households. Women constituted 88.7 percent of those who received the caregiver payments (Toksöz 2016). The pitch the government made for its project of strengthening the family appropriated a feminist slogan from the 1970s, Wages for Work, which recognized women's unpaid labor in the family and demanded compensation for it. The caregiver payment reinforced women's role as caregivers in the family, serving the political agenda of familialism in the context of globalization.

The paternalist-familialist ethos that drove the overhauling of the welfare system also offered a new direction to urban planning to multiply the number of "family values-centered spaces" in cities. In the Turkish context, family values-centered spaces indicated the availability of amenities and spaces where men, unaccompanied by their families, were not allowed. The opening of new public spaces afforded Sunni pious women new opportunities to go out and about without worrying about male presence and harassment. With the spaces reserved for women becoming more numerous and more diverse—encompassing public parks, swimming pools, beaches, and even buses—women, especially low-income Sunni women, whose mobility had hitherto been limited to the boundaries of the neighborhood and who relied mainly on women-only house gatherings for sociability opportunities, gained wider access to the urban space. In creating public venues based on gender segregation, municipalities emerged as prominent actors in organizing a range of homosocial activities for women including seminars and conferences on women's health, family, domestic violence, and motherhood, as well as social events such as concerts (Şahin 2018).

The enactment of familialist social policies was central to the electoral success of the AKP among women. Since 2002, when the AKP first came to power, the party steadfastly counted on women to generate large winning margins in elections. It received overwhelming backing from women, with half of the women in Turkey voting for the AKP in elections, and with an even greater majority amongst housewives. Indeed, housewives emerged as the largest voting group for the party, accounting for 37 percent of AKP supporters in 2017, followed by a bloc composed of workers, farmers, and shopkeepers making up 27 percent (Uncu 2018). Many women gained access to ATM cards for the first time in their lives, as well as to cash not controlled by their husbands through the implementation of cash transfers in this period (Yaraş 2019). Pious Sunni women from the popular classes appreciated the opening of gender-segregated parks, schools, and swimming pools and beaches, which enabled them to participate in and enjoy public life (Alkan-Zeybek 2011).

The electoral success of the AKP, however, cannot easily be distinguished from Erdoğan's own brand of masculinism, which strongly appealed to his support base. This is not to suggest that his political authority sprang merely from the "masculine enhancement effect" (Hustvedt 2016, 80) through which men are judged to be more credible than women due to unconscious ideas about masculinity and femininity. Rather, it means that Erdoğan differed from earlier generations of males in the political establishment in that his efforts to push masculine honor codes of the *mahalle* into governmental politics were unprecedented. Erdoğan—unlike many former political leaders who were more educated, fluent in foreign languages, and more invested in politeness and formality—had an unbridled desire for masculine power. Far from making him appear greedy or aggressive in the eyes of supporters, his masculine ambition was regarded as something that attested to political potency and command. For his supporters, Erdoğan was an uneducated man of and for the people, who belonged to and identified with the cultural tradition of the *mahalle* and lived by male honor codes. In other words, he embodied the familiar old masculine trope of the **kabadayı** (meaning tough uncle).

An exclusively masculine figure, the *kabadayı* has been associated with traditional *mahalle* structure. Popular in accounts of Ottoman everyday life, *kabadayı*s were male neighborhood residents, mostly uneducated and often shopkeepers or artisans involved in trade, who were recognized as members of good standing in the community. They gave themselves license to protect the women of the neighborhood, to keep the honor of the *mahalle*, and to punish infractions and transgressions according to masculine codes of honor. In *mahalle* life, *kabadayı*s acted as "guarantors and protectors of a normative order that was at once stifling and reassuring, constraining yet deeply familiar" (Kandiyoti 1997, 122).

Erdoğan, in a similar way, was intimidating yet trustworthy, like a *kabadayı*, in the eyes of his supporters. By strategically using the masculine repertoire of the *kabadayı*, Erdoğan transformed a primarily local gender trope into a successful political ruling strategy on a national scale, which helped him both store up political capital and cement the AKP's authoritarian regime. In his popular *What Is Populism?* Jan-Werner Müller (2016) described how this masculine posturing from male honor codes rendered substance to Erdoğan's politics: "A plucky underdog; he would always be the street fighter from Istanbul's tough neighborhood Kasımpaşa, bravely confronting the old Kemalist establishment of the Turkish republic—even long after he had begun to concentrate all political, economic, and cultural power in his own hands" (Müller 2016, 42). The awe he evoked as the desirable patriarch—a large man with an imposing body language, an audacious leader who stood up to powerful nations' hypocrisy, a man with a cause who is willing to go to prison for what he believes, and a fair ruler who restored justice by empowering the Sunni population who had been long dominated by the secular elite—was indeed drawn from the story of a young man, a *kabadayı*, who with his male gang had worked to protect the honor of the *mahalle* before rising to prominence in national politics.

His supporters, men and women alike, described him as an upright man. But for women Erdoğan also stood for the man who protected the honor of his family—the head of family and a breadwinner with integrity who never fails to take care of his family. Women who felt their husbands had failed them, who felt unappreciated or had suffered ill treatment by their husbands, were especially drawn to Erdoğan, who restored women's dignity by treating them fairly. Women went to great lengths to support him and stood up against their husbands who planned on voting for a party other than the AKP, even fighting them right at the ballot box. This was a new gender dynamic, as a civil society representative explained: "Such determination to resist the husband began with Erdoğan. Not with the AKP but Erdoğan. It is his charisma that makes all these women so determined to serve the mission of the party, disregarding its possible consequences" (quoted in Yaraş 2019, 289).

This was the gender pact Erdoğan promised by restoring the family based on the norms of male honor upon which the forces of global modernity were encroaching. This politics, however, came at a huge price: the policies that defined and catered to the needs of low-income households empowered Sunni women, but eroded the state's commitment to gender equality. Indeed, the government became less and less committed to gender equality during this era (Acar and Altunok 2013, Korkman 2016, Koyuncu and Özman 2019). Soon it would become clear that gender equality was not merely neglected by the AKP government but actively repudiated.

In July 2010, Erdoğan invited representatives of women's organizations to the Dolmabahçe Palace in Istanbul, where he professed his views on gender equality. Referring to the Islamic concept of *fitrat* (creation) as his point of reference, a notion that can be translated as God-given nature, Erdoğan stated that he did not believe in the equality of the sexes but that women and men were inherently different and complemented each other (Gazetevatan 2010). This came as quite a shock to women activists and feminists among the audience. Never before had they seen Erdoğan denounce gender inequality so staunchly. The meeting was a landmark; it announced the end of an era. The AKP government that had drafted a raft of laws in consultation with feminist lawyers and women's groups in the early 2000s was no longer willing to work together with women's organizations for gender equality.

The Moralist Arc of Authoritarianism

One murkier implication of Erdoğan's masculinist rejection of gender equality in favor of male honor was the unsettling hostility Erdoğan unleashed toward antigovernment women activists. In June 2011, Erdoğan denounced left-wing activist Dilşat Aktaş for climbing onto a police vehicle during a protest against police violence, saying, "on a TV channel I saw someone climbing on a police vehicle; if she is a girl or a woman, that I don't know. And as if climbing on the police vehicle was not vehement enough, she did not slow down, and began to attack with a stick in her hand our police who had been stationed there, holding the shield, just standing there and being patient with her" (Kazete 2018).

On that day, Dilşat Aktaş was violently beaten and had her hips broken by the police during the demonstration, causing irreparable damage to her legs. This, of course, was not the first time Erdoğan had vilified a left-wing antigovernment activist, but there was something new in his attack on Aktaş. Rather than discredit her politics, he crudely questioned her status as a virgin, pointedly commenting, "If she is a girl or a woman, that I don't know." In Turkish, the distinction between "girl" and "woman" relates to the moralized distinction between a virgin and a nonvirgin. In common usage, the word girl implies virginity.

In his denunciation, Erdoğan did not engage Dilşat Aktaş as a political opponent to be criticized, but as a moral transgressor to be shamed and humiliated. Shame-honor discourse, which had long given permission for aggression against women who committed moral infractions, was mobilized by Erdoğan to mark Dilşat Aktaş's body as violable and to make the violence she experienced at the hands of the police morally acceptable or at least negligible. Erdoğan's move foreshadowed what was to come as the AKP maneuvered toward authoritarianism: a revival of shaming, reasserting the moral authority of shame-honor as the basis for judging women's embodied actions, irrespective of whether these actions were economic, social, or political. In the hands of the AKP, shame-honor would begin to function as a gendered means of violence that would exacerbate women's embodied openness to violation and attack, allowing the AKP to skirt legal restrictions that curtailed the party's access to coercive power. As opposed to the legal order, the moral order of shame-honor unlocked hostile emotional energy against the New Woman, giving moral permission to the expressions of that hostility.

The moralistic arc of politics and what it entailed for the New Woman became increasingly discernible as the AKP consolidated its political power. An important turning point was the AKP's electoral victory in the 2011 elections. The elections marked a watershed in the history of the AKP, which, for the first time, received 49.95 percent of votes, securing the electoral majority in Turkey. Previously, the AKP relied on rather large cross-class coalitions, a political dynamic that forced the party to adopt a strategy of ruling through hegemony as opposed to coercion. In its first term in power, for instance, AKP embarked upon a series of democratization reforms, including the gender legislation. After the July 2007 elections, when the AKP assumed power with 47 percent of the vote, securing its second term in power, the party found itself in a political conundrum. The democratization process had enabled the party to gain an upper hand vis-à-vis the older secularist power bloc made up of the military and bureaucracy, while at the same time curtailing its power over opposition forces who were working to expand civil rights and freedoms. Had the AKP government played by the prevailing rules of democracy, it is almost certain that women, Kurds, Alevis, feminists, LGBTI+ and queer groups would have gained more power and pushed the government for further democratization.

The 2010 referendum, following a highly-polarized referendum process, enabled the party, through constitutional amendments, to undermine the military and judiciary's efforts to oversee the AKP government and brought the heretofore ambiguous politics of the AKP to a halt.[1] The government in this period went into overdrive to implement coercive measures. It de facto ended the EU accession process, cracked down on the secularist political establishment, heavily controlled the media, gradually suppressed political dissent, and severely curtailed freedoms in the country. By the time the AKP won its third consecutive election in 2011 with unprecedented support—receiving almost 50 percent of the vote, doubling its share against its closest opponent, the CHP—many secular citizens were already feeling besieged by AKP rule.

The national election results came as a shock to the large, secular segment of the society. On Election Day, I was at work at MajorMarket. It was a pleasant and warm Sunday, a usually quiet day in the store when well-dressed Kemalist elderly women came in for their weekly grocery shopping accompanied by younger helpers to carry the bags. When the first results came in toward the end of evening, the mood at the store palpably changed and a quiet sense of gloom descended. My fellow cashier, who was a young university student working part-time and a CHP supporter, was appalled by the results. Upon hearing that the AKP won the fifty percent of the vote, he quit fumbling with his cashier box and with a soft voice said to me: "I wasn't expecting this. I didn't think they would get this much." He looked defeated and the atmosphere in whole supermarket grew more ghostly.

In the aftermath of the AKP's victory in 2011, the party's anti-democratic activities picked up pace and the government began to turn away from, in Weberian parlance, legal-bureaucratic authority toward alternative sources of authority. Quietly dropping the term conservative democracy, the AKP increasingly appealed to the notion of the majority—based not a numerical power but rather a moralizing one—that enabled the government to introduce a variety of measures curtailing freedoms in the name of values, which Erdoğan framed as "our national values" and "our civilization."

The link between shame-honor-based morality and politics in this period became visible in popular, common political rhetoric. Political commentators on TV, for instance, observed how CHP's secular proposal for improving freedom of speech was poorly received by the "conservative *mahalle*" (referring to AKP supporters) and columnists complained about anxious secular *mahalle* residents, alluding to CHP voters who feared the erosion of the secular foundation of the Turkish Republic. Embedded in this widely popular way of talking about politics was an understanding of politics as based on the *mahalle,* or more precisely on belonging to the normative order of the *mahalle* and not on interest groups, policy, and political ideology. While the traditional *mahalle* was in a literal sense eroding—its spatial organization and social formation crumbling under global restructuring—figuratively the *mahalle* was making a comeback, extending itself from the local to the national level, becoming a conceptual metaphor for politics itself in Turkey.

Rancor and Hostility against the New Woman

Distinct from morality, moralism—which is concerned with ethical values and principles about moral conduct—can best be characterized as an orientation that manifests itself through an attitude of self-righteousness and certainty, rejecting ambiguity and urging purity (Brown 2001; Bennet and Shapiro 2013; Laursen 2013). When directed against others, the moralist orientation might quickly morph into intolerance and even punitiveness, animating a host of hostile and vengeful sentiments. Mobilized in daily interactions by individuals, moralizing sentiments can fuel reactionary politics, with moralist discourses of the twenty-first century driving antidemocratic politics across the world (Brown 2018; Yilmaz 2017).

The AKP's moral politics that shaped the post-2008 period, in a similar vein, fueled moral sentiments against the New Woman by recoupling the female body to moral precepts. A variety of issues related to women's lives and embodied capacities—such as abortion, divorce rates, and women's embodied comportment in public—veered into the orbit of moralism and were reimagined through the terms offered by shame-honor discourse, significantly increasing the New Woman's openness to violation and attack.

Take, for instance, the abortion debate which broke out in 2012 when the Health Ministry was drafting a law to restrict abortion, a law that included penalties for hospitals that carried out caesarean sections. The plan sparked a huge public outcry from the women's movement and the larger society, with thousands of pro-choice advocates taking to the streets in protest. For one thing, an anti-abortion bill was not something the public expected, because abortion had not been a subject of significant public discussion until then (Unal and Cindoglu 2013). A relatively liberal legal framework that permitted abortions until the tenth week of pregnancy had been in place since 1983, and abortion was widely accepted in society (Yalçın 2019). So, when the abortion ban plan was announced, it met with such strong resistance that it forced the government to backpedal from its initial plan to curb women's access to abortion.[2]

Erdoğan, in the meantime, stepped in to defend the proposed law, which poured more fuel on the fire, heavily antagonizing abortion advocates. In a speech he gave at the International Parliamentarians Conference on the Action Plan for Population and Development Conference on May 24, 2012, Erdoğan boldly professed: "I am a prime minister who is against caesarean section at birth. I regard abortion as a murder. No one is entitled to authorize abortion. I am asking you to tell me if there is any difference between killing a baby in the womb and killing a baby after the birth. There's no difference between the two" (NTV 2012).

This was one main plank of the AKP's moral politics-in-the-making: an attack on women's rights and gender equality by forcefully mobilizing shame-honor discourse. Erdoğan's decisive return to traditional sources of authority, as opposed to legal-bureaucratic authority, enabled him to incriminate women and feminists, as well as larger segments of society, by recasting political opposition as depraved or vile. Modesty, as the sole arbiter of femininity, was invoked to control and reprove women who did not consent to the AKP's authoritarian project. At the same time, male honor became more accentuated in politics through heightened performances of masculinity. Erdoğan came to embody the righteous masculine leader in charge of women's embodied capacities, who had a right to be incensed by the moral infractions committed under his rule.

It was during this period that Erdoğan and his government grew more uncompromising, pulling political negotiation off the table in discussions of gender policies and politics. Indeed, the AKP government, by its appeal to shame-honor precepts, was able to slice off the domain of politics characterized by open contestation for power and hegemony. At times, the AKP government's political rhetoric was hardly distinguishable from the discourse of shame-honor, with the binary it established between moral transgression and conformity setting the terms for women's embodied actions. For instance, when Parliament debated the abortion law plan, women deputies' opposition to the plan was branded as shameless moral conduct. When Aylin Nazlıaka, the main opposition CHP Ankara deputy, demanded that Erdoğan "stop watching the women's vagina," she was chastised for her "shameless conduct." Referring to Nazlıaka, Bülent Arınç, then the deputy prime minister said, "I also got extremely embarrassed during the abortion discussions when you, as a married woman with children, explicitly spoke of one of your organs [vagina]" (Hürriyet 2012). Arınç's political reprobate was a masculinist claim to monitoring women's modesty, asserting that the women's body was still a male preserve. A man, for instance, should be able to inspect a woman's moral conduct and warn her when she transgressed moral norms, despite whatever trappings of respectability she had, such as marriage and kids.

The abortion debate also marked another phase of moralism, where gendered assault was strategically used to shape the terms of the political conflict around the Kurdish question. For instance, when Erdoğan was criticized for the Turkish air strike that killed thirty-four Kurdish civilians in the border town of Roboski (Uludere in Turkish), Erdoğan struck back with fury, saying: "You always talk about Uludere. Every abortion is like an Uludere." He repeated this anti-abortion subterfuge at the AKP women's congress the following day to discredit his critics, saying, "You live and breathe Uludere. I say every abortion is an Uludere" (NTV 2012). The Uludere massacre elicited significant public reaction, both for its atrocity and also for the role of the AKP government in organizing the air strikes that would incriminate Erdoğan. His remark, drawing a parallel between abortion and violent atrocity against Kurds, was regarded as a political maneuver to deflect attention away from the AKP government's culpability.[3]

Issues like abortion or divorce, along with violence against women, motherhood, and marriage, seemed to hold great moral and political significance for Erdoğan and the AKP. For instance, despite only a modest increase in divorce rates, the AKP government launched an alarmist campaign—through the strategic use of the government-backed media—to construe divorce as an omen of impending moral decay, which would plague Turkish society and hollow out the social order. The feminist movement has, so far, been very successful in setting the terms of the political debate on violence against women, divorce, and abortion. While mainstream feminist ideals made their way into the larger society through media, social media, and fashion—becoming

hegemonic especially among younger generations of urban women—
Erdoğan crusaded against feminism, moralizing divorce along with
abortion.

In today's Turkey, an increasing number of women who weigh their
options for a decent life turn to divorce, with the prospects of autonomy
triumphing over the risks associated with ending a marriage. This sentiment resonated among my interlocutors, too. During an interview,
Nihan, a forty-year-old woman working as a secretary in Ankara, told
me that she was happily divorced. After a difficult separation process
and with the support of her employer—a female psychotherapist—she
was able to start a new chapter of her life with her young daughter. "But,"
she said, "my husband was horrible with me. He threatened me, tried to
turn our daughter into a pawn in the separation process, and he stalked
me for years when I was coming here to work."

Previously, divorce was not an option unless the husband was violent or an alcoholic or failed to measuring up to the breadwinner ideal,
because the family—as opposed to the market or the welfare state—
was the key institution that ensured women's survival in Turkey. The
aftermath of divorce was damaging for women, too, particularly since
the stigma attached to divorce laid women open to community surveillance mechanisms such as gossip, as well as to threats and violence from
their former husbands. This is likely why, when Nesrin wanted a divorce
in 2012, members of her family were truly shocked. According to the
family, her marriage was a happy one; her husband was not an alcoholic,
nor a gambler, and most importantly he had never been violent toward
Nesrin. Why would she ever want a divorce? Her logic came across as
completely foreign to her family, who nevertheless ended up supporting
Nesrin.

A young couple, Nesrin and her husband had been married for
five years and did not have children. During that time, they grew increasingly distant from each other, especially after Nesrin earned a high
school diploma and landed a job at MajorMarket. While her position
opened up a new world for her—enabling her to discover new interests,
meet new people, and acquire novel aspirations—her husband, "stayed
the same." The couple lived in a five-story *gecekondu* building owned
by the husband's extended family, and each apartment was occupied by
a member of the family. In other words, there were no outsiders in the
building; everyone had a key to each other's apartment and could enter
any apartment in the building when the need arose. For Nesrin, the lack

of boundaries and the heavy surveillance of the family became increasingly hard to endure and she felt trapped. In the meantime, she found herself growing apart from her husband; while she was immersed in an egalitarian and modern ethos at MajorMarket, he worked at a *kebap* restaurant, serving a well-off clientele comprising mostly homosocial groups of men and families. As opposed to the sales floor, the *kebap* restaurant did not promote a heterosocial work culture but was heavily shaped by codes of male honor, with all the servers being men. Nesrin divorced him because they were living in different worlds, and because she had the material and emotional resources to go through a divorce—a job to support herself, and confidence to start a new life. That was how she became the first person to divorce in her family.[4]

For Tayyip Erdoğan, on the other hand, who had severed ties with feminists and women's rights organizations, feminist propaganda was something to suppress with appeals to family and religion, as well as shame-honor morality. He wanted to "raise devout and vengeful generations," a statement that incited great furor within the larger society, especially at the time in 2012 when the AKP government had approved an education reform bill. The reforms extended compulsory school attendance from eight to twelve years, while permitting parents to move their children to vocational schools, a category which also includes the religious *İmam Hatip* schools, after only four years of education (Genckaya et al. 2015).

Alarmed by the changes in masculinities and femininities, the AKP government wanted to put more women within reach of state-controlled religion's tentacles. One major tool in this endeavor was the Presidency of Religious Affairs, the Diyanet, an administrative office founded in 1924 after the abolishment of the Islamic caliphate to regulate religion under the control of the prime minister. By drastically increasing its budget, the AKP government massively expanded the Diyanet's operations in society, whose power now achieved a capillary quality, diffusing and circulating throughout the social body (Kocamaner 2019). As a first step, the Presidency of Religious Affairs hired more female preachers, or *vaizes*, who regularly delivered seminars and organized projects for women, addressing issues related to marriage, divorce, motherhood, childcare, and disability. In addition to these projects, which often took place in mosques or local municipal cultural centers, the Presidency of Religious Affairs founded the Offices for Family Religious Guidance (Aile İrşat ve Rehberlik Büroları) as an alternative to secular couples therapy, where **vaizes** and other service providers, offered counseling to families based on Sunni values (Sancar 2016; Maritato 2018). The Presidency also set up the provincial fatwa online and telephone call service (*Alo Fetva* 190) to enable people to receive an authoritative opinion from religious experts on different matters (Kalpaklıoğlu 2021). Through these channels of call services and online websites, female preachers and religious experts employed by the Diyanet offered Islamic perspectives on subjects such as getting a tattoo, having one's hair dyed, working at a place where alcohol is sold, spending one's husband's money for personal expenses without his consent, and taking days off from fasting during Ramadan because of menstruation.

Moral Vigilantism and Shaming as a Failed Strategy

The establishment of new institutionalized channels—in which self-fashioning, physical bearing, and proper embodied conduct were discussed with reference to Sunni Islamic norms—sparked enthusiasm among the Sunni population, who readily made use of these services on a daily basis. However, this was not the only way that the AKP government invested in corporeality and everyday embodied modes of being in the post-2008 era. Erdoğan began to assume more and more the role of a moral vigilante, chastising people for their so-called moral transgressions. Laying claim assertively to male honor, he called out women for their embodied comportment in public, couples for indulging in public displays of affection, and young people for drinking alcohol and smoking cigarettes on the street. These quickly turned into venues for vicious moralization, escalating the political tensions around embodiment, manners, and conduct, which were couched in the idiom of "lifestyle" in public discourse.

Erdoğan's angry rants and self-righteous reprimanding speeches became so frequent and intense that they made his embodied existence—his ways of acting and being in the everyday world—ontologically invasive[5] in the eyes of those who did not support the AKP regime; an intrusion into their space that undermined their lived existence. Contemptuous, angry, and hostile, and punitive and insolent in his approach to others, Erdoğan appeared constantly on TV. Newspapers extensively covered his speeches in which his fury and contempt were targeted at people's embodied modes of being in everyday life. Rather than encouraging people to inhabit the world with ease and safety, Erdoğan was disruptive and unsettling. I have many times seen people, feeling suffocated and constricted, reach for the remote control to turn off the TV as soon as his face appears on the screen. In the eyes of those who did not support the AKP regime, Erdoğan was not a *kabadayı*; he was just a bully who had no respect for anyone.

In May 2013, a young couple riding the subway in Ankara were told over a loud PA speaker that they should stop kissing and conform to moral codes. The intervention, nevertheless, prompted a more conspicuous gesture of affection. A week later, dozens of couples gathered at the same subway station and launched a kissing session, a long moment of a public display of affection to protest the Ankara subway officials who had admonished the couple. When asked about the kissing incident, Erdoğan later said on TV, "A state-owned subway train has moral codes too. If these codes are violated, there is nothing wrong in making public announcements against it. And there are groups on the street with alcoholic drinks in their hands. I am asking now: Would a mother or a father, excuse me saying this but, like to see their daughter sitting on a boy's lap?" (Sözcü 2013).

The kissing protest organized in Ankara was not an isolated incident; more public performances like this one began to take place in response to the moral accusations leveled by Erdoğan. It is worth taking a moment to consider what kind of resistance strategy was implicated in public responses like kissing protests. Although Erdoğan ramped up his moral accusations, his targets, as the kissing performance demonstrated, did not necessarily feel ashamed or humiliated. They felt angry, perhaps, but not ashamed. Evidently, Erdoğan's accusations of sexual impropriety, especially against women, did not elicit a strong defensiveness among them concerning their moral chastity. To be sure, when faced with an elevated risk of losing their rights—rights that were enshrined in law—the New Women and feminists were roused to action, rallying around a common discourse of women's rights and pluralism, and protesting the incursions into their lives at marches and demonstrations. Nevertheless, the manner in which they responded to the moral politics expressed a sensibility that was distinctly not defensive. New Women, it became apparent, were not offended by the sexualized moral charges brought against them.

Feeling offended is often classified under the category of self-conscious emotions (Lewis 2008), such as humiliation, shame, embarrassment, anger, and guilt, that wound one's self-image and self-respect. One is offended when one feels injured by a social attack, except the injury is not a physical one. The offense and insult are often paired together; both emotional states are rooted in "violation of the demands of respect for the integrity of one's person" (Neu 2008, 24). But what happens when one is accused of not measuring up to norms that one does not abide by? Such an accusation can cause offense only if one has internalized the standards in question.

Such was the case for the women whom Erdoğan continually chastised. Unlike his supporters, New Women considered Erdoğan a bully, not a charismatic leader. Neither did they recognize his masculine authority. For them, the trope of the *kabadayı* that Erdoğan came to embody had completely different connotations; it was a product of a patriarchal social formation that justified male control over women's lives and bodies. Significantly, then, New Women did not feel shamed by the moral accusations he leveled against them. When Erdoğan hurled insults against women who did not get married, instead of taking offense, they organized demonstrations and chanted the slogan, "I make love but I don't marry, I get pregnant but don't have a baby." When politicians reproached them for loose morals, the women became defiant, mischievously holding placards that read "I am a slut." This sensibility marked an important change in women's embodied orientations—openness in particular—which seemed to take a pronounced turn toward assertiveness when attacked. The number of women who engaged in what conservative moralists deemed "unchaste behavior" grew bigger, their voices stronger, their attitudes more humorous, and their moods more cheerful. This would have been hardly possible had shame-honor discourse been legally intact.

When it was enshrined in law, shame-honor discourse had grave repercussions for women who were marked as immoral, opening their bodies to violence and a range of violations. Such punishment compelled women to subscribe to the terms of shame-honor discourse even when they opposed it. For instance, during the virginity test debates in the 1990s, secular groups, with the exception of radical feminists, protested the state-led virginity exams while at the same time lauding virginity as a moral virtue. Protestors, especially Kemalists, developed the idea that "virginity is not in the hymen, but in the mind," thus criticizing the virginity exams but not the underlying norm of female virginity (Parla 2001). By emphasizing personal integrity, the phrase shifted the focus of morality away from the hymen to one's code of conduct and choices; however, at the same time it continued promoting chastity as a feminine virtue.

In the 2010s, however, that was no longer the case. Now that shame-honor discourse was legally dismantled, women felt entitled to their bodily inviolability. No moral accusation could serve as a pretext for violence or hostility against them. When women carried placards that read "I am a slut," not only did they own their own sexual desires, but their embodied actions expressed that a significant change in the socio-legal order had taken place; they would no longer face serious consequences for so-called moral transgressions. Now the crowds cheerfully called for everyone to engage in public immorality, as opposed to public morality, during Pride Parades. Moral accusations were met only with a brazen attitude that mocked Erdoğan's authority and self-righteousness. After all, support for the norms of shame and honor, as well as the notion of public morality endorsed by Erdoğan, had already worn thin among the New Women, feminists, and LGBTI+ and queer communities who no longer took virginity, chastity, or public morality as reference points for their code of conduct or self-worth.

Such a shift, of course, alarmed the conservative political bloc, who grew more vigilant in the first decade of the twenty-first century about the New Woman and the new sexual mores gaining traction in the larger society, which they feared would corrupt pious women and undermine their support for the AKP.[6] But not until the AKP government burned tents at a park in Taksim, Istanbul in the spring of 2013 did it grasp the true nature of the challenge that the New Woman posed to its rule as well as moralist politics in Turkey.

Endnotes

1. As early as 2006, for instance, anti-terror laws were changed; the number and scope of crimes considered terror offences increased and political crimes were defined in ways that could easily be conflated with terror crimes (Yonucu 2018).
2. The anti-abortion initiative did not become codified, but the AKP government imposed de facto limitations making it difficult for women to access safe abortion services. Moreover, a new public health law introduced in 2012 imposed a ban on C-sections, permitting them only for strict medical reasons (Güneş-Ayata and Doğangün 2017).
3. Feminists, on the other hand, criticized the argument that Erdoğan's rhetoric around abortion and sexuality is a strategy to distract from heavy-weight political issues. For a feminist analysis, see (Korkman 2016).

4. It is, however, worth emphasizing that statistically a woman's decision to obtain divorce is strongly correlated with her educational attainment. The more educated a woman is, the higher the likelihood for her to file for divorce (Çavlin 2014).

5. In coining the term ontological invasiveness, I build on Shannon Sullivan's (2006) concept of ontological expansiveness, which refers to the unreflective habits of racialized bodies to take up space, entailing a set of power relationships that flow from racist use of space. Ontological expansiveness, in Sullivan's account, designates the way racism enables white bodies to access space. "It implicitly encourages them not to concern themselves with other people's lived existence, including the ways in which other people's existence is inhibited by white people and institutions. In this way, the nontransactional, unidirectionality of projective intentionality lends itself toward ethical solipsism" (Sullivan 2006, 163). By employing the term ontological invasiveness, I look not at the ways in which bodies literally take up space but how the embodied existence is amplified by political power, gender hierarchies, and the media infrastructure, and how it intrudes into other people's lived existence, violating and threatening their everyday modes of being and acting.

6. During this period, new public discourses around pious young Muslim women emerged that reflected growing social anxiety about the transformation of female respectability. One such discourse was *Süslüman*, a compound word made out of two terms, "*Müslüman* (Muslim) and *Süslü* (dressy)" (Yarar 2021, 217). *Süslüman* is a derogatory term used to describe young, upwardly mobile, pious women who craft new ways of being feminine through practices of consumption and the use of social media. The expression has been employed both by secularists and conservatives to mark this modality of femininity for its inclinations toward sensuous gratification, self-indulgence, and materialism.

CHAPTER 5

The New Woman in the Gezi Uprising

A New Political Actor or a Violable Subject?

On May 29, 2013, as I hurried down the hall of the law school to give the final exam for my Gender and Society class, Öykü, a student, stopped me right just outside the classroom. "What happened?" I asked, noticing tears in her eyes. **"*Hocam*"** (an honorific term in Turkish for teachers), she said, alarmed, "All my friends are at Gezi Park now, staying in the tents burnt up by the police in the early morning today and I feel so bad. I don't know if I can concentrate on the final exams right now." I hushed her, saying that everything would be alright; the people in Gezi Park were not alone and we are around for support in case of an emergency. I was able to mollify her and Öykü took the final exam. Although I sounded self-assured, I was utterly unaware of just how much support this minor action by leftists—who had occupied the park, a small patch of green at the heart of Istanbul, to protest the government's plan to turn it into a shopping mall—would attract. In less than a week, demonstrations flared across the country, with people taking to streets in almost every city, rallying day and night for the rest of the summer against the AKP government and the rule of the national patriarch. For three months in the summer of 2013, the country was seized by what people called the "Gezi spirit," a sense of fellowship, a mix of inspiration, hope, and solidarity along with resistance. According to police estimates, 3.5 million people took part in demonstrations (Amnesty International 2014). By the time the protests had largely tapered off in August 2013—leaving thousands of protestors injured and at least five dead (Amnesty International 2013)—the enormity of what had happened had still not sunk in for many. Nonetheless, it would soon become clear that nothing would ever be the same in Turkey. And for the New Woman, now a major actor engaging in grassroots political activism, it was both the best and worst of times.

Nobody expected Gezi. Nobody saw it coming, nor was anyone prepared for such a small conflict to erupt into a large-scale resistance movement, spreading across the country rapidly in a show of unprecedented solidarity among the millions disaffected and disgruntled by twelve years of AKP rule. To be sure, following 2008 when the government began to maneuver away from democracy, political protests began to increase in frequency: from less than "sixty in July 2012 to over a hundred a month from September to December 2012; from 150 in January 2013, to over 200 in March and 250 in May, spiking at over 400 protests in June 2013" (Yörük and Yüksel 2014, 12). However, nobody anticipated that the AKP government's decision to demolish a public park in Istanbul would serve as the breaking point, causing existing public grievances to explode into rebellion across the country. The ensuing public protests were unmatched in both number and diversity of the participants, who represented segments of society from Alevis to football fans, from leftists to anticapitalist Islamists, Kemalists, Kurds, and the LGBTIQ+ groups. All came together to contest the rule of the AKP government.

Uprisings rarely break out unless political systems, the courts, or other institutions fail to offer alternative routes to justice. If the AKP government had been in power, for instance, in the 1960s and 1970s, when military tutelage was at its height, disgruntled masses might have taken to the streets as well. Many protestors, however, would have called for military intervention to topple the government. This was the usual mode of internal political intervention in Turkey at that time: a military coup that effectively displaced the government in order to restore democracy and secularism, a process that only deepened the entrenchment of military tutelage. After seemingly successful military interventions, many people maintained a belief in the ability of the military to function as the guardian of secularism and a stable political order. Military tutelage, which appeared solid in the 1960s and 1970s, was, nevertheless, progressively weakened by 2013. Now the masses drew on their own resources to oust an autocrat. The popular struggle represented by the Gezi uprising not only resisted and challenged the power of the government but, perhaps more importantly, opened the door for a more thorough democratization and the emergence of an anti-authoritarian variant of secularism.

This chapter further examines the New Woman's embodied capacities, bodily gestures, orientations and disorientations, feelings, and speech acts, which took on immense political significance during the Gezi uprising in 2013, underscoring the uneasy position the New Woman came to occupy as the icon of resistance and the target of police violence. Scholars of Turkey have already established the importance of the body to the Gezi uprising: for Zeynep Gambetti (2014), the body itself was the subject of the Gezi uprising and for Banu Gökarıksel (2016), bodies at the Gezi protests "manifest as the most intimate, gendered, and sexualized sites of political resistance and repression" (Gökarıksel 2016, 242). Focusing on two dimensions of corporeal openness—one that emphasizes the body's capacity and other the body's vulnerability—I discuss two opposing visions of body politics that clashed at the Gezi uprising when everyday bodily experience became invested with politicized affects and feelings. The chapter also highlights the AKP government's incapacity to deal with the affective and embodied strategies employed by demonstrators during the protests, which prompted a shift in the government's emotional investment in moralist politics away from masculinist self-righteousness toward offendedness. It was this shift that set the stage for the return of vigilante violence against women.

The Gezi Uprising: Herstory

"I went there on the day Gezi broke out," said Nesrin, her face lighting up upon saying the word Gezi. It was a chilly March evening in 2018, five years after the Gezi uprising ended. We were in Bakırköy, an overcrowded central district on the European side of Istanbul, having coffee at one of the outdoor tables of a Starbucks packed with young people, reminiscing over our experiences of Gezi together. Nesrin continued:

> That was the day when people in Gezi Park were doing traditional folk dance, dancing *halay* to the rhythm of the *zurnas* and *davuls*. Back then I was working at a small accessories store at Levent, you

know, after I left my job at MajorMarket. Someone mentioned Gezi to me. I went there by myself, alone, because I was intrigued by what people had told me. I found that at Gezi Park people were just dancing and most of them looked like lefties and Kurds. The following day I left for a Black Sea trip but stayed glued to my phone to keep up with the news during the trip because things had become really huge and the resistance grew in size. Then I came back to Istanbul and started going to Taksim every day after work just to be a part of the events. I am so happy for having done so, for not staying at home; I now have a story to tell.

Never before in her life had Nesrin joined a demonstration. She did not have a history of activism, nor was she a member of a political party or an organization. When the protests broke out, however, she did not hesitate to join and made resistance a daily routine that she followed for the rest of the summer. Beginning from the first days of the Gezi uprising, she used social media to follow the most recent news and meet with fellow demonstrators with whom she often bonded over cigarettes or *Talcid* solutions when they needed to get pepper spray out of their eyes. When "there was too much going on", she discovered that the doors of some offices in Taksim would be open to demonstrators like her so they could hide from the intensified police attacks. Just as Nesrin felt that the Gezi uprising was a part of "herstory," so too did many women who were involved in the resistance. In fact, women joined the uprising in large numbers. Fifty-one percent of activists in the park, for instance, were women, according to a survey conducted by the polling company KONDA in 2014. The heart of resistance, protected by protestors from police intervention, Gezi Park functioned as the meeting ground for women who conceived inventive strategies for protesting against the AKP government.

In a piece aptly entitled "Law of the Father," Çağlar Keyder (2013) sketched a profile of the Gezi Park protestors, a portrayal which sheds light on the incentives for women to join the uprising:

Almost all the protestors in Gezi Park were young people with no direct experience of military rule or state repression. They were the beneficiaries of economic growth and greater openness to the world. They now wanted the basic rights that they knew existed elsewhere: they wanted to be able to defend public space against neoliberal incursion, and they refused to live under the authoritarian guidance of a self-appointed father of the country. They felt at home in a collective

way of life with gender equality and respect for diversity—a recipe
for a new covenant that makes irrelevant the pretensions of Erdoğan's
supposedly benevolent (and now wrathful) paternalism. It might once
have been possible for the political class to dismiss their demands as
the aspirations of a cosmopolitan minority in Istanbul, but their resistance found widespread (and unexpected) support in many urban
areas, with a rich mix of civil disobedience, demonstrations and street
politics. (Keyder 2013)

The Gezi protest, according to Keyder, was "the first social movement" to
grow out of the new social reality that globalization engendered in Turkey:
the capitalist restructuring promoted a corollary shift in employment patterns towards a service economy, rapid urbanization accompanied by the
spread of education, and legal reforms safeguarding the principle of gender
equality and democracy, along with the alacritous embrace of cultural diversity and equality by younger generations especially. Here it is worth re-
membering that this was the same social reality that laid the foundation for
the ascendance of the New Woman in Turkey in the global era.

The stakes for the New Woman were high now. At a time when
she was setting out to establish her place in society in the wake of the
dizzying changes brought by globalization—including the entrenchment of gender equality, new job opportunities brought by the growth
of the service industry, and the freedom from the strictures of shame-
honor discourse—the AKP government abruptly encroached upon her
life. Through a de facto ban on abortion, a legal ban on the sale of the
morning-after pill (a medication that prevents pregnancy after sex),
along with a severely moralizing discourse that aimed to discipline wom-
en's bodies with notions of chastity and modesty, the AKP government
thwarted the New Woman's capacity to thrive. In the few years prior to
the Gezi protest, the country saw blatant attempts by the AKP to muzzle
the media and restrict television content and internet use, as well as the
right to free assembly. Less than a week before the uprising, the government announced its plan to ban the sale of alcohol in shops between
10 p.m. and 6 a.m. and prohibit sponsorship of cultural events by alcohol companies. The laws were passed less than two weeks after their announcement without any public consultation. For the New Woman, this
world in the making was enervating, not least because her embodied
capacities through which she acted in the world were being infringed.
However, as the uprising would demonstrate, she was no longer willing

to shrink to fit the narrow confines of the AKP government's vision of femininity. It was through the Gezi protest that she reclaimed her space.

Openness as a Political Demand

In explaining the motives of demonstrators, Alev Çınar (2019) highlights their desire to reclaim autonomy from the familial forms of patriarchal governance that the AKP government promoted. This authoritarian, masculinist intervention was often embodied in the personhood of Tayyip Erdoğan, which explains why Nesrin brought up his name at the beginning of her account. "I joined the demonstration to say that this is our place, not Tayyip's," said Nesrin while placing both hands on the coffee table, as though to mark her own place. Nesrin was one of the hundreds of thousands of frustrated women who felt constricted by Erdoğan's ontological invasiveness. They vocalized their utter refusal to accept invasions into their lives and bodies by addressing him directly: "You cannot tell me what I can wear, eat, drink or how I can reproduce, you cannot regulate my life." These were the main concerns for the protesting groups, said one demonstrator, who remained before the bulldozer to stop it from wrecking the park on the second day of the uprising (quoted in Çınar 2019, 455). "Don't touch my home, my city, and my living space!" was another famous slogan. On the streets, women frequently chanted "Tayyip, hands off of my body!"

With globalization having opened up new possibilities for feminine existence in Turkey, the New Woman now fought to protect her bodily autonomy from encroachment by the ruling party. The embodied openness—which was an everyday bodily orientation and capacity that came easily to the New Woman—became hard to maintain with the government's attempts to impose a neoconservative gender order that pressured her to abandon those modalities. When women, in an effort to preserve their bodily autonomy, brought their embodied orientations to the resistance, a distinct vision of politics also came into view which I call a politics of embodied openness. A particular understanding of bodily autonomy underlies this politics of openness. In contrast to monadic and atomistic understandings of the body and the self that prevail in liberal thought, the politics of openness brought to the fore the intersubjective and relational capacities of the body. The New Woman, by re-enacting her everyday bodily orientations in the context of political resistance, was thus able to articulate her political demands: a firm openness to the world and a desire for sustained engagement with others.

Perhaps nowhere was this political vision clearer than in the embodied experience of Ceyda Sungur, who became popularly known as "the woman in red" during the Gezi resistance. On May 28, 2013, the second day of demonstrations and before events had spiraled into a nation-wide resistance movement, Ceyda, then a graduate student, was at Gezi Park with a small group of people to protest the demolition of the park. Little did she know that she would soon emerge as an icon of the Gezi uprising. When police began spraying protestors with pepper spray, a photographer captured the moment when Ceyda was brutalized: a policeman wearing a gas mask vigorously sprayed her in the face, drenching her, while Ceyda stood firm, her feet planted solidly on the ground and one hand holding the strap of her tote bag, her red dress slightly flared, with her head turned away and her wavy black hair flowing. As soon as the photo was circulated on social media (the mainstream media and press were heavily censored), Ceyda instantly became the emblem of dissent,

The famous picture, popularly known as "the woman in red", was taken at the beginning of the Gezi protest. Istanbul, 2013 (Photo by Osman Orsal).

with her image printed on badges, graffitied on walls, and posted on Facebook profiles; people both inside and outside Turkey expressed solidarity with the Gezi protestors by wearing a red dress.

Ceyda's image powerfully juxtaposed the deeply entrenched reality of women's violability in Turkey—aggravated by the police brutality that targeted the New Woman—against women's firm intentions to open up to and engage the world on their own terms. The image grabbed people's attention immediately; many felt drawn to Ceyda, as though wanting to absorb her embodied response—her poise and bearing in the face of police brutality. "Look at her, she does not even flinch," was the sentence I often heard from others who saw the photo. It seemed that what moved people to veneration was not only Ceyda's courage in standing up for what she believed in, but her embodied response: the habitual and unreflective way her body reacted to the immediate violence she faced. Despite the force of the pepper spray, she did not shrink, cower, or seek to escape; instead, she remained rooted and balanced, her body continuing to express her political intention. What the famous image featured was not a woman cowed by police violence, but one who, like a fluid figure of insubordination, gracefully whirled in the face of police brutality. In fact, in the following days, a whirling dervish in red skirts and wearing a gas mask, inspired by Ceyda, performed a ritual dance at Gezi Park.

If the body is the locus of intentionality, as phenomenology has long taught, Ceyda's embodied response was a feat of agency in a world that did not affirm the openness of women's bodies. In such a world, Ceyda persisted, carrying her body not as a fragile burden, but as a medium of capacities, converting her intentions into actions and her bodily gestures into political demands. In fact, during the Gezi uprising, phenomenologically speaking, women's bodies robustly projected a modality of openness. To begin with, the frustrating sense of constriction women experienced due to the AKP government's authoritarian rule vanished when the resistance took off and women acquired a sense of spaciousness. Openness was psychological too; protestors were able to cultivate relations of care and solidarity among themselves. Nesrin told me how fulfilling it was for her to be at Taksim during the uprising and that she went there almost every day. "I would just go to Taksim and sit with people whom I haven't met before," she said. "We shared everything; food and cigarettes, and there was no sexual harassment going on. I was totally amazed at how people treated each other."

Women who participated in the resistance often continued doing in Gezi Park what they had been doing in their everyday lives: gathering with friends and reading books, doing yoga in groups, and taking care of their children. All of these mundane activities assumed a new phenomenological and political significance when done during the protest. Reading books in front of police barricades demonstrated a refusal to be intimidated. Taking care of children meant forming a human shield around them to protect them from police brutality. Organizing collective *iftars* at night on the street to break the Ramadan fast meant an insistence on a firm openness to the world, a desire for collectivity and sustained engagement with others. In re-enacting their daily habits and routines in the context of the protest, women were able to articulate what bodily openness meant for them—the body's ability to open up to the world for connection, encounters, and contact: Its capacity to create an opening in the domain of politics, building a sense of open-endedness at a time when the authoritarian government wanted to impose a sense of finality. And its capacity to foster a sense of possibility and opportunity, enabling women to resist a world that instilled a sense of powerlessness.

The resistance in general, and for women in particular, evoked immense excitement and joy among millions. Demonstrators' acts of solidarity animated embodied life, counteracting feelings of insufficiency, constriction, and powerlessness that the increasing authoritarianism produced. It was as if the Gezi uprisings had revealed a "golden shadow" in protestors that they had not even known existed. The golden shadow—a collection of abilities, capacities, and creative urges one possesses yet which have not yet manifested, according to Carl Jung (1959) —takes up residence in the inner recesses of the psyche. It often gets projected onto others whom one admires for manifesting, potential that one, in fact, has but is not yet aware of. During the Gezi protest, a similar dynamic became evident, with people unleashing their own creative capacities and valor all the while revering other protestors who inspired courage and hope. However, they did not realize, themselves, that what they were doing was also courageous and inventive. Nesrin, for instance, who went to Taksim almost every day despite her heavy work schedule, told me in excitement that she was in awe of women she met during Gezi: "Those women were so strong, Esra," she said, exhaling her cigarette and shivering in the chill night. "Imagine gathering together every day demonstrating, during daytime to relieve your children of the protest, so that kids can go back home and sleep for a bit. Seeing this, you overflow with energy—having been pepper sprayed by the police just cheers you up, doesn't discourage you."

The resistance did not have a leader and was highly decentralized. According to Eslen-Ziya and Erhart, this granted the uprising post-heroic qualities, which, unlike masculinist and authoritarian forms of control, promote "leadership that focuses on networks of communication, and is relational and less hierarchical" (Eslen-Ziya and Erhart 2015, 472). Social media was the main vehicle of mass mobilization. Tech-savvy young generations used it to document police violence and violations, to creatively mock the government, and to organize and assemble the protestors.

Women, in particular, promoted gender egalitarianism and, in an effort to combat sexism among the protestors themselves, created new modes of expression and a new vocabulary for resistance. Feminists, for instance, built a women's tent in Gezi Park called "the zone without Tayyip and without harassment," which functioned as a meeting point for women (Turkmen 2018). Women were also active in the public forums held at night in the city parks throughout Turkey. They gave talks expressing their desires for their environment, for their right to the city, and their resentment of violations of personal and social space, in addition to offering opinions on gender problems that had long plagued the country: violence against women, division among secular and headscarf-wearing women, and the indifference of Turkish women to the political struggles of Kurdish women (Rahte and Tokdoğan 2014). During the resistance, they had to confront the pervasive use of sexist slogans and slurs. To redress the situation, women activists came up with creative solutions: one group painted over slurs that had been spray painted on a wall in the Taksim area and replaced them with nonsexist graffiti (Korkman Kurtulus and Aciksoz 2013); queer groups organized a workshop in Gezi Park and generated a list of inventive slogans to use at demonstrations, drawing heavily on the vocabulary of the LGBTIQ+ communities (Zengin 2013).

All of these modes of resistance and community-making generated a novel emotional state for women—a sense of security, solidarity, and joy that was reflected in the playful inventiveness of their chants and slogans: "If you have gas, I have waterproof mascara!" read one that commonly was spray painted on walls. Another one frequently resounded through the Taksim district when women chanted in the streets: "Tayyip run run run, women are arriving!" A slogan painted on a wall around Gezi Park summed up women's attitude vis-à-vis Erdoğan's political authority: "Tayyip, I have three children not because you wanted me to, but because I have had sex as often as I wanted."

Fighting Openness with Violence

On May 31, 2013, one of the first days of the resistance before thousands massed on the streets, Lobna Allami, a Turkish-Jordanian woman, was hit on the head by a tear gas bomb during a sit-in at Taksim Square protesting the government's plans for Gezi Park. There were around five hundred people at the protest and Allami, then thirty-four, was sitting on the grass, singing along and smoking a cigarette when the police, without any warning, attacked with tear gas and water cannons (t24 2013a). When she arrived at the hospital, Allami was unconscious and had a fractured skull and severe head trauma. Her life-threatening injuries required a long hospital stay, during which she was kept in an induced coma for a month. Allami, who regressed to the state of five-year-old as a result of her injuries, had three brain surgeries and other extensive treatments (Arman 2013). Over the next two years, she regained some speech and eyesight, but doctors said it could take years to gain full recovery of her speech and mobility. An examination of her wounds indicated the injury was caused by a teargas canister fired from close range.

On the day Allami was injured, the image of her body in a red T-shirt and denim shorts lying on the ground, convulsing, with a puddle of blood on the side of her face became etched into the minds of many. People now realized the lengths to which the AKP government would go to repress the Gezi uprising. From the start, the government had taken coercive actions with little attempt to initiate a dialogue with protestors or to allay public frustration. Police violence was pervasive; they heavily relied on the use of water cannons, pepper spray, and tear gas merely to disperse nonviolent protestors. Crackdowns in the streets saw the police armed with rubber bullets, water-tanks, and scorpions (police command cars) attacking protestors and using violent tactics such as beating and kettling. In the wake of the protests, the Turkish Medical Association reported that as of July 10, 2013, more than eight thousand people had been injured at demonstrations, more than sixty-one severely (Amnesty International 2013).

Coercion and violence proved to be the AKP government's main containment strategy against the protestors. Many women like Ceyda

Sungur and Lobna Allami were brutalized by the police. Given that women's historically and politically constituted violability had been heightened by the government's regressive gender politics, police violence was inevitably directed to subjugate women's bodies, in some cases fatally. The largely male police forces, which were given license to brutalize protestors, readily treated women's bodies as a site for violence and injury. In fact, women's violability took on a disturbing character. When paired with hostile government attitudes, the violence against women quickly degenerated into a spectacle, with numerous public displays of the punitive power by male law enforcement over women. Video footage uploaded to the internet, and shared via social media, attested to the fact that police targeted protestors even after they had left the protest scene. For instance, Başak Özçelik, a university student, posted pictures on Twitter revealing large bruises on her legs and arms after she was battered by twenty police officers and men in plain clothes while sitting on some grass with friends following a protest in Gündoğan Square. Although she attempted to flee, the men continued to beat her with batons and sticks, breaking her leg and arm (t24 2013b). The police also attacked small groups of individuals caught in the vicinity of protests. One recorded incident showed young people being violently attacked by riot police as they walked along a seaside promenade known as Kordon in Izmir. While three policemen used their batons to strike a young man and woman on their head and arms, another policeman yanked a passing young woman by the hair (Haberturk 2013). Law enforcement officials also were reported to have sexually harassed women demonstrators who were detained. According to a 2013 report by Amnesty International, many women held by the police mentioned the repeated use of sexual insults and the threat of sexual violence, while some reported actual sexual assaults.

Understanding police violence only as a containment strategy, however, would be to adopt a narrow view, since this approach does not account for the linkages between bodies, politics, and violence during the Gezi protest. For the women who joined the Gezi protest, their bodies were not only the medium for making political demands but also the political demand itself. They demanded that feminine embodiment no longer be tied to violability, abuse, and violence. They demanded that bodily openness be an ability and a resource, not a weakness. While the politics of openness affirmed the capacity of women's bodily openness, the AKP government forcefully denied women's demands. More disconcerting than the AKP's rejection was perhaps the *way* the AKP rejected women's embodied openness. The government fought back with police violence and seized on women's embodied openness as an occasion to inflict harm on them. Police violence, in this sense, dramatically heightened the AKP's politics in that women's bodies were intrinsically associated with violence and violations, a process that marked the New Woman as a violable feminine subject.

Counter-Mobilization by the AKP: A Strange Blend of Power and Powerlessness

Police violence was by no means the only method the AKP government employed to crack down on the resistance. Soon after the protests fired up, the government unfurled a counter-mobilization campaign aiming to vilify and criminalize the protestors. Erdoğan, who led the campaign, effectively fanned the flames of resentment among his base against the protestors through his hectoring demeanor and overweening masculine posturing. The campaign started with Erdoğan's derogation of protestors, but quickly flamed out when the protestors responded with humor and creativity. In the first week of the protests, Erdoğan scoffed at Gezi demonstrators, branding them *Çapulcu,* indicating a crowd of marauders or bums who have no credible political demands but want only to loot. This label, along with others used by Erdoğan such as "vandal" and "extremist," failed to have the intended effect. Instead of being stigmatized by it, demonstrators embraced it, and in less than a week, it became a globally recognized popular phrase. Soon after Erdoğan's speech, a video was uploaded on YouTube, a wittily adapted version of the song "Party Rock Anthem" by the American duo LMFAO that includes the lyrics "everyday I'm shuffling." The video had the title "Everyday I'm chapulling - Tayyip feat. Bülent," which referred to the first names of the prime minister and the deputy prime minister, respectively. The video went viral on the social media and the term chapulling, an anglicized version of the word *çapulcu*, became globally popular as an English verb meaning to disrupt the order through humor. A few days later intellectual Noam Chomsky shared a video in which he stated his support for Gezi with a banner in the background that read: "I am also a capulcu in solidarity." The following day singer Patti Smith shared a picture of herself on Instagram holding a placard that said, "We are all chapulchu."

The AKP government's vulnerability to mockery had previously been exposed by the feminist and queer movements, who subversively reclaimed derogatory terms like slut and *ibne* (faggot). The government now floundered during the Gezi protests too. Amid growing support for the resistance, the AKP found itself in a powerless, if not a helpless, position to outsmart the inventive tactics deployed by the mass resistance movement, which not only opposed the government's policies but also was deeply at odds with AKP's masculinist notion of authoritarian politics embedded in the shame and honor codes. The government reacted from a position of power in its reliance on police violence to restore authority, but to the extent that it failed to stigmatize and impose labels on the protestors, it had no capacity to exercise symbolic violence over them.

The AKP's lack of power to classify, stigmatize, and label the protestors was significant. And the more acutely the government became aware of its impotence, the more outrageously Erdoğan reacted to the Gezi protestors. From then on, a new moral framing began to emerge: The AKP, instead of acting from a position of power, switched to a position of powerlessness to intensify the violence used against the protestors. The self-righteousness that fueled the moral politics of the post–2008 period was replaced by a sense of aggrieved indignation. Offendedness, an emotion of injury, now animated the AKP government's counter-mobilization campaign to ostracize and discredit protestors. This interesting blend of powerlessness and power that characterized the new stage in the AKP's government's moral politics would prove to be a lasting strategy, altering the course of moral politics away from exercising moral authority to evoking moral injury.

One such attempt was the Respect for National Will[1], a series of mass rallies organized by the AKP and led by Erdoğan that took place across Turkey during June 2013. In those rallies, Erdoğan demonstrated the extent of the AKP's popularity by drawing millions of his supporters into the streets. The government rallies helped the AKP to frame the Gezi protest as an offense against the legitimate authority of the government, an injury that was inflicted on the nation and an outrageous and disrespectful attack on Erdoğan, who alone embodied the national will. Speaking at these rallies, Erdoğan emphasized the need for Turkey to stand united against the attacks. Referring to the protests, he said: "You saw the game played against our nation, you felt the trap, you understood the real target of the attacks," (World Bulletin 2013).[2] The government's call for respect for the national will had strong denunciatory overtones. Within this framework, Gezi protestors were outsiders, assaulting the nation itself.

The defense the AKP government took during the Gezi uprising was formulated in not only national but also religious terms. For instance, at a speech Erdoğan delivered before Parliament on June 11, 2013, he accused the Gezi protestors of insulting the sacred values of Islam. Addressing the protestors, he said: "You step into a *camii* with your shoes on, you drink (alcohol) there, and you will commit this assault on this country's religious sanctuaries, in the name of what? In the name of the environment! We have in our hands now, the video footage. We will share it." The video footage Erdoğan claimed to possess, however, was never released.

Perhaps the most disturbing allegations against Gezi protestors for breaching morality took place when, in June 2013, news about an incident of vigilante violence made headlines. The news revealed to a shocked public the gruesome details concerning a young woman wearing a headscarf who was viciously assaulted by male protestors. Known as the Kabataş incident, the only eyewitness to the alleged crime was the victim herself, a young woman who claimed to have been attacked by a gang of seventy male protestors in the centrally located neighborhood of Kabataş in Istanbul. The woman claimed that half-naked men wearing black leather pants and leather gloves first verbally harassed her, then beat her, crushing the stroller carrying her baby. After urinating on her and her six-month-old child, the men left the woman lying on the street unconscious. When a small number of journalists from the mainstream media testified that they had seen video footage of the incident, AKP officials lashed out against the Gezi Park protestors. Erdoğan seized the moment and accused the Gezi protestors of moral turpitude, galvanizing his political base by declaring: "They harassed and beat my fellow head scarf-wearing sisters," using his usual paternal and yet enraged intonation (NTV 2013). It was not until two years after the Kabataş event that the video footage was finally leaked to the press, which showed that the allegations were grossly distorted and many parts entirely fabricated. The footage showed a group of six young men who seemed to be walking past the young woman and verbally harassing her.

. . .

In a famous 1996 essay entitled "Taking Offense," JM Coetzee presents an unorthodox analysis of state censorship in relation to the state being offended and powerless. "The powerlessness of a subordinated religious sect or ethnic minority is easy to see," he writes. "But when at the other extreme a national government or dominant church or powerful class is offended by some or other teaching or representation to the extent that it sets about suppressing it, how can I claim that it reacts out of powerlessness?" (Coetzee 1996, 5). The crux of his argument is that taking offense is in fact a sign of powerlessness. "The experience or premonition of being robbed of power seems to me intrinsic to all instances of taking offense," he writes, explaining the emotional logic of censorship in apartheid South Africa (Coetzee 1996, 3). In a similar vein, the AKP government, like many other powerful institutions that failed to establish cultural hegemony, was quick to take offense and came to invest in the feeling of offendedness as a political strategy to put a stop to the resistance.

Erdoğan's strategy was neither unprecedented nor ingenious. Historically, Islamist right-wing politics in Turkey has fed on feelings of injury (Yilmaz 2017). This politics, building on the notion of a wounded collective self, traced the original injury back to the fall of Ottoman Empire and the foundation of a secular republic, which abolished the institution of the caliphate and sharia law (Tokdoğan 2018). For the Islamist right wing, whose political power ebbed away following the foundation of the secular republic, the strict control of the secular state over Sunni Islam was deeply upsetting. The Islamist right wing framed the secular takeover as a gross moral offense, a huge wrong committed by the new Turkish state that inflicted a collective wound on Muslims. This narrative also dictated that the injury imposed by the secular republic rightfully demanded a moral reaction.

During the period when Islamists—who presented themselves as conservative democrats—were no longer deprived of political power but ruled the country, the AKP rekindled the old flame by evoking the feeling of injury, especially when launching political attacks on the secular military and bureaucracy. During the Gezi protest, however, the government stoked the feeling of injury by reframing it in terms of disrespecting the national will. The call to "Respect the National Will" became so effective that, even after a failed coup attempt in July 2016, national will–themed rallies were organized by the AKP, and bridges and squares were renamed with reference to the national will (Bilgiç 2018).

During Gezi, the AKP used various tactics to contain the resistance. The government denied the right to protest in Gezi Park and Taksim Square, presented the Gezi resistance as a coup attempt against the

Erdoğan regime, and Erdoğan declared the demonstrators terrorists. Of all these tactics, it was the framing of the resistance as a moral insult to the national will and Muslims that proved most effective. The lure of moralization lies in the ambiguity with which it blends power and powerlessness and the opportunity to seek retaliation under the cloak of moral outrage. The offended party—that is, Erdoğan—came across as a righteous leader of high moral principle rather than a macho bully moving aggressively against a grassroots movement. The state, likewise, presented itself as a bulwark protecting society from the forces of moral degeneration and subversion. In such appeals to morality, political leaders did not occupy the position of authority, as Erdoğan had when he denounced Dilşat Aktaş, a left-wing woman activist, for unchaste behavior in 2011. This time the AKP government acted from a position of powerlessness, professing offense in order to unleash violence against the Gezi protestors.

The strategy enabled the AKP to mobilize its base against the resistance. After all, the nation—represented by the half of society who had voted for the AKP—was entitled to defend itself against those who threatened it. Such a strategy of incitement translated into collusion between police forces and civilian men. Indeed, incidents in which police officers acted in partnership with civilians to batter protestors, or those suspected of joining demonstrations supporting the Gezi protests, were justified by political authorities on the grounds that the nation was defending itself. For those who did not subscribe to the AKP government's interpretation, however, such collusion was deeply disturbing. One of the young women I interviewed, Hale, a Starbucks worker, told me how unsettling it was for her to see a man she had flirted with join the police in assaulting protestors in Ankara. He later deluged her with text messages attacking Hale for her alleged moral degeneration.

> H: I was flirting with this guy during Gezi Park events. We were not steady though, just flirting. One day, I, with my father, walked up to this square to withdraw money from an ATM and saw a group of policemen coming over towards us to beat the protestors in the vicinity. And there he was! He was with the police, throwing stones at people. It was so bizarre. I said to myself, what's going on! He saw me, too. We didn't talk.
>
> E: Do you think he was attacking Gezi protestors?

H: Yeah! He was with police ganging up against protestors, attacking people! And at night a message popped up on my
screen. "What a slut you are!" the message said. It was from
him. It made me feel terrible, as if I had done something
terrible and degenerate, as if I were this mature woman, not
a young girl. He kept texting all night, writing things like:
"You are supporting Gezi, you are anti-police!" I told him
that I was not there to protest but he kept going, flooding me
with messages like, 'You don't even fast during the month of
Ramadan. You are an atheist and don't believe in God.' I was
speechless. I had a completely different idea of him before. I
thought he was a good guy.

The man who denounced Hale did so by subjecting her embodied existence and actions to shame-honor morality, taking her pre-
sumed political stance as a sign of moral degeneration. The fervor in
which men like him embraced shame-honor-based morality cannot,
however, be understood independently of the AKP's efforts to reroute
Turkey toward an autocracy. Indeed, shame-honor morality, more so than
the notion of national will, facilitated collusion between men and the AKP
government in the aftermath of Gezi. By revitalizing the traditional *mahalle* culture, in which men had acted as informal guardians protecting
the normative order of the neighborhood, the AKP government actively
sought the collaboration of particular groups of men at the local level to
intensify its authoritarian control of urban space.

Intensified Moral Vigilance

In the wake of the Gezi uprising, the AKP government took upon
itself the task of masculinist enforcement of morality, with an alarmist
sense of vigilance to protect the society from so-called moral harms.
Diligent efforts were put forth to push particular practices—such as
the consumption of alcoholic beverages, abortion, women's sexuality,
and co-ed living—out of political discussion by framing them as moral
transgressions. Although the government was the main actor execut-
ing the masculinist enforcement of morality, the involvement of the
local male community in the *mahalle* was publicly encouraged through
discursive means. In 2014, for instance, Erdoğan praised shopkeepers
(*esnaf*) and artisans (*zanaatkâr*) for the role they had played in the history of Turkey, helping the state to protect the social order:

In our civilization, in our national and civilizational spirit, the shop-keeper, the artisan is the soldier and the fighter when necessary, he is the hero, veteran, and the martyr who defends the land if need be. He is the police who restores order and the judge who secures justice, and a compassionate brother when need be. You cannot write him off as merely a cab driver or chauffeur. He is the trusty brother and the guardian of the *mahalle*. You cannot write him off as *bakkal* (a corner store owner), *kasap* (a butcher) and *manav* (a grocer). He is the spirit of the *mahalle*. He is the conscience of our street and our quarter. If you erased *esnaf* (shopkeepers), there would be nothing left in the history of Turkey. (CNN Türk 2014)

The AKP also invoked the shame-honor-based order of the *mahalle* and the masculine guardianship it entailed as political solutions to gender issues such as violence against women. For instance, in 2015, an AKP deputy, İsmet Uçma, proposed reactivating the honor of the *mahalle* as a strategy to mitigate violence against women in the country. Speaking at a meeting of the Commission for Preventing Violence against Women, which was established within the National Assembly as part of political efforts to tackle gender violence, İsmet Uçma, instead of presenting a policy proposal, posed honor as a solution: "We can develop something like *mahallenin namusu* (honor of the neighborhood)," he said. "When something happens to a resident, everyone steps in to protect the victim and wipe out the perpetrator," (Kazete 2015).

In the meantime, government pundits appeared on TV and other media to repudiate the persistent criticisms leveled against Erdoğan's authoritarian rule by portraying Erdoğan as a father figure of the traditional Turkish family, a move that obscured his workings of political power. Pundits lauded the moral authority of Erdoğan through populist claims about Turkey, which they pointed out was actually part of the Middle East, where there was not a strong affinity toward Scandinavian-style democracy. Erdoğan was merely acting like a traditional father who cared for the whole society and meddled in everything, including people's dietary habits, something which was understandable given the traditional father's authority in Turkish culture. This rhetoric had no weight among Gezi supporters, however, who were critical of the patriarchal family as well as the political rule of the patriarch. The government, nonetheless, insisted on revitalizing it in public discourse, mostly because the rhetoric about the gendered order of the *mahalle* and the family was a source of power, a cultural means that the AKP used to attain its political goal of authoritarian rule.

One area that the AKP government clamped down on was mixed-gender college student accommodations. Concerned by the increasing autonomy and liberation of educated young people who supported the Gezi resistance, Erdoğan, in November 2013, expressed the AKP government's discomfort with co-ed dormitories at public universities and off-campus housing. The co-ed living arrangements, Erdoğan declared, were clearly morally dubious and required the intervention of the state. "Nobody knows what takes places in those houses," he remarked in a speech. "All kinds of dubious things may happen [in those houses]. . . . Then, parents cry out, saying, 'Where is the state?' These steps are being taken in order to show that the state is there" (quoted in Cindoglu and Unal 2017, 46). Soon after Erdoğan's statements, dorms that were previously co-ed started to separate male and female students, and many landlords who had rented apartments to mixed-gender roommates started to terminate their contracts. On numerous other occasions, Erdoğan similarly asserted that it was the duty of the state to protect the honor of the nation and the youth from alcohol, gambling, and narcotics.

It was not just college student accommodations that were targeted by the AKP government in the wake of the Gezi. The construction of studio apartments—1+1 apartments in Turkish phrasing—and single-person households also became subject to moral vigilance. Government-backed media reported that studio apartments for singles had become hotbeds of prostitution and moral corruption. An interview published in Star News featured an academic who claimed that while 1+1 apartments were acceptable in regions with a high density of college students, their proliferation across the country would put the Turkish family system at risk. "Unless necessary measures are taken," he warned, "it will lead to the dissolution of our social order" (Star 2015).

Here it is worth mentioning that the construction of 1+1 apartments in the 2000s did not take place independently of the AKP government. Turkey's housing agency TOKI (Turkey's Mass Housing Administration), backed by the AKP government, was directly involved in construction of these apartments in large urban areas. As Turkey went through a major urban transformation led by the AKP government in the early 2000s, TOKI emerged as a major player in AKP's urban policy. The party, in fact, secured its hegemonic position in electoral politics by way of governmental housing projects, which supplied mass housing as well as construction-related jobs and contracts. When, however, the AKP government's liberal politics reached certain cultural limits, features of its urban policy were reversed. In May 2015, Ayşenur İslam, then minister of family and social policy, declared the AKP government's decision to halt TOKI's construction of 1+1 apartments "in order to protect the integrity of the family" (Hürriyet 2015).

The Gezi protests came as a shock to the AKP government, which was not prepared for a mass uprising involving many different segments of society using inventive strategies that featured both local and global practices such as humor and yoga. As the government struggled to suppress the resistance, a decisive shift took place from hegemony to violent domination, from disciplinary power to retribution, and from persuasion to downright coercion (Keyder 2013). Likewise, with the failure of the most prominent aspect of moralist politics and the emergence of Erdoğan as a moral guardian of the normative order, a new strategy emerged that operated mainly along the lines of taking offense. In an effort to mobilize civilians, especially local men, to quell the Gezi uprising, the government implicitly encouraged them to assume the role of moral guardians of women. These changes supercharged politics, allying moralism with violence, severely disorienting New Women in the future. Shame-honor-based morality would become a gendered means of violence when vigilante men took justice into their own hands and attacked women in public places for their alleged moral infractions.

Endnotes

1. The notion of national will has always been fundamental to Turkey's center-right discursive repertoire (Bilgiç 2018). Historically, the Islamist right-wing parties identified themselves with the nation as opposed to the state. The latter was historically a stronghold of secular military forces and bureaucracy that dictated its will from above. The AKP, which came to power through democratic elections, deemed itself the manifestation of the will of the nation, as opposed to the former Kemalist secular establishment, which lacked popular support.

2. These mass rallies were supported by the members of the (MHP) Nationalist Action Party, Turkey's nationalist opposition party, the country's third-largest political party. By drawing on this support, the AKP government framed the protest as an attack on the larger society and national will, not merely on the government.

CHAPTER 6

The New Woman against the Vigilante Man

Violence, Orientations, and Disorientations

When vigilante violence against women first broke out in large cities, rupturing the fabric of everyday life for the New Woman, it had been more than three years since the Gezi protests ended. The democratic rights that protestors had exercised were severely curtailed because the AKP government had suspended democracy and imposed a state of emergency after a failed coup attempt in July 2016 that killed 265 people and wounded 1,400 (New York Times 2016). In fact, many tumultuous changes took place in those years in addition to the failed coup attempt: Erdoğan was elected president in 2014, increasing his powers with an absolute majority of the vote in the first round of elections; the mainstream media became fully government-controlled; the country weathered the largest suicide bombings in its history; the military launched invasions of Kurdish cities; the separation of powers that lies at the heart of a democratic regime was drastically compromised; and violence against women became explosive.

This final chapter takes the story of the New Woman in the global era forward to the current populist moment to show how feminine bodies that posed a threat to the AKP's authoritarian political initiatives were increasingly marked by performative violence, provoked by the AKP's moralist politics as well as a new gender justice paradigm the party introduced after the Gezi uprisings. It focuses on incidents of vigilante violence, investigating how the New Woman's body became the site of performative violence. By closely examining the moralized ways women's bodies are subjected to vigilante violence, the chapter demonstrates the collusion between vigilante men and the AKP. It also analyzes both individual and collective responses—including disorientation, fear, and reorientation—that feminine bodies express when confronted with the violence and punitive orientation of the populist moment. Unlike the earlier period of global capitalist reconstruction, in which economic liberalism was accompanied with political liberalism—a period when the New Woman was integral to the economic fortune of Turkey—the new populist moment vigorously rejected the New Woman. Global capitalist reconstruction was far from immune to sexism and gender hierarchies, but the New Woman was able to push beyond the strictures of class and gender to generate new bodily and emotional modes of being feminine. In the populist moment, however, these modalities of being feminine came under attack, often through violent means enabled and fueled by the affective intensities of shame and honor. In protesting the violence, the New Woman would renew and revive political resistance against the authoritarian rule in Turkey.

Performative Violence and Moral Vigilance under AKP Rule

So-called punishment of women by men for their alleged offenses against morality used to be a widespread misogynistic practice in Turkey. It was historically enabled by the shame and honor discourse, in which men—by virtue of having been granted de facto power to control women's bodies and sexuality—threatened to harm and penalize women if they transgressed moral norms. Vigilantism, however, did not always come cloaked in morality.[1] In the 1990s, for instance, when the secular state upheld a headscarf ban in government offices, hospitals, universities, and schools, vigilantism in large cities in western Turkey, the stronghold of elites, took the form of secularist vigilance against women who wore headscarves in public places. College students entering campus were bullied by professors and women walking on the street were verbally harassed by men and women alike.

Moral vigilantism resurfaced in 2006, this time exclusively targeting transwomen who had to survive brutal attacks in Ankara. The next vigilante attack against transwomen was reported in Istanbul in 2012 (Savcı 2021). In the meantime, specific districts of Istanbul, especially those strongly leaning toward the AKP government, where the urban gentrification process initiated an influx of upper-middle class residents and new commercial establishments such as art galleries, bars, and restaurants, began to emerge as loci of vigilante practices (Polat 2021). One such district was Tophane, where cafes and art galleries involved in so-called immoral activities, such as serving alcohol during an art exhibition, were threatened by a group of residents in the fall of 2010.[2] During the same period, mixed-gender groups that were consuming alcohol in public were intimidated by local small business owners (Başaran 2015). These incidents found an explicit moral justification in the populist political vision the AKP government endorsed and, hence, were openly avowed. In June 2016, for instance, when neighborhood men ransacked a music store and beat Seogu Lee, the store's owner, who had organized a Radiohead night where alcohol was served, Erdoğan commented that it was wrong for the neighborhood residents to forcefully intervene but it was equally wrong for people to drink alcohol on the street during the month of Ramadan (Hürriyet 2016a).

Vigilante violence that exclusively targeted women broke out after the democracy vigils of 2016. Instigated by Erdoğan, the vigils started on the night of July 15, 2016, after a faction of the Turkish military initiated a coup against the AKP government.[3] That night, Erdoğan appeared on a live CNNTürk broadcast and called on the people to go out, violate curfew, resist the traitors, and stop the attempted coup. Erdoğan's call was met with enthusiasm by AKP supporters, and large masses of men and women took to the streets to join the vigils. Men readily took on the role of vigilantes protecting the national will as well as the political regime against the so-called corrupt traitors. Held nightly for weeks in urban streets and squares, the vigils drew thousands of participants who came together to express the national will against the putschists. Islamic calls (**Sala**) were recited from mosques, not to call prayer but to spark civilian resistance against the attempted coup and urge believers to pledge allegiance to the AKP regime. Never before in the history of the Turkish Republic had a government called the masses to the streets to display the national will against military intervention.

The first vigilante attack against a woman for an alleged moral transgression was reported just a few weeks after the vigils ended. On September 12, 2016, an Istanbul nurse was violently attacked on a public bus for wearing shorts. The male perpetrator defended himself in court by claiming that his moral and national sentiments were particularly intense at the time of the incident, and the piece of clothing the woman was wearing offended him morally. His statement went as follows:

> It was the Feast of Sacrifice Day. My national and moral sentiments were heightened and intense. Every single day, some moral values in our country are made to erode further. It was one of those days. I don't think my action was right. I don't think it was constructive. The woman's way of dressing was not normal. It offended my moral feelings. A woman should appear chaste and in order to do that, she should dress according to the norms and position herself accordingly. If she had been dressed decently, we would not have been morally offended and would not have acted this way. We would have been less offended if she had at least put on trousers or a tracksuit. They are ruining our mental and spiritual chemical balance. I have been fasting for the last four years. However, because of these people, I cannot turn towards the eternal life and cannot have a peaceful religious life. (Terzi v. Çakıroğlu 2016)

On that morning Ayşegül Terzi, a twenty-three-year-old recently graduated delivery nurse, left the hospital around 7:45 a.m. when her night shift was over. On her way out, she saw a colleague, a nurse who suggested Ayşegül stay at the hospital since her next shift would be that night. It was the first day of sacrificial Muslim holiday and Ayşegül wanted to exchange *bairam* greetings with her father, so she took the bus home, where she lived with her parents. On the bus, she was listening to music and checking her messages, reading the *bairam* greetings popping up on the screen of her cell phone. The last thing she remembered was suddenly being hit in the face and flung to the bus window, her head smashing hard against the glass.

The person who attacked Terzi was a thirty-five-year-old man, Abdullah Çakıroğlu, who worked as a security guard in Istanbul. On that morning Abdullah Çakıroğlu left his workplace around 8:00 a.m. and boarded the bus to return home where he lived with his uncle, his siblings, and their spouses. After a while he noticed a woman who was unknown to him. He recounted the event at court in the following way:

> The woman was wearing a short skirt. She was sitting on a seat in an obscene way with her legs pointing towards the edge of the seat and at the same time looking at me with a saucy attitude. In that moment, I lost my self-control. I thought that the values of the country we live in as well as the values of the society were being trodden underfoot, I also thought that the woman disrespected people around her as much

as herself by dressing up in the way she did, my moral side weighed heavily and I got to my feet in that moment, did something, an involuntary move, and I threw a kick to her face. . . . About eight to ten passengers huddled around me and attacked me, hit my face and eyes. The driver stopped the bus and in that moment I flung myself out of the bus. People got off too and kept harassing me. When I got a moment, I snuck off. I walked back home. When I got back home my shirt was torn; I told my family that I got stung by a wasp. Later, I got back to my daily routine. A few days after the incident, I received calls from friends and family, telling me that they saw me on the internet. I watched the video on the internet. My face was not visible, the kick was obviously visible. I thought they would not file a report and hence I didn't go to the police. (Terzi v. Çakıroğlu 2016)

Between September 2016 and July 2018, at least nineteen cases of vigilante violence against women were documented in Turkey. İpek Atcan, a twenty-two-year-old music writer, was kicked while she was waiting for the subway in Istanbul. The male perpetrator yelled at her: "You can't sit here with your legs crossed like that!" (Hürriyet 2016b). Canan Kaymakçı, an Istanbul woman, was harassed by a man on the street for wearing "provocative clothing" and "turning people on" (Yarın Haber 2017). Another woman in Istanbul was attacked by a man in a supermarket for her so-called inappropriate walking style (Siyasi Haber 2016). The man inside the store shouted at the woman and ordered her to "walk properly." He then attacked her, breaking the woman's nose and bruising her arms.

In all these incidents, vigilantes, almost exclusively male, meted out violent punishments to women they did not know personally for their alleged moral transgressions, transgressions as innocuous as wearing shorts on public transport, walking in the supermarket, smoking cigarettes in a park, wearing a sleeveless shirt on the street, sitting cross-legged in public, and exercising in the park. It soon became clear that vigilante violence did not target women across the board but rather those whose embodied existence did not conform to the codes of feminine propriety. The particular ways these women inhabited the city—their orientations, including demeanor, posture, confidence, and clothes—seemed to offend certain men, who took it upon themselves to punish them for their alleged immoral behavior.

Sometimes the perpetrators were the very police officers that women approached to file a harassment complaint. For instance, on August 9,

2017, two young women in Izmir were assaulted by male police officers on the street after they requested to file a report of sexual harassment against other men who had harassed them. The two women were walking on the street in Alsancak—the liveliest and most vibrant neighborhood of the city that is packed with bars and restaurants—when two men on a motorbike groped them. The women decided to report the incident and headed to the police station. On their way, they ran into two police officers whom they approached for help, but instead the officers scolded them for their outfits and said: "You actually deserve more with these outfits. Look at yourselves." When one of the women told the police to watch his mouth, he punched her in the face and dragged her on the ground (t24 2017). Later the women took the case to the court, and the police officers received sentences.

The public was accustomed to hearing news about male violence against women but, in this period, vigilante violence took place in the most unexpected places: large cities such as Izmir, Antalya, Istanbul, Bursa, and Adana. The New Woman who had long found comfort in big cities thanks to lax gender norms now risked violence by the resurgence of vigilantism there. In Istanbul, for instance, Çağla Köse was asked to leave a public park by security on account of her so-called morally unacceptable outfit. On July 29, 2017, Çağla was lounging with her dog and a female friend at Maçka Park, a public park in the close vicinity of Gezi Park, when she was stopped by the security guard on her way to the restroom. The male security asked her to leave because her outfit, he said, offended families at the park. When Çağla told the security guard to not meddle in her affairs, he grew infuriated: "You dress up like this and you get raped, then you blame it on us, telling people around that nobody protected you!" he shouted at her. Then he called the police. Upon seeing the security shouting at her, people in the park went over to support Çağla. The young woman later took the case to the court (Bianet 2017).

These violent practices of vigilantism proliferated in the context of the state of emergency imposed after the coup attempt in July 2016, which authorized a wide array of violations and exclusions women endured. Many women saw their rights and freedoms refracted primarily by the emergency decrees that the AKP government issued under emergency rule, which remained effective until July 2018. The AKP government, with the help of the emergency decrees, had exclusive authority over the dismissal of public employees and the closure of institutions and associations deemed to be affiliated with so-called terrorist organizations. In 2017, The Confederation of Public Employees Trade Unions reported that 25,523 out of 110,971 public employees laid off by the emergency decrees were women, who constituted at least twenty-three percent of all the dismissed employees under emergency rule (KESK 2017). During the same period, eleven women's associations were closed (Kerestecioğlu 2017) and numerous female news agencies were outlawed (Kivilcim 2018). The closure of numerous organizations in Kurdish cities and towns reversed the decades-long efforts of the Kurdish women's movement to build organizations and institutions such as women's centers and shelters (Kivilcim 2018). The increased military attacks in Kurdish cities disproportionately affected women, subjecting them to intensified violence (Göksel 2018), and women's and LGBTIQ+ organizations drew attention to an alarming uptick in homophobia, transphobia, and violence against women at large in the country (Kivilcim 2018).

By 2018, violence against women had become much more prevalent in the country. The number of women murdered by men, according to data provided by We Will Stop Femicide Platform, was 80 in 2008 and more than quadrupled to 440 in 2018. A study on domestic violence against women published by Hacettepe University in 2014 documented that 36 percent of women reported having been subjected to physical violence by husbands or intimate partners (HUIPS 2014). Violence against women, in addition to being more prevalent, increasingly acquired a performative dimension. Changes in the patterns of male violence against women led to the creation of new categories used in the classification of data on the issue. For instance, Bianet, an independent Turkish press agency that kept records of male violence in Turkey, created a new statistical category in 2016 under the heading "murders committed in public spaces" due to a spike in public incidents of male violence against women. According to data from Bianet, of all intentional killings of women covered in the media in 2016, 13.5 percent were committed in public spaces—the streets, shopping malls, and workplaces— in the presence of witnesses. In just a year, the percent of murders committed in public spaces jumped to 17 percent.[4] Feminist activists and lawyers I interviewed also drew attention to the performativity of male violence. Moreover, one feminist activist told me that the techniques men used to kill women had recently become more gruesome and extreme. "Now," she said, "men are killing women by using torture methods, with intense hatred, for instance by using lethal electroshock weapons. Or else, they kill women by placing explosive devices in women's cars."

In February 2015, news outlets reported that Özgecan Aslan, a twenty-year-old university student majoring in psychology had been murdered by the driver of the minibus she had been riding in Mersin, a large city by the Mediterranean. The driver had first attempted to rape her but she resisted him with pepper spray. He then stabbed the young woman several times and bludgeoned her to death with an iron rod. Afterward, he enlisted the help of his own father and a friend to burn her body and bury it in a forest after amputating her hands with the aim of hiding traces of his DNA left under fingernails as she scratched him during the struggle.

Horrified and infuriated by the gruesome brutality of Özgecan's murder, thousands of women and men hit the streets and held large rallies in numerous Turkish cities, including Istanbul and Ankara, chanting the slogan of solidarity, "You Will Never Walk Alone." Women's rights activists claimed that the legal system and public policy framework were geared toward eliminating violence against women in the county but were not used effectively. For instance, in 2011, the government signed the Council of Europe Convention on Preventing and Combating Violence Against Women and Domestic Violence. Known as the Istanbul Convention, the agreement mandated that ratifying countries combat gender-based violence, provide adequate protection and services for violence survivors, and ensure the prosecution of perpetrators. Legislation was introduced in 2012 to adopt the convention. The AKP government enacted Law Number 6248—the Law to Protect the Family and Prevent Violence Against Women—in an effort to mitigate violence against women in the country. Despite the new legislation, however, the violence escalated.

In the aftermath of Özgecan's murder, fear and shock continued to prevail among women, although street demonstrations helped foster a sense of solidarity. The explosion of performative violence made women acutely aware of how violable their bodies had been made over the last years. With the AKP government failing to take action against the violence, women were largely left to their own devices. Afraid of venturing out alone, they developed personal strategies to protect themselves. Younger women, for instance, resorted to online applications, which enabled them to share their location with friends and activate a fake phone call in case of danger.

The New Woman: Disoriented and Frightened

After the attack on the bus, the next thing Ayşegül Terzi knew was that she was in a hospital being taken for a CT head scan. Following a head-to-toe examination, she learned that she had soft-tissue trauma and acute stress disorder. In the following days, Ayşegül began to have flashbacks of those traumatic moments. She recalled a girl with long hair who hollered "This could have happened to me!" inside the bus after the attack. Every time Ayşegül remembered something about the attack, she was overcome with chest pain and grew nervous. In the following weeks, she never left the house, often awoke in the middle of the night, experienced crying fits, and had nightmares in which she was being kicked by someone. She was unable to be alone or go back to her everyday life. She lost her appetite, and whenever she recounted the incident to someone, she found herself crying involuntarily. People advised her to stand tall, but she felt she could not. For the first time in her life, she heard her father weep (Terzi v. Çakıroğlu 2016).

Being targeted by violence is a deeply disturbing experience that one cannot easily shake off, resulting in shock and fear as well as the loss of a sense of safety and security. In Ayşegül's case, the violence fractured her ordinary sense of being in time and space as well as how to relate to others, obstructing her everyday habits and affective orientations. Violence, in other words, severely disoriented her. The disorientation was aggravated by the formal complaint process she experienced. When Ayşegül first went to the police station to file a complaint, she was told that the police were unavailable due to the *bairam* holiday. Upon hearing that, Ayşegül asked what it would take for police to assist her: "Am I supposed to be dead?" (Terzi v. Çakıroğlu 2016).

Disorientations, according to Sara Ahmed, can be understood in relation to "failed orientations" (Ahmed 2006, 159). Orientations—including embodied and emotional attitudes, gestures, beliefs, and habits—enable us to dwell in a space with relative ease and comfort, creating patterns of relating to others in ways that feel safe, while disorientations break apart these unreflective manners of being in the world. Disorientations "disrupt everyday sensuous and affective habits of being embodied, moving in space, and relating to others. In such cases, how individuals should act, how others will respond, what is appropriate, healthy, or normal becomes uncertain" (Harbin 2016, xviii). Experiences of illness, trauma, migration, war, and violence— all can be severely disorientating, making it "difficult for individuals to know how to go on. They often involve feeling deeply out of place, unfamiliar, or not at home" (Harbin 2016, 2).

Ayşegül's emotional trauma following the vigilante violence directed at her body illustrates how her orientation was shattered, engendering profound disorientation. It altered her everyday bodily way of existence. Her daily routine was disrupted; she could not go back to work or to her everyday life; her body was unable to occupy space with ease and comfort.

She did not leave her home because the violence had shattered her understanding of the world as a place where she could operate with at least a minimum sense of security. With her familiar sense of the world and relating to it obliterated, she also lost her bearings on how to move on.

Disorientation also renders intelligible the New Woman's embodied way of being in today's Turkey from a phenomenological perspective. The corporeal and emotional experiences of feminine bodies that were not acknowledging feminine modesty endured severe disorientations in the post-2008 period when the AKP government pursued authoritarian rule with the aid of shame-honor discourse. Especially after the outbreak of vigilante violence, disorientation evolved into an everyday corporeal mode of being for women in urban contexts. Not only were women abruptly robbed of their familiar ways of being in the world—their corporeal habits of approaching others and the comfort of inhabiting their own bodies—but they also lost their sense of safety and direction, unsure how to proceed.

This was further exacerbated by the escalation of violence in the country during the same period due to several ongoing internal conflicts, including political conflicts between the Turkish state and the Kurdish movement, the split between the AKP and its long-term partner the Gülen movement (the followers of Gülen, a self-exiled religious figure), the oppressive one-man rule after the coup, the increasing presence of ISIS in the country, and the ongoing war in neighboring Syria. In 2016 alone, for instance, there were at least twenty bombings reported across the country, five of them being suicide bombs that left hundreds dead or wounded (DW 2017).

Helin, who worked at a human rights organization in Ankara, told me over tea how utterly discombobulating and disorienting it felt to navigate everyday life in the city of Ankara, where there were three deadly bombings in 2015 and 2016, killing 172 people and leaving several hundred wounded:

> There were bombings and we narrowly survived them. People narrowly survived all of these explosions. It was a pure stroke of luck that we survived them. . . For the last few years, it is so difficult to go out at night. You take the minibus and feel scared. You constantly worry whether you will safely make it to the last stop. Will the driver do something to hurt me? Or else, will he change direction in a moment and drive somewhere else? It could happen to any woman. Any man could do this; not every man is decent, not only ignorant men but also very educated men do these kinds of things.

When I asked her to describe the effects of fear she experienced, she replied, "Oh! To live in fear all the time is terrible. At night, you put your head on your pillow and the fear is still with you. You keep asking yourself if all this will be over or not. Is it going to get better or worse? People cannot make plans for the future any longer. You don't know what will happen to you in the next two years." The nebulous feeling of uncertainty and fear that shrouded Helin's everyday existence stemmed from an unpredictable daily life where things could change from one moment to another, a situation generally unknown in countries where the rule of law and stable democracy prevail. Helin's feelings of uncertainty and fear that arose in response to inhabiting a world characterized by violence and fragility was common among other women, too. In fact, all the women I talked to in 2017 and 2018 were affected in similar ways with the threat of violence, and actual violence, undermining their everyday embodied and affective habits of moving through space and relating to others.

Being queer or lesbian in a context where it is not safe to be publicly out, brought even more risk of violence and harassment. Ferda, who worked at a café in Ankara, recounted how the whole atmosphere of the city, especially in neighborhoods that had accepted her in the past, had become strikingly oppressive over the last few years due to Turkey's lurching into a dictatorship after the failed coup attempt:

> After 2015, the police and those fascists were emboldened because they were exempted from punishment. Back in 2012, we organized LGBT demonstrations in Kızılay; now we can't. I worked at Queerfest but now we cannot even organize movie screenings in Ankara because the Ankara governorship banned all LGBT activities in the city. I used to hold my girlfriend's hand and walk along Konur Street until a few years ago but now they erected a police station over there. The whole vibe changed on the street. There were lots of places owned by left-wing people; now the neighborhood is packed with shady night clubs and *kebap* stores. The police presence was not so strong before. For the past few years, it makes me very uneasy to hold Ahu's hand while walking on the street. Now men walking behind us brazenly throw terrible insults at us. When they see us walking together holding hands they say out loud, "Oh these two! I can fuck them together really hard." Now, I also know that if I called the police nothing would change.

Protestors display a placard that reads "If You're Afraid of The Dark at Night, We'll Set This City on Fire" at the Feminist Night Walk. Istanbul, 2022 (Photo by Mehmet Temel-Aktivist Kamera).

The Curious Link between Justice and Vigilantism

Vigilante man, who does not tolerate transgressions, hardly resembles the sovereign man. Rather, he is driven with a resentful desire to restore his masculine authority, expecting impunity for his acts in the populist moment. Vigilante men took offense at women who did not recognize male authority, inciting many to the breaking point for violence. A close look reveals that male vigilantes were more likely to resort to physical violence when women confronted them by talking or fighting back—acts which conveyed women's autonomy and refusal of men's claims to moral authority. Consider Abdullah Çakıroğlu again, who attacked Ayşegül Terzi on a public bus. His description of the attack tells us that what threw him into a rage was not simply her alleged violation of moral norms, but the fact that Ayşegül Terzi confronted him: "The way she sat was obscene. When I told her to sit properly, she made a facial gesture which meant, none of your business. I wasn't able to stomach that. It was an involuntary reflex what I did. . . . I warned the plaintiff but she didn't care and didn't change the way she sat. Then this event occurred" (Terzi v. Çakıroğlu 2016). Similarly, Dilay Özel, a twenty-year-old woman, was attacked on the street in Antalya, along with her aunt and her mother, by men after the women challenged them and told them to mind their own business (Cumhuriyet 2017).

The AKP government was aware of many men's feelings of disempowerment, as well as the threats that improvements in gender equality posed to some men's masculine authority in the country. In 2015, in search of a new gender contract, the party introduced a framework for gender justice. The AKP—the acronym stands for Justice and Development Party—came to power on the promise of restoring justice in the country, although what "justice" meant was never clearly articulated. The influence of the concept of justice, however, stretches far beyond the AKP in Turkish politics. The concept appears throughout the history of the modern Turkish Republic, with the majority of right-wing political parties drawing on the discourse of justice to articulate their political vision, whereas left-wing politics and social-democratic parties have primarily embraced the discourse of equality and freedom (Bora 2019). For example, the centrist right-wing Justice Party was founded in 1961 and was prominent throughout the 1960s and 1970s. Islamist Necmettin Erbakan's Welfare Party, founded in 1983, appealed to Sunni populations through the populist "Just Order" program, a form of popular rule that sought to fuse economic redistribution with Islamic morality.

Justice as used in the right-wing political framework is not necessarily connected with the modern understanding of justice, which entails the rule of law. Rather, as a state philosophy, it tends to harken back to the imperial Ottoman notion of justice, a concept that denotes a particular relationship between the ruler and the ruled. Drawn from the Qur'an, the Ottoman notion of justice, which set behavioral norms for all spheres of life, including economics and politics, represents an alternative to secular law (Mardin 1991). Justice here refers to the distinct way the ruler treats the empire's subjects, with fair treatment that generates a virtuous justice circle. A functional solidarity, a desired balance among the groups and classes in the society, emerges from this just rule (Tuğ 2017). A distinguishing characteristic of the Ottoman notion of justice is that it accommodated entrenched social hierarchies by promising those at the bottom of the hierarchy a paternalistic type of protection. Justice that entails fair treatment, for instance, stipulates that non-Muslims, common people, and women—those at the very bottom—should be shielded from brutal treatment as long as they know their place in the hierarchy and do not challenge the status quo (Eldem 2017). When they do, justice requires punishment, because the notion of fair treatment is founded on the idea that, if an offender breaks the order, she suffers in return.

This notion of justice—in which distinctions between fair treatment and brutal forms of mistreatment are blurred—allowed Ottoman Muslims, as opposed to non-Muslims, to advance their claims as belonging to the community of the just, a moral community that contrasted with outside, non-moral communities (Mardin 1991). This version of justice, however, began to lose its command over politics in the late nineteenth century. In 1856, the Islahat Fermanı (Royal Edict of Reform) marked a momentous shift, replacing Ottoman justice with the principle of equality, which, in particular, meant acknowledging legal equality between Muslims and non-Muslims (İrem 2008).

It is against this backdrop of anti-egalitarian historical relations that the gender justice[5] paradigm was introduced in the aftermath of the Gezi uprisings and promoted through new civil society organizations founded in this period (Diner 2018). Unlike the contemporary global understanding of gender justice, the AKP's gender justice paradigm promoted neither human rights nor gender equality. Like its imperial

Ottoman counterpart, AKP's gender justice was built on the inherent differences/hierarchies that separated social groups. Such was the discursive strategy the AKP pursued with the aim of restoring eroded gender inequalities: justice discourse, by explicitly referring to the God-given, natural differences between men and women, reasserted male authority.

The concept was outlined in an article penned by the founding president of the Women and Democracy Association (KADEM)—an organization established to disseminate and popularize the AKP's gender politics and gender justice discourse—in the following way: "This framework centers on justice, in opposition to the approach that seeks to establish 'equality' enshrining the same rights and responsibilities for men and women in social life" (Yılmaz 2015, 107). While at first, the notion of justice seemed to complement a reductive understanding of gender equality, which did not recognize differences between men and women, it soon became clear that gender justice grants men a higher rank. This, according to the author, follows from natural differences between man and woman: "Some differences inherent in men and women may require that men could be regarded as *primus inter pares* (first among equals) in some cases" (Yılmaz 2015, 114).[6]

Gender justice discourse was also predicated on an understanding of fair treatment that split women into two categories: those who deserved benign protection and those who did not. Because fairness was a virtue of those located at the higher echelons of the hierarchy, such as God and the ruler, fair treatment became the bastion of men by the same logic. As one of the myriad ways male honor manifested itself, fair treatment directed that women were to be protected by men as long as they squarely complied with gender norms, which mandated women to live according to their *fitrat* (inherent nature).

Fair treatment had a relatively benign aspect that was characterized by masculinist protectionism, a bias which underscored AKP social policies and welfare assistance in the global era. Underprivileged women whose homes lacked a male breadwinner gained access to welfare assistance as mothers, widows, and caretakers within this logic of fair treatment. At the same time, this notion of fair treatment bred punitive masculinities and a proclivity to violence that the government relied on to maintain its domination over the society. Masculinist resentment and practices against women and their bodies were made morally permissible within the logic of fair treatment, which facilitated the recasting of certain women—who neither acknowledged nor complied with the moral authority of men—as undeserving (of male protection). For these women, including the New Woman, fair treatment entailed punishment instead of protection. Within the logic of gender justice, punishment, after all, was indeed a form of fair treatment reserved for those women who transgressed moral norms.

Women Claw Back: Fighting for the Body's Inviolability

On August 5, 2017, I arrived at Kuğulu Park, a public park located in one of the Ankara's downtown neighborhoods where secular middle classes historically resided, a park which had been occupied by demonstrators during the Gezi uprising. It was around 3 p.m. and many women, old and young, had turned up in shorts and t-shirts, holding placards reading "Don't Mess with My Outfit." People seemed jovial and carefree, chatting with friends, taking selfies together, smoking, and at times posing casually for the press. Two women in their sixties—one in a stylish straw hat with a large brim, the other with a very short haircut, both flashing big smiles and an easy attitude—were holding up a banner that read: "No Bra, No Master."

On another corner, a young woman carrying her baby was approached by deputy Aylin Nazlıaka from the secular CHP, the main opposition party. The two women posed for the media while police officers, scattered among the demonstrators in groups of three or four, casually observed. Having survived a dark period of bombings, including one targeting a pro-Kurdish peace rally in 2015 where more than a hundred demonstrators were killed, the women demonstrators in Ankara seemed to cherish the opportunity to protest without fear for their lives. The gathering seemed to energize them, and the atmosphere was relaxed and hopeful. "We

Don't Mess with My Outfit Demonstration. Ankara, 2017 (Photo by author).

are not silent! Enough is enough, we are here and will be holding tight onto our lives!" read the handouts that were passed around that day.

Before leaving the demonstration, I approached a small group of police officers, a woman and three men, and asked how they felt about the protest, after identifying myself. The woman officer seemed reluctant to answer and just smiled, without saying anything. The officer next to her jumped in: "Oh! I support their cause," he said. "The same thing could have happened to my sister and even to my mother, yeah I support them." When I glanced back at the woman, she nodded in agreement with her colleague, and said, "Obviously, I support them."

Almost a week before, on July 29, 2017, hundreds of women in Istanbul joined the protest against the rise in vigilante violence. They marched under the slogan "Don't Mess with My Outfit," carrying denim shorts on hangers, an item of clothing vigilante men found morally offensive. Soon, demonstrations dubbed "Don't Mess with My Outfit" spread to other big cities. Women hit the streets to protest both the violence and the oppressive measures the AKP government was planning to introduce, including lowering the marriage age—which would legalize child marriage—and implementing "pink wagons" (that is, designated areas for women in public transport vehicles)—which might lead to gender segregation in public spaces.

From its inception, the wave of demonstrations in the summer of 2017 aimed at reaching out to and mobilizing all women, not just particular groups. Miniskirts and shorts were likely to emerge as the latest partisan flashpoint in Turkey, because women's clothing has always been a contentious issue in mainstream politics between the conservative and secularist parties. The issue would play into the hands of the CHP. The tendency of mainstream secular political actors to hijack feminist agendas gave even feminists some trepidation about organizing demonstrations against vigilante violence. Nevertheless, they refused to allow the instrumentalization of vigilantism in the service of the CHP's political agenda. United around the inviolability of *all* women's bodies—as opposed to fighting for the rights of only a particular group of women— feminists defended women's embodied existence against the threats from AKP rule. Women demanded safety from violence and violations for all women. At street demonstrations, they embraced different pieces of clothing, including headscarves, shorts, and skirts, that represented different visions of femininity.

An important locus of women's advocacy centered on vigilante violence court trials. Although the practice of vigilantism under Turkish law is punishable as a criminal act, Turkish courts in cases of domestic violence against women tended to grant leniency to men. Often feminist lawyers took up vigilantism cases in order to prevent the courts from handing down reduced sentences to male assailants. In addition, women's organizations monitored court trials and pushed back against the judiciary's masculinist bias for the assailants. Feminists' involvement in court trials also minimized political efforts to exploit vigilantism for partisan gain. For instance, despite the efforts of the CHP deputy Aylin Nazlıaka to portray the Terzi trial as "a trial of secularism" and convince people that fighting for secularism—not feminism—was the way to prevent vigilante violence, her intervention did not affect the course of women's activism. Feminists' sustained efforts to raise public awareness about vigilante cases have proven to be successful. More and more young women have spoken out about the vigilante violence they have faced. Amplifying their voices through social media, women have also communicated their firm intention not to forego their own bodily modes of inhabiting the world.

One of those women was Asena Melisa Sağlam, who was attacked for wearing shorts on a minibus during the month of Ramadan in 2017. Asena became a symbol of defiance during this period by speaking out for women's bodily inviolability and by encouraging other women to do so. Named among the BBC's list of the world's one hundred most influential and inspirational women in 2017—for tackling the biggest issues confronting them such as the glass ceiling, female illiteracy, harassment in public spaces, and sexism in sport— Asena voiced a sentiment shared by millions when she commented about women's speaking out: "There's nothing to be ashamed of. We shouldn't feel intimidated. When we are scared, we gave them more power. It's time we all speak up against such attacks" (BBC 2017).

A few weeks after the "Don't Mess with My Outfit" demonstration in Kuğulu Park in Ankara, women gathered together at Seğmenler Park—a patch of green close to Kuğulu Park—for a forum to share frustrations and ideas for moving forward and organizing greater political opposition to the AKP government's gender politics. In a period when dissidents were being arrested and opposition movements forcibly suppressed, it was feminists' and women's activism that broke the silence and the oppressive environment in the country that was still being ruled by the emergency laws. Pushing back against the severe disorientation of the last few years, women reoriented themselves and spelled out their political project explicitly: a united resistance against the rule of Erdoğan who, in their view, was the main actor making women's existence more violable.

During the forum, a woman who was employed as a public park maintenance worker by the Ankara municipality told the crowd that her years-long experience as a working-class woman taught her the importance of perseverance and believing in oneself. "If we, as women, believed in ourselves," she said, "we could create a country for ourselves." Another woman, whom I had seen at the first demonstration in Kuğulu Park a few weeks before, reported that after a picture of her holding the placard reading "No Bra, No Master" hit social media, she was flooded with messages—a deluge of insults as well as a wave of support and encouragement. "I will keep doing what I have been doing all along," she said before finishing her talk.

The confidence and the conviction with which women activists spoke—besides greatly adding to the hopeful mood that allowed women to re-orient themselves after a disruptive period— hinted at something else, something bigger, in the making: the New Women's increasingly prominent presence in grassroots politics. Indeed, New Women, in this politically tense atmosphere, grew into one of the most visible grassroots oppositions to the AKP. This was partly related to the crushing of organized political opposition in Turkey by a wave of government repression. In the absence of other political opposition, women's mobilization gained momentum, giving the opposition a fresh impetus. This, to be sure, does not entirely explain why women's street demonstrations reinvigorated the antigovernment protests. The new momentum achieved in grassroots opposition had to do, more than anything else, with the New Woman's singularity. The New Woman rose in strength and visibility thanks to the embodied and emotional resources she commanded, ones she now utilized as political tools to exhibit a bold determination to resist authoritarian rule. It was this singularity the New Women manifested at a crucial time in the history of Turkey that gave the women's protests a distinctly confrontational and fresh edge in the populist moment.

The New Woman's singularity derives from her social origins: she emerged in a period when legal and social changes have, in many respects, freed women's bodies from the obligations of feminine modesty. For this reason, she is not predisposed to accede to masculinist control based on shame-honor discourse, which seeks to restrict her bodily autonomy and threaten her very mode of being feminine. Feeling entitled to her bodily mode of being, she is, almost automatically, able to react to incursions because she was born into a world where moralized understandings of shame and honor had already lost traction. When vigilante violence erupted in large cities as men inflicted harm on New Women's bodies in the name of moral norms, New Women were quick to fight back against this coercive power. But more importantly, women fought back *as* New Women, bringing their gendered predispositions to their struggle, mobilizing them as a resource for political action, and creating a cultural-political orientation of their own. This push back reflected a repudiation of enforced feminine modesty, a strong rejection of moralist politics, a dismissal of attempted shaming of women, irreverence for masculinist authorities and their claims to male surveillance, an unflagging defense of women's bodily inviolability, and a solid aversion to the moralist *mahalle* and what it represented in politics.

Such predispositions defined the singularity of the New Woman, who now harnessed these in the service of effective opposition, generating political consequences in three distinct ways. First of all, because her embodied orientations inclined her toward repudiating masculinist claims to authority rather than conformity, New Women were placed in a unique position to undermine Erdoğan, whose political rule was distinctly built upon his masculinist authority. In a period where the cult around Erdoğan was at its height, with one-man rule in the making and no other male politician able to edge him out, New Women's posture vis-à-vis Erdoğan— ranging from flat-out ire to mockery— proved to be powerful. Confronted with New Women, who remained completely impervious to his hectoring attempts at shaming, Erdoğan's masculine authority faltered. His shaming strategy had already repeatedly proven to be entirely ineffective as a mechanism of social control over New Women, something that Erdoğan was nowhere near equipped to handle. Having failed to invent another strategy to discipline New Women, Erdoğan had no option but to resort to more repression and violence.

Second, women's fight went beyond the narrow limits of vigilante violence and challenged the AKP's authoritarian project itself. Once New

Women rose up against vigilante violence, they also confronted head-on the AKP's authoritarianism. The key here was the moralist politics that New Women robustly rejected. Moralism, after all, was pivotal both to vigilante violence and to the AKP's politics. Because the authoritarian regime was led by a self-professed patriarch and grounded in moralist premises of shame and honor, New Women's resistance against male dominance and moralism translated into a powerful resistance to the authoritarian regime.

Third, New Women's fight against moralism reshaped secularism in Turkey by furnishing its politics with a distinctly anti-authoritarian argument. The women protesting vigilante violence were overwhelmingly secular. A distinct yet popular understanding of secularism prevailed among these women, who, accordingly, focused their efforts to reject the legal, social, and cultural enforcement of religious morality. These efforts, as opposed to the long-standing secularist tradition represented by the Turkish military, were neither imposed from above nor did they display authoritarian tendencies aimed at erasing the public presence of Islam. Rather, the women's efforts represented an anti-authoritarian and democratic secularism coming from below. In the absence of military tutelage, by which the military advanced its political power through assuming the role of the guardian of secularism, women emerged as independent grassroots actors with considerable capacity to make a difference. They reshaped the politics of secularism away from its traditional militarist and nationalist entanglements, while at the same time resisting Sunni domination. The political opposition slowly came to understand the distinctiveness of New Women. At first, women drew respect for their resilience and fearlessness. About a year later, magazine articles with headlines such as "These Women Are Turkey's Last Hope" (Nawa 2019) reflected increasing public awareness of the New Woman's prominence in the resistance against authoritarianism.

Later the same week as the women's conference in Seğmenler Park, I met Ayşen, a young college student and activist from We Will Stop Femicide Platform. At a popular café in Konur Sokak, less than a hundred feet away from a mobile police station that was erected in the wake of emergency rule, we talked about the women's struggle and the AKP's politics over dinner. Turkey, according to her, was at a critical juncture. The AKP was laying groundwork that would change the gender order of society at the roots. While it was frightening to think that the

AKP-led transformation might be a lasting one, women's resistance in contemporary Turkey was a source of optimism for the future. She summed up the predicament the New Woman faced in the populist moment:

> A big problem now is that the AKP rollbacks on women's rights and all our previous gains are now up for discussion. This is a very regressive situation. I think we are now on a threshold. It is of utmost importance that we defend our rights and protect previous gains as women. It seems to me we are succeeding in doing that. Women's resistance is not weak—this gives me hope. All the violence, murders of women, and attacks on the street are for one reason: to erase women from public life, to remove them forcefully from life. Women's struggle is now about trying to stay alive, living freely in daily life, and being a part of life. Because women are making inroads into life, we face attacks.

Endnotes

1. For studies that examine different forms of vigilantism in contemporary Turkey, see Yonucu (2018) and Saglam (2021).
2. Two years before that, news about a vigilante incident—discussed in Chapter 5—captured headlines in June 2013 during the Gezi resistance. Although it proved to be largely a fabricated story, it nevertheless stoked the supercharged moral politics that Erdoğan had escalated.
3. For a fuller discussion of the gendered implications of the failed coup attempt and its immediate aftermath, please see Arat (2017), Başdaş (2017), and Korkman (2017).
4. Çiçek Tahaoğlu (personal communication, March 21, 2018), then an editor from Bianet, provided the data.
5. In the early 2000s, when the AKP first came to power, the notion of justice advocated by the party—breaking away from conventional right-wing Islamist politics—promised to correct the injustices of past militarist rule and Kemalist authoritarianism, emphasizing the fair treatment of popular classes through an array of paternalist welfare policies. However, beginning with the party's turn to authoritarianism, justice began to take on hostile and vengeful undertones, with the government singling out those groups who deserved punishment or penalty.
6. It is not difficult to imagine a myriad of ways in which gender justice paradigms can go awry and undercut gender equality in social life. To begin

with, the emphasis on embodied gender differences serves to reinforce an ideology of familialism, which regards the family unit as the primary ordering element of society and predicates the social relationship between men and women on familial relations exclusively. After all, the view that a woman and a man complement each other follows directly from the spousal model. This familialism also entails a heterosexual, gendered division of labor, in which women are heavily burdened with a host of reproductive tasks, whereas men, freed from those tasks, are granted certain privileges, such as the privilege to act as *primus inter pares*.

The New Woman and Feminism in Uncertain Times

This book has presented an account of a feminine response to Turkey's experience of globalization, examining what possibilities emerged in urban contexts for women's everyday bodily being as global inflows of capital and power, growing masculinist forces of populist authoritarianism, and the energies unleashed by grassroots oppositions have acted on gendered bodies with different intensity. Placing the figure of the New Woman at the center of analysis reveals connections between neoliberal capitalist globalization, the cultural politics of feminine respectability, urban sociality, and women's agency, as well as populist and authoritarian politics that have not been fully appreciated in contemporary studies of gender and politics.

The emergence of the New Woman in the global era asks us to pay close attention to some defining moments for women in Turkey, in which new gendered ways of being have been enabled by, or materialized out of, the socio-economic and cultural reconfiguration of Turkey in the post-1980s era. This was a period of global capitalist restructuring marked by notable social changes in the country, including emerging neoliberal policies, Turkey's attempts to join the European Union, the declining influence of Kemalist ideology, growing Islamization of the public sphere, the emergence of radical feminist groups and LGBTIQ+ movements and their strong resistance to the ruling party's neoconservative gender politics, increasing visibility of nonnormative genders and sexualities, and legal changes in the Civil and Penal Codes towards gender equality. All of these complex processes have reconfigured what I call the cultural politics of embarrassment, in which particular understandings of femininity, along with historically informed interpretations of modesty and respectability, set the cultural standards which define feminine embodiment. In the early 2000s, when the legal framework of gender equality offered by the new Penal Code and Civil Code granted women new bodily autonomy, the cultural politics of embarrassment and conceptions of what it meant to be modest and respectable—which had already been undermined by large-scale social and economic transformations and the sustained activism of women's groups over the last decades—decisively lost their legal underpinnings.

Accompanying this transformation was a change in the way gendered emotions were experienced: feelings that defined what could be expected of women—embarrassment and the emotional disciplinary mechanism of shaming in particular—and the affective components of feminine respectability lost their intensity and force, making possible new bodily capacities and new forms of bodily living. The New Woman reflects these new affective capacities and corporeal ways of being in the world at a moment when the limiting forces of shame and embarrassment are fading. One of the gendered shifts brought by globalization in Turkey that has not received enough scholarly attention has been the transformation of shame-honor discourse under global capitalist restructuring and its recent mobilization in national politics by the ruling party. A feminist phenomenological analysis of shame-honor discourse reveals links between the emergence of New Women from popular classes, the weakening of masculine authority, new dynamics of the urban capitalist economy, the contemporary backlash against women, and right-wing authoritarian populism in Turkey.

In tracing the rise of New Woman, I place a particular emphasis on the expansion of the service economy in urban Turkey, which, along with some other important social trends, signals a larger shift in the gender order of the country in the global era: more women working outside the home, rising education levels and reduced fertility rates for women, and the nuclear family household becoming the norm, all framed by a strong legislative framework rooted in gender equality.

A focus on the service economy that considers both macro and micro dynamics lends substance to my argument about contributive links between the increasing prominence of the service economy as a site for women's work, the emergence of new bodily modalities of femininity, and the New Woman's role in the resistance against the AKP government's authoritarian rule in Turkey. When the old world of industrial production—which was historically characterized by a predominantly male labor force and workplace discipline organized largely around the binaries of shame-honor—started to attenuate, the expansion of the service economy under neoliberal global capitalism more decisively affected the gendered dynamics of urban life in Turkey. Many underprivileged women were able to increase their presence in the wider urban life-worlds of the twenty-first century by making use of the employment opportunities in the service economy, while the labor and sociality of service work welcomed their embodied habits. This was the new gendered social order that the urban service economy generated. When Turkey's politics took a turn towards authoritarianism, unleashing a backlash against gender equality, all of these gendered dynamics—including the New Woman's bodily autonomy—became markedly at odds with the neoconservative gender order that the AKP government wanted to impose.

The rise of the New Woman provides a critical prism for understanding the specific relationship between feminine agency and embodiment during the global capitalist restructuring in Turkey. In this historical moment, when feminine embodiment was no longer ineluctably tied to violence and abuse, the New Woman's ability to forge a new relationship to her body, to the world, and to others materialized into a distinct orientation towards openness. This is the feminist vision that the New Woman in Turkey communicates: the feminine body's ability to undo rigid, watchful, and guarded modes of being in the world; its power to enact a sense of openness and to bring about a sense of open-endedness, as opposed to it being closed off and defensive; the body's willingness to contest the legitimacy and validity of shame and honor precepts; and its ability to tap into the new emotional and embodied energies required to navigate the economic terrain of exploitation and marginalization that women open themselves up to in the vicissitudes of the market. Despite the ruling party's top-down imposition of a neoconservative gender agenda and heavy reliance on moralist discourses of honor and shame, these new modalities prevailed and facilitated a collective ability to effectively say no to the government's vision of politics, which the Gezi uprising illustrated in 2013. The body was an important resource that women demonstrators used during the Gezi protest. In addition to bringing their bodies to the action, women carried to the resistance their pre-reflective and emotional ways of inhabiting urban space and their habitual ways of approaching others. Beyond their mundane context, these embodied and affective orientations revealed a vision of politics that affirms the capacity of women's bodily openness, which aspires towards a more inclusive community and society.

The New Woman is also pivotal in understanding the backlash to women's empowerment under globalization, which swiftly shifted Turkey's political orientation away from neoliberalism to right-wing authoritarian populism. Particularly important here is the re-launch of shame-honor discourse in the service of authoritarian populism. Threatened by increasing demands for liberty and equality from large segments of society—including women, Kurds, the Left, and LGBTIQ+— the AKP government embarked on an authoritarian project in 2008, infusing everyday political rhetoric with the terms of shame-honor discourse. Male honor was used aggressively to buttress the political authority of Erdoğan to such an extent that masculinism became inseparable from the AKP's authoritarianism. Erdoğan relied on shame and shaming to morally disavow women's rights groups and feminists, characterizing them as alien and threatening to the religious and cultural order of society. As the New Woman waded through this politically fraught process, her embodied orientations became a focus of populist political backlash, promoted by right-wing expressions of masculinist discontent. This backlash put her in danger of intensified vigilantism and violence. At the same time, her presence became more authoritative in the feminist resistance and grassroots opposition to the ruling party, eventually making her the face of potent opposition to the AKP's authoritarian regime.

. . .

After her divorce, Nesrin experienced violence at the hands of her new boyfriend, when he tried to assault her at home one night after drinking too many beers. When he became aggressive, she locked herself in the bathroom and waited there until almost dawn, then he finally left her apartment. "Then, I saw all the things he smashed inside the apartment. I called the police as well as my father," she said to me. "That was one thing he was not expecting. He thought I would not be able to tell my father what happened. He thought I could never get the support of my family, he thought I'd hide my relationship from my father as a divorced woman having an affair. Well, I got their full support." It is true that many women might choose to remain silent in such circumstances because the revelation of a sexual affair could incite violence against them by their own family members. However, despite this, an increasing number of women are speaking up against partner violence. Nesrin was one of them. She left her boyfriend. Violence may have momentarily disoriented her, but she got back on her feet and continued her life as usual.

Women defend their embodied openness not only by speaking out but also by creating new terms, understandings, and concepts to describe the different forms of opposition they experience to their newly embodied openness. After all, violence is not the only form of aggression that men resort to when responding to women's openness in intimate relations. New words for different forms of emotional abuse, often formulated and circulated by psychologists and gender rights activists—such as gaslighting (a form of psychological manipulation in which the victim begins to doubt her sanity), love-bombing (demonstrating extreme love and affection as a way of controlling another), and ghosting (a form of emotional abuse where one halts all communication with the other without explanation)—help young women to articulate the aggression that adversely affects their openness. The abuses that many young women have experienced in intimate relationships cannot be separated from women's historically constituted violability. Women are exposed to these forms of power and abuses of vulnerability when they open themselves to new forms of intimate relations, ranging from casual dating to committed relationships. The effort to name and describe these experiences helps establish openness as an inviolable modality of being feminine.

Under the AKP's authoritarian project, however, containment of New Women seems to be the new goal. With the authoritarian populist turn of the AKP—despite the government remaining fully committed to the neoliberal capitalist economy and continuing to uphold the principles of trade openness—it grew increasingly hostile to New Women's phenomenological openness. The party's persistent preoccupation with controlling the New Woman is a sign of her growing power—she cannot be ignored, so the old patterns of male domination are reactivated in an effort to control her. One of the most recent initiatives of the AKP came in 2017 with the decision of the Ministry of Interior to revive the old institution of *bekçi* (traditional neighborhood guards), as a security force to control public spaces in metropolitan cities. *Bekçi*, who used to patrol residential neighborhoods in urban areas, had been effectively obsolete as a force for decades and were fully abolished in 2008 (TRT-World 2020). Given the advanced level of modern surveillance techniques, the reinstatement of traditional male officers on foot patrol was puzzling. Nevertheless, Istanbul became the first city to return to foot patrol, with seven hundred new recruits in 2017. Across the country, seven thousand *bekçi* were hired in 2017 and seven thousand more in 2018 (Haberturk 2018).

However obsolete it might appear, the institution of *bekçi* fits squarely with the AKP's strategy of re-mobilizing elements of shame-honor to pressure the New Woman. Indeed, complaints from women and members of the LGBTIQ+ community who were stopped and searched on the streets indicate that the actions of the *bekçi* are often related to the monitoring of morality and decency (Batuman and Erkip 2019, 9-10). The male prerogative of protecting the neighborhood's honor (*mahallenin namusu*), which petered out after the large-scale social changes of recent decades, was reawakened with the reintroduction of the *bekçi* a policing strategy in which individuals were coerced into behaving in conformity with gendered norms of "public morality."

The implementation of the *bekçi* system in cities in today's Turkey does not seem to be a temporary measure, since the AKP government continues to support the system through investment and redefinition of its policing priorities. In June 2020, for instance, Parliament approved a government-proposed bill that granted *bekçi*s broader powers, including the authority to use firearms, stop vehicles, carry out ID checks, and conduct body searches (TRT-World 2020). The bill drew swift reaction from the main opposition party, the CHP, and the Peoples' Democratic Party (HDP), which both voted against the proposal and called out morality policing as the real issue lurking behind the reintroduction of *bekçi*s in public life. They especially criticized the clause authorizing *bekçi*s to alert police in cases of suspicious activity—such as illegal drug making or using, gambling, and prostitution—as setting the stage for egregious police intervention into private lives, especially of unmarried women. An Istanbul lawyer, Cesim Parlak, pointed out the gendered implications of the new bill: "With this new bill, *bekçi*s are granted authority to meddle into any activity or behavior they deem improper in public areas such as markets, parks, gardens, strolling areas, and entertainment venues. Besides, the wording of the regulation about 'those locations where the *bekçi* suspects illegal prostitution' is so vague that this can easily lead to neighborhood guards watching single women as well as women who live alone in the neighborhood" (Ileri Haber 2020).

In March 2021, almost a year after *bekçi*s were granted broader powers by the parliament, the AKP government took fresh aim at the existing legal framework on violence against women and announced Turkey's unilateral withdrawal from the Council of Europe Convention on Preventing and Combating Violence Against Women and Domestic Violence, popularly known as the Istanbul Convention. Signed by the AKP government in 2011, the Convention covered thirty-four European countries and provided an international legal framework that connected practical measures to tackle violence against women with the larger politics of gender equality. Energetic political campaigns led by feminists, women's rights groups, and LGBTIQ+ activists spurred the ratification process, making Turkey the first country to adopt the Convention in 2012, a landmark moment for women's rights and feminist movements in Turkey. For Erdoğan, however, the Convention was seen as a regulation imposed by the West—emboldening LGBTIQ+ groups to advance their political agendas—posing a threat to the integrity of the Turkish family. Erdoğan justified the withdrawal decision by saying, "I am of the opinion that we are highly capable to draft texts which honor human dignity, put the family at the center, and which are appropriate for our social fabric. Instead of translated texts, we need to determine our frame on our own" (Duvar English 2020). In the months following the AKP government's announcement, protests erupted across the largest cities in Turkey, opposing the government's decision to pull out of the Convention. Along with the public protests, the AKP government faced criticism even from pro-government organizations. The most important was the Women and Democracy Association (KADEM), which advocated the gender justice paradigm for women's welfare in Turkey. Despite the close ties between the AKP government and KADEM, the organization released a public statement expressing full support for the Istanbul Convention.

If the *bekçi* system reinstated the masculinist enforcement of morality in public, the withdrawal from the Istanbul Convention made the AKP government's anti–gender equality stance even clearer. Taken together, these two actions exemplify the AKP's backlash against the politics of gender equality and women's empowerment in the global era, morally repudiating the new bodily possibilities of being feminine and making women vulnerable to violence. The restoration of *bekçi* in the urban landscape forges new connections between the male gaze, masculinist surveillance of women's bodies, and feminine modesty. Similarly, the government's withdrawal from the Istanbul Convention—stripping women of their rights—is yet another attempt to narrow down the multiple modalities of being feminine that complex forces of globalization have enabled. The aftermath of these political decisions illustrates the government's increasingly restrictive vision of the world, which does not accommodate the most basic rights of women, such as dwelling in everyday spaces of life with ease and comfort, and creating patterns of relating to others that feel safe. Phenomenologically speaking, the understanding of the body that informs these regulations is not one that affords women a sense of autonomy in their everyday lives, but one that makes them acutely aware of their vulnerability and violability.

As of now, much of what the AKP government has done to contain the New Woman through repression seems to have failed to change how New Women see themselves or how they orient themselves to the world. Instead, women feel suffocated and constrained by the mounting political pressure, and their sense of entitlement to political rights and civil freedoms is stronger. One powerful expression of women's tenacity is the ongoing street demonstrations. These demonstrations, in which women often confront the police who respond the protests violently, not only attract more and more women but also elicit admiration from others who are growingly discontented with the AKP regime. Nuri, a sixty-four-year-old man, for example, described his impressions of the night he saw young women march in Ankara during the March 8, International Women's Day, traditional night walk:

> On that night my brothers wanted to watch a soccer game on TV at a restaurant and asked me to join them. We went to Sakarya Street where there were tight police controls, with every street corner taken over by the police checking people's bags and everything. The presence of many young female cops caught my attention. Many cops had guns. I didn't exactly know where the women's march would take place that night. Luckily, they just marched by our restaurant. Well, I got a feeling when I saw them. It made me shiver to see them march like that. They are all very young, young women I mean. They don't give a damn about the police. It was obvious that they had long overcome the fear. And it was something wondrous to see. Just when women were marching, people sitting at the tables, dining at restaurants started clapping and cheering, giving a collective round of applause for the women. The police could not do anything, could not intervene. Women were like, 'This is our right; no one can stop us.' After the march was over the police captured a woman but they were not able to keep her because all the women rushed on to get her back from the police. It was so good. I wasn't expecting this. And the turnout was good, there were more than a thousand women there. I'd say the average age of the women was twenty-five that night. There were women with headscarves among them, too.

Nuri is a leftist political exile who fled Turkey following the military coup in 1980 and has been living in Berlin ever since. Since the late 1990s, after he was permitted to return, he has visited Turkey every year to see friends and family. In 2020, when he flew back to Berlin the day after witnessing the women's traditional night walk, he was visibly excited. "We keep hearing about this, but seeing the women's march for yourself is something different, very powerful," he said to me. Nuri is one of many who admire women's struggle in today's Turkey. This is also reflected in his changing political interests: he now follows closely the heated debates around women's rights, violence against women, and the government's withdrawal from the Istanbul Convention. People like Nuri, who once considered the women's struggle an insignificant political movement or regarded feminism as a political ideology that pits women against men, have changed. Now, in their eyes, the New Woman in Turkey is a political force to reckon with.

A woman encircled by the police is taken into custody at the Women's Protest in Solidarity with the Chilean Feminist Collective LasTesis. Istanbul, 2019 (Photo by Mehmet Temel-Aktivist Kamera).

GLOSSARY OF TURKISH TERMS

....

Ar A moral term used for shame and its capacity to guide one's moral conduct. *Ar* prevents one from committing wrong or immoral deeds and facilitates feelings of shame in cases of moral transgressions.

Ayran A popular cold and salty beverage made out of plain yogurt.

Bacı Informal form of address used for women, which translates as sister and denotes a low-status kin position. In daily interactions it is used to create a fictive sense of familiarity based on familial ties.

Bakkal A corner store.

Bayram A nationwide religious or non-religious festival or holiday often celebrated as a public holiday.

Bekçi Watchman, a state-authorized security force that maintains control and surveillance in neighborhoods and public spaces in cities.

Camii A mosque.

Çapulcu Literally a crowd of marauders. The word was used by Erdoğan during the Gezi uprising in 2013 to cast the demonstrators as bums or looters with no credible political demands. Demonstrators reclaimed the word and referred to themselves as "*Çapulcu*" following Erdoğan's verbal attacks.

Davul A cylinder-shaped, double-headed drum used in folk music. It is suspended on the shoulder and played with sticks.

Esnaf Shopkeepers.

Fetva Fatwa. Qualified opinions delivered by religious scholars on any kind of legal or practical issue with regard to Islamic conventions.

Fıtrat An Islamic notion that can be understood as God-given nature.

Gecekondu   A compound word which literally translates as "built overnight." The term is used to describe the informal housing system created by newly-arrived migrants in cities beginning from the 1950s with the onset of industrialization in the country.

Genel Ahlak   Public morality. The term is also recognized in the current Turkish Penal Code, which includes a section entitled "Offences against Public Morality."

Halay   A generic term for popular folk dances where people form lines or move in circles, holding hands or standing close to each other, often with their shoulders touching.

Hayâ   A moral term used for prospective shame, which motivates one to avoid or escape a situation that might generate feelings of shame.

Hayâsızca hareketler   Shameless behaviors.

Hoca   An honorific used for teachers and professors in both secular and Islamic settings as well as for prayer leaders at mosque.

Irz   An Ottoman-Turkish word that can be translated as honor and purity.

Irza geçmek   A phrasal verb that literally means "violating one's honor." An old-fashioned word used for rape, depicting it as a moral injury.

İbne   A derogatory word used to denote a gay man. The word has been recently reclaimed by some members of the LGBTIQ+ communities in Turkey although it should be avoided by those outside of the community.

İftar   The meal eaten after sunset to break the daily fast during the month of Ramadan.

İmam   A male religious leader, for Sunni Muslims in Turkey, who leads Islamic worship services as well as prayers in mosque and offers guidance to the community.

İmam Hatip   Middle and high schools that are part of the public school system in Turkey, where a science curriculum is combined with Sunni Islam teachings.

Kabadayı   A compound word to refer to a tough guy. In particular, the word describes a form of masculinity animated by masculine codes of honor dating back to the Ottoman Empire.

Kadın   Woman. The word sometimes refers to an adult female with prior sexual experience.

Kasap   A butcher or a butcher store.

Kebap   Refers to a wide variety of dishes with meat, often combined with vegetables and flat bread, where the meat is grilled.

Kemalist   Often describes a person with secularist, nationalist views committed to the Turkish state's official ideology of Kemalism, named after Mustafa Kemal Atatürk, who founded the Turkish Republic in 1923.

Kız   Girl. The word is sometimes used to denote the status of virginity.

Mahalle   Neigborhood.

Mahallenin namusu   A phrase that literally translates as the neighborhood's honor. The term reflects an understanding of the neighborhood as a moral community.

Manav   Grocer or a grocery shop.

Muhallebici   Pudding shop.

Muhtar   Local authority, often the head of the neighborhood.

Namusuyla yaşamak   An idiom which could mean living with honor and integrity or earning an honest penny.

Pazar   Outdoor fresh market.

Sala   Muslim call to Friday prayers and funeral prayers.

Süslüman   A derogatory term used to describe young, upwardly mobile, pious women. The term *Süslüman* is built by combining *Müslüman* (Muslim) and *Süslü* (dressy).

TOMA   A shortened form of the phrase Mass Incident Intervention Vehicle.

Vaize   A female preacher in Sunni Islam.

Zanaatkâr   Artisans.

Zurna   A conical-shaped woodwind instrument popularly used in folk music.

REFERENCES
....

Abu-Lughod, Lila. *Veiled Sentiments: Honor and Poetry in a Bedouin Society*. Berkeley: University of California Press, 1986.

Abu-Lughod, Lila. "The Romance of Resistance: Tracing Transformations of Power through Bedouin Women." *American Ethnologist* 17, no. 1 (1990): 41–55.

Abu-Lughod, Lila. "Modesty Discourses: An Overview." In *Encyclopedia of Women & Islamic Cultures: Volume II Family, Law and Politics*, edited by Suad Joseph, 494–497. Leiden and Boston: Brill, 2005.

Acar, Feride, and Gülbanu Altunok. "Understanding Gender Equality Demands in Turkey: Foundations and Boundaries of Women's Movements." In *Gender and Society in Turkey: The Impact of Neoliberal Policies, Political Islam and EU Accession*, edited by Saniye Dedeoğlu and AdemY. Elveren, 31–47. London and New York: IB Tauris, 2012.

Acar, Feride, and Gülbanu Altunok. "The 'Politics of Intimate' at the Intersection of Neo-liberalism and Neo-conservatism in Contemporary Turkey." *Women's Studies International Forum* 41, part. 1 (November December 2013): 14–23, Pergamon.

Ağaoğlu, Adalet. *Ölmeye Yatmak*. Istanbul: Türkiye İş Bankası Kültür, 2011. First published 1973.

Ağaoğlu, Adalet. *Bir Düğün Gecesi*. Istanbul: Türkiye İş Bankası Kültür, 2012. First published 1979.

Ağaoğlu, Adalet. *Hayır*. Istanbul: Everest, 2012. First published 1987.

Ahmed, Sara. *Queer Phenomenology: Orientations, Objects, Others*. Durham: Duke University Press, 2006.

Aile ve Sosyal Politikalar Bakanlığı. *Türkiye'de Kadın İşgücü Profili İstatistiklerinin Analizi*. Ankara: 2014. https://dspace.ceid.org.tr/xmlui/bitstream/handle/1/355/ekutuphane3.5.1.5.1.pdf?sequence=1&isAllowed=y

Akkan, Başak. "The Politics of Care in Turkey: Sacred Familialism in a Changing Political Context." *Social Politics: International Studies in Gender, State & Society* 25, no. 1 (2018): 72–91.

Aktaş, Cihan. *Bacı'dan Bayan'a: İslâmcı Kadınların Kamusal Alan Tecrübesi*. Istanbul: Kapı Yayınları, 2005.

Al-Ali, Nadje, and Latif Tas. "Reconsidering Nationalism and Feminism: The Kurdish Political Movement in Turkey." *Nations and Nationalism.* 24, no. 2 (2018): 453–473.

Alcoff, Linda Martín. *Visible Identities: Race, Gender, and the Self.* New York: Oxford University Press, 2005.

Alkan Zeybek, Hilal. "Bir Aile Mekanında Cinsiyet, Cinsellik ve Güvenlik." In *Neoliberalizm ve Mahremiyet: Türkiye'de Beden, Sağlık ve Cinsellik,* edited by Cenk Özbay, Ayşecan Terzioğlu, and Yeşim Yasin, 227–243. Istanbul: Metis, 2011.

Allen, Amy. *The Politics of Our Selves: Power, Autonomy, and Gender in Contemporary Critical Theory.* New York: Columbia University Press, 2008.

Al-Saji, Alia. "The Racialization of Muslim Veils: A Philosophical Analysis." *Philosophy & Social Criticism* 36, no. 8 (2010): 875–902.

Amnesty International. *Gezi Park Protests: Brutal Denial of the Right to Peaceful Assembly in Turkey.* 2013. https://www.amnesty.org/download/Documents/12000/eur440222013en. pdf

Amnesty International. *Adding Injustice to the Injury: One Year on from the Gezi Park Protests in Turkey.* 2014. https://www.amnesty.org/download/Documents/8000/eur440102014en. pdf

Arat, Yeşim. "From Emancipation to Liberation: The Changing Role of Women in Turkey's Public Realm." *Journal of International Affairs* 54, no.1 (2000): 107–123.

Arat, Yeşim. *Rethinking Islam and Liberal Democracy: Islamist Women in Turkish Politics.* Albany: State University of New York Press, 2005.

Arat, Yeşim. "Men's Coups, Women's Troubles." *Journal of Middle East Women's Studies* 13, no. 1 (2017): 175–177.

Arman, Ayşe. "35'tim, 5 Yaşıma Döndüm Artık Türkiye'yi İstemiyorum." *Hürriyet,* November 24, 2013. https://www.hurriyet.com.tr/gundem/35-tim-5-yasima-dondum-artik-turkiye-yi-istemiyorum-25190881

Arslan, Ayşe. "Kapitalist Ataerkinin Ablukasında Kadınların Sınıf Deneyimleri: İzmir Konfeksiyon Sektöründe Üretim Süreçlerinin ve Gündelik Hayatın Cinsiyetçi Yapısı." *Praksis* 52, no.1 (2020): 135–155.

Atay, Hazal. "Kürtaj Yasasının Arkeolojisi: Türkiye'de Kürtaj Düzenlemeleri, Edimleri, Kısıtları ve Mücadele Alanları." *Fe Dergi* 9, no. 2 (2017): 1–16.

Baran, Zeyno. *Torn Country: Turkey between Secularism and Islamism.* Stanford: Hoover Institution Press, 2010.

Bartky, Sandra Lee. *Femininity and Domination: Studies in the Phenomenology of Oppression.* New York: Routledge, 1990.

Başaran, Pelin. "Türkiye'de 'Toplumsal Hassasiyetler' ve Tophane Vakası." *T24,* May 27, 2015. https://t24.com.tr/haber/tophaneli-kendi-adaletini-kendi-uyguluyor,298293

Başdaş, Begüm. "Unity in Rupture: Women against the Coup Attempt in Turkey." *Journal of Middle East Women's Studies* 13, no. 1 (2017): 186–188.

Batuman, Bülent, and Feyzan Erkip. "'Night Hawks' Watching Over the City: Redeployment of Night Watchmen and the Politics of Public Space in Turkey." *Space and Culture* 22, no.4 (2019):1–14.

BBC. "Erdoğan: Anneliği Reddeden Kadın, Eksiktir, Yarımdır," June 5, 2016. https://www.bbc.com/turkce/haberler/2016/06/160605_erdogan_kadin

BBC. "100 Women: The Woman Attacked for Wearing Shorts." October 18, 2017. https://www.bbc.com/news/av/world-41628298/100-women-the-woman-attacked-for-wearing-shorts

Behar, Cem. *A Neighborhood in Ottoman Istanbul: Fruit Vendors and Civil Servants in the Kasap İlyas Mahalle.* Albany: State University of New York Press, 2003.

Bennett, Jane, and Michael J. Shapiro. "Introduction." In *The Politics of Moralizing,* edited by Jane Bennett and Michael J. Shapiro, 1–9. New York and London: Routledge, 2013.

Benson, Susan Porter. *Counter Cultures: Saleswomen, Managers, and Customers in American Department Stores 1890–1940.* Urbana: University of Illinois Press, 1986.

Beşpınar, F. Umut. "Questioning Agency and Empowerment: Women's Work-Related Strategies and Social Class in Urban Turkey." *Women's Studies International Forum* 33, no. 6 (2010): 523–32, Pergamon.

Bianet. "Kadın Bakanlığı Kaldırıldı, Kadın Örgütleri Öfkeli." June 8, 2011. https://m.bianet. org/bianet/kadin/130585-kadin-bakanligi-kaldirildi-kadin-orgutleri-ofkeli

Bianet. "Women Policies Erased from Political Agenda." June 9, 2011. http://bianet.org/english/women/130607-2011

Bianet. "Woman Harassed by Security Staff Faces Prosecution for 'Insulting Public Officer.'" October 7, 2017. http://bianet.org/english/print/190400-woman-harassed-by-security-staff-faces-prosecution-for-insulting-public-officer

Bilgiç, Ali. "Reclaiming the National Will: Resilience of Turkish Authoritarian Neoliberalism After Gezi." *South European Society and Politics* 23, no. 2 (2018): 259–80.

Birgün. "Devletin Kadın Politikası Artık Yok." June 10, 2011. https://www.birgun.net/haber/devletin-kadin-politikasi-artik-yok-58802

Bora, Aksu, and Asena Günal. *90'larda Türkiye'de Feminizm.* Istanbul: İletişim, 2002.

Bora, Tanıl. "Analar, Bacılar, Orospular: Türk Milliyetçi-Muhafazakâr Söyleminde Kadın." In *Şerif Mardin'e Armağan,* edited by Ahmet Öncü and Orhan Tekelioğlu, 241–281. Istanbul: İletişim, 2005.

Bora, Tanıl. "Adalet Dairesi." *Birikim Dergi,* March 13, 2019. https://www.birikimdergisi.com/haftalik/9401/adalet-dairesi#.XOFqBFIzZdg

Borsuk, Imren, and Ensari Eroglu. "Displacement and Asset Transformation from Inner-City Squatter Settlement into Peripheral Mass Housing." *European Urban and Regional Studies* 27, no. 2 (2020): 142–55.

Bourdieu, Pierre. *Distinction: A Social Critique of the Judgement of Taste.* Translated by Richard Nice. Massachusetts: Harvard University Press, 1984.

Bourdieu, Pierre. *Masculine Domination.* Stanford University Press, 2001.

Bourdieu, Pierre, and Loic Wacquant. *An Invitation to Reflexive Sociology.* Cambridge: Polity Press, 1992.

Boserup, Ester. *Women's Role in Economic Development.* London: Allen and Unwin, 1970.

Boyar, Ebru. "An Imagined Moral Community: Ottoman Female Public Presence, Honour, and Marginality." In *Ottoman Women in Public Space,* edited by Ebru Boyar and Kate Fleet, 187–229. Leiden and Boston: Brill, 2016.

Brown, Wendy. *Politics Out of History.* Princeton: Princeton University Press, 2001.

Brown, Wendy. "Neoliberalism's Frankenstein: Authoritarian Freedom in Twenty-First Century Democracies." *Critical Times* 1, no. 1 (2018): 60–79.

Buğra, Ayşe, and Çağlar Keyder. "The Turkish Welfare Regime in Transformation." *Journal of European Social Policy* 16, no. 3 (2006): 211–28.

Buğra, Ayşe, and Burcu Yakut-Çakar. "Structural Change, the Social Policy Environment and Female Employment in Turkey." *Development and Change* 41, no. 3 (2010): 517–38.

Buğra, Ayşe, and Yalçın Özkan. "Modernization, Religious Conservatism, and Female Employment through Economic Development in Turkey." In *Trajectories of Female*

Employment in Mediterranean, edited by Ayşe. Buğra and Yalçın Özkan, 91–113. New York: Palgrave Macmillan, 2012.

Butler, Judith. *Gender Trouble: Feminism and the Subversion of Identity.* New York and London: Routledge, 1990.

Butler, Judith. *Precarious Life: The Powers of Mourning and Violence.* London and New York: Verso, 2004.

Cakir, Burcin. "Gendering the Empire: The Discourse on the New Woman and Emergence of Ottoman Feminism, 1860–1918." In *Women's Emancipation Writing at the Fin de Siècle,* edited by Shabliy, Elena V., Dmitriï Nikolaevich Kurochkin, and Karen O'Donnell, 120–157. New York: Routledge, 2018.

Caldwell, John, C. "A Theory of Fertility: From High Plateau to Destabilization." *Population and Development Review* 4, no. 4 (1978): 553–77.

Cindoglu, Dilek. *Headscarf Ban and Discrimination: Professional Headscarved Women in the Labor Market.* Istanbul: TESEV Publications, 2011. https://www.tesev.org.tr/wp-content/uploads/report_Headscarf_Ban_And_Discrimination.pdf

Cindoglu, Dilek, and Didem Unal. "Gender and Sexuality in the Authoritarian Discursive Strategies of 'New Turkey'." *European Journal of Women's Studies* 24, no. 1 (2017): 39–54.

CNN Türk. "Erdoğan: 'Esnaf Gerektiğinde Asker, Polis ve Hakimdir'." November 26, 2014. https://www.cnnturk.com/haber/turkiye/erdogan-esnaf-gerektiginde-asker-polis-ve-hakimdir

Coetzee, J.M. *Giving Offense: Essays on Censorship.* London and Chicago: The University of Chicago Press, 1996.

Cohn, Dvera, Jeffrey S. Passel, Wendy Wang, and Gretchen Livingston. "Barely half of US adults are married–A record low." Pew Research Center, 2011. https://www.pewresearch.org/social-trends/2011/12/14/barely-half-of-u-s-adults-are-married-a-record-low/

Coole, Diana. "Rethinking Agency: A Phenomenological Approach to Embodiment and Agentic Capacities." *Political Studies* 53, no. 1 (2005): 124–42.

Cumhuriyet. "Son Bir Hafta İçinde Bekâret Kontrolüne Gönderilen 8 Kızdan 3'ü İntihar Girişiminde Bulundu, 2'si Öldü." May 9, 1992. https://egazete.cumhuriyet.com.tr/katalog/192/1992/5/9/3

Cumhuriyet. "Laf Attı, Boğazında Sigara Söndürdü, Serbest Kaldı." May 16, 2017. http://www.cumhuriyet.com.tr/haber/turkiye/742031/Laf_atti_bogazinda_sigara_sondurdu_serbest_kaldi.html

Cunningham, Gail. *The New Woman and the Victorian Novel.* London: Macmillan Press, 1978.

Çağlayan, Handan. *Women in the Kurdish Movement: Mothers, Comrades, Goddesses.* Cham: Palgrave Macmillan, 2019.

Çarkoğlu, Aslı, Nilufer Kafescioğlu, and A Aslı Akdaş-Mitrani. "Review of Explicit Family Policies in Turkey from a Systemic Perspective." *Journal of Child and Family Studies* 21, no.1 (February 2012): 42–52.

Çavlin, Alanur. "Türkiye'de Boşanma." In *Türkiye Aile Yapısı Araştırması: Tespitler, Öneriler.* Araştırma ve Sosyal Politika Serisi. TC Aile ve Sosyal Politikalar Bakanlığı, 196–207. Istanbul, 2014.

Çınar, Alev. "Negotiating the Foundations of the Modern State: the Emasculated Citizen and the Call for a Post-Patriarchal State at Gezi Protest." *Theory and Society* 48, no. 3 (2019): 453–82.

Delaney, Carol. *The Seed and the Soil: Gender and Cosmology in Turkish Village Society.* California: University of California Press, 1991.

Dillon, Martin C. *Merleau-Ponty's Ontology*. 2nd ed. Evanston: Northwestern University Press, 1997.

Diner, Cagla. "Gender Politics and GONGOS in Turkey." *Turkish Policy Quarterly* 16, no.4 (2018): 101–108.

Diner, Cagla and Şule Toktaş. "Waves of Feminism in Turkey: Kemalist, Islamist and Kurdish Women's Movements in an Era of Globalization." *Journal of Balkan and Near Eastern Studies* 12, no. 1 (March 2010): 1–57.

Dolezal, Luna. *The Body and Shame: Phenomenology, Feminism, and the Socially Shaped Body*. Lanham: Lexington Books, 2015.

Dong, Madeleine, Y. "Who Is Afraid of the Modern Girl?" In *The Modern Girl Around the World: Consumption, Modernity, and Globalization*, edited by Alys Eve Weinbaum, Lynn M. Thomas, Priti Ramamurthy, Uta G. Poiger, Madeleine Yue Dong, and Tani E. Barlow, 194–209. Durham: Duke University Press, 2008.

Duvar English. "Erdoğan Signals Withdrawal of Turkey from Istanbul Convention." August 13, 2020. https://www.duvarenglish.com/women/2020/08/13/erdogan-signals-withdrawal-of-turkey-from-istanbul-convention

Düzkan, Ayşe. "Sevgili Stella." *Feminist* 7, (March 1990): 23–24.

DW. "2016'da Türkiye'yi Sarsan Saldırılar." January 1, 2017. https://www.dw.com/tr/2016da-t%C3%BCrkiyeyi-sarsan-sald%C4%B1r%C4%B1lar/a-36966926.

Ehrenreich, Barbara and Arlie R. Hochschild, eds. *Global Woman: Nannies, Maids, and Sex Workers in the New Economy*. New York: Metropolitan Books, 2003.

Ekal, Berna. "Women's Shelters and Municipalities in Turkey: Between Solidarity and Benevolence." *EchoGéo* 16, (March-May 2011): 1–15.

Ekmekçioğlu, Lerna. *Recovering Armenia: The Limits of Belonging in Post-Genocide Turkey*. Palo Alto: Stanford University Press, 2016.

Elaman-Garner, Sevinç. "The New Turkish Woman and Her Discontents: The Contradictory Depictions of the (A) sexual Zeyno in Halide Edib Adıvar's Kalp Ağrısı (Heartache 1924)." *Journal of Turkish Literature* 10, (2013): 20–40.

Eldem, Edhem. "Osmanlı İmparatorluğu'ndan Günümüze Adalet, Hukuk, Eşitlik ve Siyaset." *Toplumsal Tarih* 288, (December 2017): 24–37.

Emen-Gökatalay, Gözde. "Popularizing and Promoting Nene Hatun as an Iconic Turkish Mother in Early Cold War Turkey." *Journal of Middle East Women's Studies* 17, no. 1 (2021): 43–63.

England, Paula. "Emerging Theories of Care Work." *Annual Review of Sociology* 31, (2005): 381–99.

Enstad, Nan. *Ladies of Labor, Girls of Adventure: Working Women, Popular Culture, and Labor Politics at the Turn of the Twentieth Century*. New York: Columbia University Press, 1999.

Erinc, Miray. "The Conflict between Education and Female Labour in Turkey: Understanding Turkey's Non-Compliance with the U-shape Hypothesis." *Journal of Balkan and Near Eastern Studies* 19, no. 5 (2017): 571–89.

Ersun, Nur, and İ. Kahraman Arslan. "Değişen Rekabet Koşullarında Geleneksel Gıda Perakendecilerinin Rekabet Gücünün Artırılması." *İstanbul Ticaret Üniversitesi Sosyal Bilimler Dergisi* 7, no. 13 (Spring 2008): 49–67.

Esim, Simel, and Dilek Cindoglu. "Women's Organizations in 1990s Turkey: Predicaments and Prospects." *Middle Eastern Studies* 35, no. 1 (1999): 178–88.

Eslen-Ziya, Hande, and Itır Erhart. "Toward Postheroic Leadership: A Case Study of Gezi's Collaborating Multiple Leaders." *Leadership* 11, no. 4 (2015): 471–88.

Esping-Andersen, Gøsta. *The Three Worlds of Welfare Capitalism*. Cambridge, UK: Polity Press, 1990.

Esping-Andersen, Gøsta. *Social Foundations of Post-Industrial Economies*. Oxford and New York: Oxford University Press, 1999.

Fernández-Kelly, Maria Patricia. *For We are Sold, I and My People: Women and Industry in Mexico's Frontier*. Albany: State University of New York Press, 1984.

Ferrante, Elena. *The Story of a New Name*. Translated by Ann Goldstein. New York: Europa Editions, 2013.

Foucault, Michel. *Power/Knowledge: Selected Interviews and Other Writings, 1972-1977*. New York: Pantheon, 1980.

Freedman, Alisa, Laura Miller, and Christine R. Yano, eds. *Modern Girls on the Go: Gender, Mobility, and Labor in Japan*. California: Stanford University Press, 2013.

Freeman, Carla. *High Tech and High Heels in the Global Economy*. Durham: Duke University Press, 2000.

Frevert, Ute. *Women in German History: From Bourgeois Emancipation to Sexual Liberation*. Translated by Stuart McKinnon-Evans. Oxford and New York: Berg Publishers, 1989.

Frevert, Ute. *A Nation in Barracks: Modern Germany, Military Conscription, and Civil Society*. Oxford and New York: Berg Publishers, 2004.

Frevert, Ute. *Emotions in History—Lost and Found*. Budapest: Central European University Press, 2011.

Fuchs, Victor. *The Service Economy*. Columbia University Press: New York, 1968.

Gambetti, Zeynep. "Occupy Gezi as Politics of the Body." In *The Making of a Protest Movement in Turkey: #occupygezi*, edited by Umut Özkırımlı, 89-102. Basingstoke: Palgrave Macmillan, 2014.

Gatens, Moira. *Imaginary Bodies: Ethics, Power and Corporeality*. London and New York: Routledge, 2003.

Gazetevatan. "'Kadınla Erkek Eşit Olamaz!'" July 20, 2010. http://www.gazetevatan. com/-kadinla-erkek-esit-olamaz-318006-siyaset/

Genckaya, Ömer, Subidey Togan, Ludwig Schulz, and Roy Karadag. *Sustainable Governance Indicators: 2015 Turkey Report*. Bertelsmann Schiftung, Güterslohp, 2015.

Goffman, Erving. "Embarrassment and Social Organization." *American Journal of Sociology* 62, no. 3 (1956): 264-71.

Goffman, Erving. "The Interaction Order: American Sociological Association, 1982 Presidential Address." *American Sociological Review* 48, no. 1 (1983): 1-17.

Goldin, Claudia. "The U-shaped Female Labor Force Function in Economic Development And Economic History." In *Investment in Women's Human Capital and Economic Development*, edited by Paul T. Schultz, 61-90. Chicago: University of Chicago Press, 1995.

Gole, Nilufer. *The Forbidden Modern: Civilization and Veiling*. Ann Arbor: University of Michigan Press, 1996.

Goral, Ozgur Sevgi. "Memory as Experience in Times of Perpetual Violence: The Challenge of Saturday Mothers vis-à-vis Cultural Aphasia." *Kurdish Studies* 9, no. 1 (2021): 77-95.

Gökarıksel, Banu. "Intimate Politics of Protest: Gendering Embodiments and Redefining Spaces in Istanbul's Taksim Park and the Arab Revolutions." In *Freedom without Permission: Bodies and Space in the Arab Revolutions*, edited by Frances S., Hasso and Zakia Salime, 221-58. Durham: Duke University Press, 2016.

Göksel, Nisa. "Peace and Beyond: Women's Activist Alliances under Turkey's 'Regime of Emergency.'" *Critical Times* 1, no. 1 (2018): 149-157.

Göksel, Nisa. "Gendering Resistance: Multiple Faces of the Kurdish Women's Struggle." *Sociological Forum* 34, (2019): 1112-1131.

Grosz, Elizabeth. *Volatile Bodies: Toward a Corporeal Feminism*. Bloomington: Indiana University Press, 1994.

Gündüz-Hoşgör, Ayşe. and Jereon Smits. "Variation in Labor Market Participation of Married Women in Turkey." *Women's Studies International Forum* 31, (March-April 2008): 104–17.

Güneş-Ayata, Ayşe, and Gökten Doğangün. "Gender Politics of the AKP: Restoration of Religio-Conservative Gender Climate." *Journal of Balkan and Near Eastern Studies* 19, no. 6 (2017): 610–27.

Haberturk. "O Polislerle İlgili Karar Verildi." June 12, 2013. https://www.haberturk.com/video/haber/izle/o-polislerle-ilgili-karar-verildi/91119

Haberturk. "7 Bin Bekçi Alımı İçin Ön Başvuru Başladı." June 8, 2018. https://www.haberturk.com/ankara-haberleri/15618258-7-bin-bekci-alimi-icin-on-basvuru-basladi

Harbin, Ami. *Disorientation and Moral life.* New York: Oxford University Press, 2016.

Harris, Anita. *Future Girl: Young Women in the Twenty-First Century.* New York: Routledge, 2004.

HUIPS. *Research on Domestic Violence Against Women in Turkey.* Ankara: 2014 https://fs.hacettepe.edu.tr/hips/dosyalar/Araştırmalar%20-%20raporlar/Aile%20içi%20Şiddet%20Araştırmaları/2014_english_main_report_kyais.pdf

Hustvedt, Siri. *A Woman Looking at Men Looking at Women: Essays on Art, Sex, and the Mind.* New York: Simon and Schuster, 2016.

Hürriyet. "Esnafa 30 Maddelik Paket Açtı, Alışveriş Merkezinde Pazar Tatiline Vize Vermedi. April 11, 2010. https://www.hurriyet.com.tr/ekonomi/esnafa-30-maddelik-paket-acti-alisveris-merkezinde-pazar-tatiline-vize-vermedi-14382855

Hürriyet. "Deputy PM Argues with Opposition Deputy Over the Word 'Vagina'." December 12, 2012. https://www.hurriyetdailynews.com/deputy-pm-argues-with-opposition-deputy-over-the-word-vagina-36683

Hürriyet. "Bakan Açıkladı: TOKİ'de Artık 1+1 Evlere İzin Verilmeyecek." May 28, 2015. https://www.hurriyet.com.tr/ekonomi/bakan-acikladi-tokide-artik-1-1-evlere-izin verilmeyecek-29127554

Hürriyet. "Ramazan'da Alkol Gerekçesiyle Saldırıya Uğrayan Koreli Plakçı Dükkanını Kapattı." June 18, 2016a. https://www.hurriyet.com.tr/gundem/ramazanda-alkol-gerekcesiyle-saldiriya-ugrayan koreli-plakci-dukkanini-kapatti-40119187

Hürriyet. "İpek Atcan'a Metroda Tekmeli Saldırı." November 29, 2016b. http://www.hurriyet.com.tr/gundem/ipek-atcana-metroda-tekmeli-saldiri-40292008

IHA. "Erdoğan'dan 8 Mart Konuşması." March 7, 2008. https://www.iha.com.tr/haber-erdogandan-8-mart-konusmasi-14935/

İleri Haber. "'Bekçiler, Yalnız Yaşayan Kadınların Evlerini Gözetleme Yetkisine Sahip Oldu.'" June 19, 2020. https://ilerihaber.org/icerik/bekciler-yalniz-yasayan-kadinlarin-evlerini-gozetleme yetkisine-sahip-oldu-114255.html

İlkkaracan, Pınar. "Reforming the Penal Code in Turkey: The Campaign for the Reform of the Turkish Penal Code from a Gender Perspective." *Institute of Development Studies* (2007): 1–28. https://www.ids.ac.uk/files/dmfile/PinarIlkkaracanGaventaMay2007final.doc

Inglehart, Ronald, and Pippa Norris. *Rising Tide: Gender Equality and Cultural Change Around the World.* New York: Cambridge University Press, 2003.

İrem, Nazım. "Klasik Osmanlı Rejimi ve 1939 Gülhane Kırılması." *Muhafazakâr Düşünce Dergisi* 4, no.15 (Winter 2008): 147–72.

Jelnov, Pavel. "The Marriage Age U-Shape." IZA Discussion Papers, No. 12356, Institute of Labor Economics (IZA), Bonn, 2019: 1–20.

Jones, Carla. 2010. "Materializing Piety: Gendered Anxieties about Faithful Consumption in Contemporary Urban Indonesia." *American Ethnologist* 37(4): 617–37.

Jung, G Carl. *The Archetypes and the Collective Unconscious.* 2nd Edition. Translated by R.F. C. Hull. Princeton: Princeton University, 1959.

Kalpaklıoğlu, Burcu. "Guiding the Female Body through the *Alo Fetva* Hotline: The Female Preachers' Fatwas on Religious Marriage, Religious Divorce and Sexual Life." In *The Politics of the Female Body in Contemporary Turkey: Reproduction, Maternity, Sexuality,* edited by Hilal Alkan, Ayşe Dayı, Sezin Topcu and Betül Yarar, 233–54. London: I.B.Tauris, 2021.

Kandiyoti, Deniz. "Bargaining with Patriarchy." *Gender & Society,* 2, no. 3, (1988): 274–90.

Kandiyoti, Deniz. "Gendering the Modern: On Missing Dimensions in the Study of Turkish Modernity." In *Rethinking Modernity and National Identity in Turkey,* edited by Sibel Bozdoğan and Reşat Kasaba, 113–32. Seattle and London: University of Washington Press, 1997.

Kandiyoti, Deniz. "Gender and Women's Studies in Turkey: A Moment for Reflection." *New Perspectives on Turkey* 43, (2010): 165–76.

Kandiyoti, Deniz. "Locating the Politics of Gender: Patriarchy, Neo-Liberal Governance and Violence in Turkey." *Research and Policy on Turkey* 1, no. 2 (2016): 103–18.

Karakışla, Yavuz Selim. *Osmanlı İmparatorluğu'nda Savaş Yılları ve Çalışan Kadınlar Kadınları Çalıştırma Cemiyeti (1916–1923).* Istanbul: İletişim, 2015.

Karaman, Emine Rezzan. "Remember, S/he Was Here Once: Mothers Call for Justice and Peace in Turkey." *Journal of Middle East Women's Studies* 12, no. 3 (2016): 382–410.

Karaömerlioğlu, Asım. "Türkiye'de Kürtajın Kısa Tarihi." *Bianet,* July 25, 2012. http://bianet. org/bianet/siyaset/139903-turkiyede-kurtajin-kisa-tarihi

Kazete. "AKP'li Uçma, Mahallenin Namusu İçin Uçtu!" January 29, 2015. https://kazete.com. tr/haber/akpli-ucma-mahallenin-namusu-icin-uctu-34409

Kazete. "Erdoğan'ın 'Kadın mıdır, Kız mıdır' Dediği Dilşat Aktaş Gözaltında." February 22, 2018. https://kazete.com.tr/haber/erdoganin-kadin-midir-kiz-midir-dedigi-dilsat-aktas-gozaltinda 55868

KESK. *OHAL-KHK Rejimi İhraç Kurultayı.* Ankara, 2017. http://www.kesk.org.tr/wp-content/uploads/2017/06/OHAL-KHKrejimi_ihracKurultayi.pdf

Kerestecioğlu, Filiz. *Report on Women's Human Rights Violations in Turkey.* Istanbul, 2017. https://hdp.org.tr/en/report-on-women-s-rights-violations-in-turkey/10887/

Keyder, Çağlar. "Globalization and Social Exclusion in Istanbul." *International Journal of Urban and Regional Research* 29, no. 1 (2005): 124–34.

Keyder, Çağlar. "Law of the Father." *LRB Blog,* June 19, 2013. https://www.lrb.co.uk/blog/2013/june/law-of-the-father

Kılıç, Azer. "The Gender Dimension of Social Policy Reform in Turkey: Towards Equal Citizenship?" *Social Policy & Administration* 42, no. 5 (2008): 487–503.

Kılıç, Azer. "Gender, Family and Children at the Crossroads of Social Policy Reform in Turkey: Alternating between Familialism and Individualism." In *Children, Gender and Families in Mediterranean Welfare States,* edited by Mimi Ajzenstadt and John Gapp, 165–79. Dordrecht: Springer, 2010.

Kivilcim, Zeynep. "Gendering the State of Emergency Regime in Turkey." *Les cahiers du CEDREF,* 22 (2018): 94–108.

Kocamaner, Hikmet. "Regulating the Family through Religion: Secularism, Islam, and the Politics of the Family in Contemporary Turkey." *American Ethnologist* 46, no. 4 (2019): 495–508.

Koç, İsmet. "Türkiye'de Doğurganlık Seviyesi ve Örüntüsünün Değişimi: 1968-2011." In *Türkiye Aile Yapısı Araştırması: Tespitler, Öneriler.* Araştırma ve Sosyal Politika Serisi. TC Aile ve Sosyal Politikalar Bakanlığı, 170–195. Istanbul, 2014a.

Koç, İsmet. "Türkiye'de Aile Yapısının Değişimi: 1968-2011." In *Türkiye Aile Yapısı Araştırması: Tespitler, Öneriler*. Araştırma ve Sosyal Politika Serisi. TC Aile ve Sosyal Politikalar Bakanlığı, 24–55. Istanbul, 2014b.

Kogacioglu, Dicle. "The Tradition Effect: Framing Honor Crimes in Turkey." *Differences: A Journal of Feminist Cultural Studies* 15, no. 2 (2004): 119–151.

KONDA. *Gezi Parkı Araştırması*, 2014. http://konda.com.tr/tr/raporlar/KONDA_GeziRaporu2014.pdf

Korkman, Zeynep Kurtuluş. "Politics of Intimacy in Turkey: A Distraction from 'Real' Politics?." *Journal of Middle East Women's Studies* 12, no. 1 (2016): 112–21.

Korkman, Zeynep Kurtuluş. "Castration, Sexual Violence, and Feminist Politics in Post–Coup Attempt Turkey." *Journal of Middle East Women's Studies* 13, no. 1 (2017): 181–185.

Korkman, Zeynep Kurtulus and Can Aciksoz. "Erdogan's Masculinity and the Language of the Gezi Resistance." *Jadalliya*, 22 June, 2013. https://www.jadaliyya.com/Details/28822

Korpi, Walter. "Faces of Inequality: Gender, Class and Patterns of Inequalities in Different Types of Welfare States." *Social Politics* 7, (2000): 127–91.

Koyuncu, Berrin, and Aylin Özman. "Women's Rights Organizations and Turkish State in the Post-2011 Era: Ideological Disengagement versus Conservative Alignment." *Turkish Studies* 20, no. 5 (2019): 728–53.

Lasco, Chante. "Virginity Testing in Turkey: A Violation of Women's Human Rights." *Human Rights Brief* 9, no. 3 (2002): 10–13.

Laursen, John Christian. "Michael Oakeshott, Wendy Brown, and Paradoxes of Anti-Moralism." *Agora: Papeles de filosofía* 32, no. 2 (2013): 67–80.

Levine, E. Bruce. "Presidential Misogyny: From Jefferson to Trump." *CounterPunch Magazine*, July 4, 2017. https://www.counterpunch.org/2017/07/04/presidential-misogyny-from-jefferson-to-trump/

Lévy-Aksu, Noémi. *Osmanlı İstanbulu'nda Asayiş*. Translated by Serra Akyüz. İstanbul: İletişim, 2017.

Lewis, Michael. "Self-Conscious Emotions: Embarrassment, Pride, Shame, and Guilt." In *Handbook of Emotions*, 3rd ed., edited by Michael Lewis, Jeannette M. Haviland-Jones and Lisa Feldman Barrett, 742–56. New York: Guilford Press, 2008.

Lutz, Catherine. *Unnatural Emotions: Everyday Sentiments on a Micronesian Atoll and Their Challenge to Western Theory*. Chicago: University of Chicago Press, 1998.

Mahmood, Saba. "Feminist Theory, Embodiment, and the Docile Agent: Some Reflections of the Egyptian Islamic Revival." *Cultural Anthropology* 16, no. 2 (2001): 202–36.

Mahmood, Saba. *Politics of Piety: The Islamic Revival and the Feminist Subject*. Princeton: Princeton University Press, 2005.

Makal, Ahmet. "Türkiye'de Erken Cumhuriyet Döneminde Kadın Emeği." *Çalışma ve Toplum* 2, no. 25 (2010): 13–40.

Mardin, Şerif. "The Just and the Unjust." *Daedalus* 120, no.3 (Summer 1991): 113–29.

Maritato, Chiara. "Expanding Religion and Islamic Morality in Turkey: The Role of the Diyanet's Women Preachers." *Anthropology of the Middle East* 13, no. 2 (2018): 43–60.

Marshall, Gül Aldikaçtı. "Ideology, Progress, and Dialogue: A Comparison of Feminist and Islamist Women's Approaches to the Issues of Head Covering and Work in Turkey." *Gender & Society* 19, no. 1 (2005): 104–20.

Marshall, Gül Aldikaçtı. *Shaping Gender Policy in Turkey: Grassroots Women Activists, the European Union, and the Turkish State*. Albany: State University of New York Press, 2013.

Mc Robbie, Angela. *The Aftermath of Feminism: Gender, Culture and Social Change*. London: Sage, 2008.

McNay, Lois. *Gender and Agency: Reconfiguring the Subject in Feminist and Social Theory.* Cambridge: Wiley, 2000.

Merleau-Ponty, Maurice. *Phenomenology of Perception.* Translated by Donald A. Landes. Oxford: Routlegde, 2013. First published 1945 by Gallimard (Paris).

Milliyet. "Arınç'tan İlginç Açıklama," July 28, 2014. https://www.milliyet.com.tr/siyaset/arinctan-ilginc-aciklama-1918060

Moghadam, Valetine. "Patriarchy in Transition: Women and the Changing Family in the Middle East." *Journal of Comparative Family Studies* 35, (2004): 137–62.

Müller, Jan-Werner. *What is Populism?* Philadelphia: University of Pennsylvania Press, 2016.

Nawa, Fariba. "Authoritarian Governments Are Rolling Back Women's Rights. These Women Are Turkey's Last Hope." *Refinery 29,* March 7, 2019. https://www.refinery29.com/en-us/2019/03/225814/turkey-feminism-international-womens day-march-8

Neu, Jerome. *Sticks and Stones: The Philosophy of Insults.* New York: Oxford University Press, 2008.

New York Times. "The Arc of a Coup Attempt in Turkey." July 16, 2016. https://www.nytimes.com/interactive/2016/07/16/world/europe/turkey-coup-photos.html

Ngo, Helen. *The Habits of Racism: A Phenomenology of Racism and Racialized Embodiment.* Lanham: Lexington Books, 2017.

Ngo, Helen. "Critical Phenomenology and the Banality of White Supremacy." *Philosophy Compass* 17, no. 2 (2022): 1–15.

NTV. "'Her Kürtaj bir Uludere'dir'" May 26, 2012. https://www.ntv.com.tr/turkiye/her-kurtaj-bir-uluderedir,z1M5Y2zmwEu6drogItVkiA

NTV. "Erdoğan: Başörtülülere Saldırdılar." June 9, 2013. https://www.ntv.com.tr/turkiye/erdogan-basortululere-saldirdilar,MY8fETQDTESWrDoEc5_tbQ

Ong, Aihwa. *Spirits of Resistance and Capitalist Discipline: Factory Women in Malaysia.* Albany: University of New York Press, 1987.

Orloff, Ann Shola. "From Maternalism to 'Employment for All': State Policies to Promote Women's Employment across the Affluent Democracies." In *The State After Statism: New State Activities in the Age of Liberalization,* edited by Jonah D. Levy, 230–70. Cambridge, MA: Harvard University Press, 2006.

Ovadia, Stella. "Bütün Kadınlar 438'e Karşı." *Feminist* 7, (March 1990): 21–22.

Ovadia, Stella. "Muhafazakâr Yahudi Aile Çevresinden Kadınların Kurtuluşu Hareketinin Kadın Çevresi'ne." *Çatlak Zemin,* April 24, 2019. https://www.catlakzemin.com/muhafazakar-yahudi-aile-cevresinden-kadinlarin-kurtulusu-hareketinin-kadin-cevresine/

Ozbay, Cenk. "Men Are Less Manly, Women Are More Feminine: Shopping Mall as a Site For Gender Crisis in Istanbul." In *Gender and Sexuality in Muslim Cultures,* edited by Gul Ozyegin, 73–95. Burlington: Ashgate, 2015.

Ozyegin, Gul. "Virginal Facades: Sexual Freedom and Guilt among Young Turkish Women." *European Journal of Women's Studies* 16, no. 2 (2009): 103–23.

Ozyegin, Gul. *New Desires, New Selves: Sex, Love, and Piety among Turkish Youth.* New York and London: NYU Press, 2015.

Özkazanç, Alev. "Anti-Gender Movements in Europe and the Case of Turkey." *Baltic Worlds* 13 (2020): 45–55.

Özyürek, Esra. *Nostalgia for the Modern: State Secularism and Everyday Politics in Turkey.* Durham: Duke University Press, 2006.

Pak, Soon-Yong. "Cultural Politics and Vocational Religious Education: The Case of Turkey." *Comparative Education* 40, no. 3 (2004): 321–41.

Parla, Ayse. "The 'Honor' of the State: Virginity Examinations in Turkey." *Feminist Studies* 27, no. 1 (2001): 65–88.

Parla, Ayse. "Revisiting 'Honor' Through Migrant Vulnerabilities in Turkey." *History and Anthropology* 31, no. 1 (2020): 84–104.

Peiss, Kathy. *Cheap Amusements: Working Women and Leisure in Turn-of-the-Century New York.* Philadelphia: Temple University Press, 1986.

Peristiany, G. John, ed. *Honour and Shame. The Values of Mediterranean Society.* Chicago: University of Chicago Press, 1966.

Polat, Defne Kadıoğlu. "'No One is Larger than the State.' Consent, Dissent, and Vigilant Violence during Turkey's Neoliberal Urban Transition." *Southeast European and Black Sea Studies* 21, no. 2 (2021): 189–211.

Quataert, Donald. *Ottoman Manufacturing in the Age of the Industrial Revolution.* (Cambridge Middle East Library, number 30.) Cambridge: Cambridge University Press, 2002.

Rahte, Emek Caylı, and Nagehan Tokdoğan. "Sokakta Kadın Olmak, Alanda ve Gezi'de, Gecede ve Gündüzde." *Moment Dergi* 1, no. 1 (2014): 69–86.

Ramamurthy, Priti. "All-Consuming Nationalism: The Indian Modern Girl in the 1920s and 1930s." In *The Modern Girl Around the World: Consumption, Modernity, and Globalization,* edited by Alys Eve Weinbaum, Lynn M. Thomas, Priti Ramamurthy, Uta G. Poiger, Madeleine Yue Dong, and Tani E. Barlow, 147–73. Durham: Duke University Press, 2008.

Reich, Willhelm. *Character Analysis.* 1945. 3rd Edition. Translated by Vincent R. Carfango. New York: Farrar, Straus and Giroux, 1972.

Ricoeur, Paul. *Reflections on the Just.* Translated by David Pellauer. Chicago: University of Chicago Press, 2007.

Rosaldo, Michelle. "Toward an Anthropology of Self and Feeling." In *Culture Theory: Essays on Mind, Self, and Emotion,* edited by Richard A. Shweder and Robert A. LeVine, 137–57. New York: Cambridge University Press, 1984.

Rowbotham, Sheila. *Dreamers of a New Day: Women Who Invented the Twentieth Century.* London: Verso, 2010.

Rowe, Victoria. *A History of Armenian Women's Writing, 1880–1922.* London: Cambridge Scholars, 2003.

Saglam, Erol. "Taking the Matter into Your Own Hands: Ethnographic Insights into Societal Violence and the Reconfigurations of the State in Contemporary Turkey." *Southeast European and Black Sea Studies* 21, no. 2 (2021): 213–230.

Salamon, Gayle, Gail Weiss, and Ann V. Murphy, eds. *50 Concepts for a Critical Phenomenology.* Evanston: Northwestern University Press, 2019.

Salzinger, Leslie. *Genders in Production: Making Workers in Mexico's Global Factories.* Berkeley: University of California Press, 2003.

Salzinger, Leslie. "Afterword: Gender and Globalization in Uncertain Times." *Qualitative Sociology* 39, no. 4 (2016): 439–42.

Sancar, Serpil. *Türk Modernleşmesinin Cinsiyeti: Erkekler Devlet, Kadınlar Aile Kurar.* Istanbul: İletişim, 2012.

Sancar, Serpil. "'Diyanet'in Kadınlaşması'": Diyanet İşleri Başkanlığı'nın Yeni Kadın ve Aile Politikası." In *Kadın Odaklı,* edited by Çiğdem Kağıtçıbaşı, Dilek Barlas, Hülya Şimga, Murat Önok, and Zeynep Gülru Göker, 203–39. Istanbul: Koç, 2016.

Sarıoğlu, Esra. "Gendering the Organization of Home-Based Work in Turkey: Classical versus Familial Patriarchy." *Gender, Work & Organization* 20, no. 5 (2013): 479–97.

Sarıoğlu, Esra. "Finding the Modern Women Workers in Global Era: Hiring and Training Practices in the Corporate Retail Sector in Turkey." *Fe Dergi: Feminist* 6, 1 (2014): 143-153.

Sarıoğlu, Esra. "New Imaginaries of Gender in Turkey's Service Economy: Women Workers and Identity Making on the Sales Floor." *Women's Studies International Forum* 54, (January-February 2016): 39–47.

Sarıtaş, Ezgi, and Yelda Şahin. "Ellili Yıllarda Kadın Hareketi." In *Türkiye'nin 1950'li Yılları*, edited by Tanıl Bora, 627–66. Istanbul: İletişim.

Sassen, Saskia. *Globalization and Its Discontents: Essays on the New Mobility of People and Money.* New York: New Press, 1998.

Savcı, Evren. "Subjects of Rights and Subjects of Cruelty: The Production of an Islamic Backlash against Homosexuality in Turkey." In *Perverse Politics? Feminism, Anti-Imperialism, Multiplicity*, edited by Ann Shoha Orloff, Raka Ray, and Evren Savcı, 159–86, Massachusetts: Emerald, 2016.

Savcı, Evren. *Queer in Translation: Sexual Politics under Neoliberal Islam.* Durham: Duke University Press, 2021.

Sehlikoglu, Sertaç. "The Daring Mahrem: Changing Dynamics of Public Sexuality in Turkey." In *Gender and Sexuality in Muslim Cultures*, edited by Gul Ozyegin, 235–52. Burlington: Ashgate, 2015.

Serdengeçti, Osman Yüksel. *Mabetsiz Şehir.* 1949. Reprint, Istanbul: Görüş, 1992.

Silverman, Debora. "The 'New Woman,' Feminism, and the Decorative Arts in Fin-de Siecle France." In *Eroticism and the Body Politic*, edited by Lynn Hunt, 144–63. Baltimore: The Johns Hopkins University Press, 1991.

Sirman, Nükhet. "Feminism in Turkey: A Short History." *New Perspectives on Turkey* 3, no. 1, (Fall 1989): 1–34.

Sirman, Nükhet. "Contextualizing Honour." *European Journal of Turkish Studies. Social Sciences on Contemporary Turkey* 18, (2014): 1–7.

Siyasi Haber. "İstanbu'da bir Markette 'Düzgün Yürü' Diyen Erkek, 53 Yaşındaki Kadına Saldırdı." October 20, 2016. http://siyasihaber4.org/istanbuda-bir-markette-duzgun-yuru-diyen-erkek-53-yasindaki-kadina-saldirdi

Skeggs, Beverley. *Formations of Class and Gender: Becoming Respectable.* London; Thousand Oaks; New Delhi: Sage, 1997.

Sözcü. "Erdoğan: 'Erkek Kız Aynı Bankta Oturursa...'" June 2, 2013. https://www.sozcu.com.tr/2013/gundem/erdogan-erkek-kiz-ayni-bankta-oturursa-306232/

Stansell, Christine. *City of Women: Sex and Class in New York, 1789–1860.* New York: Knopf, 1986.

Stansell, Christine. *American Moderns: Bohemian New York and the Creation of a New Century.* New York: Henry Holt, 2000.

Star. "Oda Azaldı Boşanma Arttı." April 18, 2015. https://www.star.com.tr/pazar/oda-azaldi-bosanma-artti-haber-1021919/

Stevens, Sarah E. "Figuring Modernity: The New Woman and the Modern Girl in Republican China." *NWSA Journal* 15, no. 3 (Fall 2003): 82–103.

Sullivan, Shannon. *Revealing Whiteness: The Unconscious Habits of Racial Privilege.* Bloomington: Indiana University Press, 2006.

Sullivan, Shannon. *Good White People: The Problem with Middle-Class White Anti-Racism.* Albany: State University of New York Press, 2014.

Sullivan, Shannon. *The Physiology of Sexist and Racist Oppression.* New York: Oxford University Press, 2015.

Süral, Nurhan, and Mustafa Kiliçoğlu, M. "Prohibiting Sexual Harassment in the Workplace in Turkey." *Middle Eastern Studies* 47, no.4 (2011): 655–62.

Szanto, Thomas, and Hilge Landweer, eds. *The Routledge Handbook of Phenomenology of Emotion.* New York: Routledge, 2020.

Şahin, Öznur. "From Home to City: Gender Segregation, Homosociality and Publicness in Istanbul." *Gender, Place & Culture* 25, no. 5 (2018): 743–57.

Şener, Meltem Yılmaz. "Conditional Cash Transfers in Turkey: A Case to Reflect on the AKP's Approach to Gender and Social Policy." *Research and Policy on Turkey* 1, no. 2 (2016): 164–78.

Şişman, Nazife. *Emanetten Mülke: Kadın Bedeninin Yeniden İnşası.* Istanbul: İz, 2003.

t24. "Gezi'de Yaralanan Lobna 12 Gündür Gözlerini Açamadı." June 12, 2013a. https://t24. com.tr/haber/gezi-parki-eylemlerinde-yaralanan-lobna-allami-yurumeye basladi,233252

t24. "İzmir'de Gezi Parkı Eyleminde Polisten Gördüğü Şiddetin Fotoğrafını Paylaştı." June, 6 2013b. https://t24.com.tr/haber/izmirde-gezi-parki-eyleminde-polisten-gordugu-siddetin fotografini-paylasti,231427

t24. "İzmir'de Tacize Uğrayan Kadını Döven Polis Hakkında Soruşturma Başlatıldı." August 13, 2017. https://t24.com.tr/haber/izmirde-tacize-ugrayan-kadini-doven-polis-hakkinda sorusturma baslatildi,419571

TBMM. *Report of the Parliamentary Investigation Commission for the Coups and the Memorandums.* Vol. 1. Ankara: TBMM, 2012.

TDHS (Hacettepe University Institute of Population Studies). "2013 Turkey Demographic and Health Survey". Hacettepe University Institute of Population Studies, T.R. Ministry of Development and TÜBİTAK, Ankara, Turkey, 2014.

Tekeli, Şirin. "Europe, European Feminism, and Women in Turkey." *Women's Studies International Forum* 15, no. 1 (1992): 139–43.

Thistle, Susan. *From Marriage to the Market: The Transformation of Women's Lives and Work.* Berkeley: University of California Press, 2006.

Thomas, Lynn, M. "The Modern Girl and Racial Respectability in 1930s South Africa" In *The Modern Girl Around the World: Consumption, Modernity, and Globalization,* edited by Alys Eve Weinbaum, Lynn M. Thomas, Priti Ramamurthy, Uta G. Poiger, Madeleine Yue Dong, and Tani E. Barlow, 96–119. Durham: Duke University Press, 2008.

Throop, C. Jason. "Being Open to the World." *HAU: Journal of Ethnographic Theory* 8, no. 1-2 (2018): 197–210.

Tokdoğan, Nagehan. *Yeni Osmanlıcılık: Hınç, Nostalji, Narsisizm.* Istanbul: İletişim, 2018.

Toksöz, Gülay. "Transition from 'Woman' to 'Family': An Analysis of AKP Era Employment Policies from a Gender Perspective." *Journal für Entwicklungspolitik* 32, no. 1/2 (2016): 64–83.

Tomkins, Silvan. *Affect Imagery Consciousness Volume II The Negative Affects.* New York: Springer, 1963.

Tomkins, Silvan. *Affect Imagery Consciousness Volume III The Negative Affects: Anger and Fear.* New York: Springer, 1991.

Toprak Zafer. *Türkiye'de Yeni Hayat & İnkılap ve Travma 1908–1928.* Istanbul: Doğan Kitap, 2017.

Trtworld. "Turkey's Neighbourhood Watchmen Get More Powers, Wider Remit." June 11, 2020. https://www.trtworld.com/turkey/turkey-s-neighbourhood-watchmen-get-more-powers-wider-remit-37184

Tsing, Anna Lowenhaupt. *The Mushroom at the End of the World: On the Possibility of Life in Capitalist Ruins.* Princeton & Oxford: Princeton University Press, 2015.

Tuğ, Başak. *Politics of Honor in Ottoman Anatolia: Sexual Violence and Socio-Legal Surveillance in the Eighteenth Century.* Leiden and Boston: Brill, 2017.

Tuncer, Selda. *Women and Public Space in Turkey: Gender, Modernity and the Urban Experience.* London and New York: Bloomsbury Publishing, 2018.

Turkmen, Buket. "'The Gezi Revolt and the Solidarist Individualism of 'Çapulcu' Women (marauder)." *Les cahiers du CEDREF* 22, (2018): 109–27.

TURKSTAT. "Education Statistics." (Schooling Ratio by Educational Year and Level of Education, 1997–2018). http://www.turkstat.gov.tr/PreTablo.do?alt_id=1018

TURKSTAT. "Labour Force Statistics Database." (Non-Institutional Population by Year and Labour Force Status, Urban and Female). http://www.turkstat.gov.tr/PreTablo.do?alt_id=1007

TURKSTAT. "Evlenme ve Boşanma İstatistikleri 2020." February 25, 2021. https://data.tuik.gov.tr/Bulten/GetBultenPdf?id=37211.

Unal, Didem, and Dilek Cindoglu. "Reproductive Citizenship in Turkey: Abortion Chronicles." *Women's Studies International Forum* 38, (May-June 2013): 21–31.

Uncu, Baran Alp. "KONDA Seçmen kümeleri: AK Parti seçmenleri." *KONDA Araştırma ve Danışmanlık,* 2018. https://konda.com.tr/wp-content/uploads/2018/05/KONDA_SecmenKumeleri_AkParti_Secmenleri_Mayis2018.pdf

Ünlü, Barış. *Türklük Sözleşmesi: Oluşumu, İşleyişi ve Krizi.* Ankara: Dipnot, 2018.

Ünsal, Özlem, and Tuna Kuyucu. "Challenging the Neoliberal Urban Regime: Regeneration and Resistance in Başıbüyük and Tarlabaşı." In *Orienting Istanbul: Cultural Capital of Europe?,* edited by Deniz Göktürk, Levent Soysal, Ipek Tureli, 51–70. London: Routledge, 2010.

Üstündağ, Nazan. "Mother, Politician, and Guerilla: The Emergence of a New Political Imagination in Kurdistan through Women's Bodies and Speech." *differences* 30, no. 2 (2019): 115–145.

Walkerdine, Valerie, Helen Lucey, and June Melody. *Growing up Girl: Psychosocial Explorations of Gender and Class.* London: Palgrave Macmillan, 2001.

Warhurst, Chris, Paul Thompson, and Dennis P. Nickson. "Labor Process Theory: Putting the Materialism Back into the Meaning of Service Work." In *Service Work,* edited by Cameron MacDonald and Marek Korczynski, 91–112. New York: Routledge, 2009.

Watkins, Susan. 2018. "Which Feminisms?." *New Left Review* 109: 5–76.

Weinbaum, Alys Eve, Lynn M. Thomas, Priti Ramamurthy, Uta G. Poiger, Madeleine Yue Dong, and Tani E. Barlow, eds. *The Modern Girl around the World: Consumption, Modernity, and Globalization.* Durham: Duke University Press, 2008.

Weiss, Gail. "A Genealogy of Women's (Un)Ethical Bodies." In *New Feminist Perspectives on Embodiment,* edited by Clara Fischer and Luna Dolezal, 17–36.Basingstoke: Palgrave Macmillan, 2018.

White, Jenny. "State Feminism, Modernization, and the Turkish Republican Woman." *NWSA Journal* 15, no.3 (2003): 145–59.

White, Jenny. *Money Makes us Relatives: Women's Labor in Urban Turkey.* 2nd Edition. London: Routledge, 2004.

Wikan, Unni. "Shame and Honour: A Contestable Pair." *Man* 19, No. 4 (December 1984): 635–52.

World Bulletin. "Respect to National Will Rally Held in Ankara." June 15, 2013. https://www.worldbulletin.net/politics/respect-to-national-will-rally-held-in-ankara h111207.html

Yalçın, Türkân. *Türk Ceza Hukukunda Kadın.* Ankara: Savaş Yayınevi, 2019.

Yancy, George. *Black Bodies, White Gazes: The Continuing Significance of Race.* Lanham: Rowman and Littlefield, 2008.

Yarar, Betül. "Disciplining Pious Female Bodies/Sexualities in the Authoritarian Times of Turkey: An Analysis of Public Moral Discourses on the *Süslümans*. In *The Politics of the Female Body in Contemporary Turkey: Reproduction, Maternity, Sexuality*, edited by Hilal Alkan, Ayşe Dayı, Sezin Topcu and Betül Yarar, 205–31. London: I.B.Tauris, 2021.

Yaraş, Sezen. "The Making of the 'New'Patriarch in Women's Self-Narrations of Political Empowerment: The Case of Local Female AKP Politicians in the Aftermath of 2009 Elections." *Turkish Studies* 20, no. 2 (2019): 273–96.

Yarın Haber. "Eminönü'de bir Kadına Kıyafeti Bahanesiyle Sözlü Saldırı: Milleti Azdırıyorsun" June 29, 2017. http://yarinhaber.net/kadin/55507/eminonude-bir-kadina-kiyafeti-bahanesiyle-sozlu-saldiri-milleti-azdiriyorsun

Yazici, Berna. "The Return to the Family: Welfare, State, and Politics of the Family in Turkey." *Anthropological Quarterly* 85, no.1 (Winter 2012): 103–40.

Yıldırım, Kadir. *Osmanlı'da İşçiler (1870–1922) Çalışma Hayatı, Örgütler, Grevler*. Istanbul: İletişim, 2013.

Yılmaz, Sare. "A New Momentum: Gender Justice in the Women's Movement." *Turkish Policy Quarterly* 13, no.4 (2015): 107–15.

Yılmaz, Zehra. "The AKP and its Family Policy in the Re-establishment Process of Authoritativeness in Turkey." In *Authoritarianism in the Middle East; Authoritarianism in the Middle East: Before and After the Arab Uprisings*, edited by Bakis J. Karakoç and Jülide Karakoç, 150–71. London: Palgrave Macmillan, 2015.

Yilmaz, Zafer. "The AKP and the Spirit of the 'New' Turkey: Imagined Victim, Reactionary Mood, and Resentful Sovereign." *Turkish Studies* 18, no. 3 (2017): 482–513.

Yonucu, Deniz. "Urban Vigilantism: A Study of Anti-Terror Law, Politics and Policing in Istanbul." *International Journal of Urban and Regional Research* 42, no. 3 (2018): 408–22.

Young, Iris Marion. "Throwing Like a Girl: A Phenomenology of Feminine Body Comportment, Motility, and Spatiality." *Human Studies* 3, no. 1 (1980): 137–56.

Young, Iris Marion. *On Female Body Experience: "Throwing Like a Girl" and Other Essays*. New York: Oxford University Press, 2005.

Yörük, Erdem, and Murat Yüksel. "Class and Politics in Turkey's Gezi Protests." *New Left Review* 89, no. 1 (2014): 103–23.

Zamudio, M. Margaret, and Michael Lichter. "Bad Attitudes and Good Soldiers: Soft Skills as a Code for Tractability in the Hiring of Immigrant Latina/os over Native Blacks in the Hotel Industry." *Social Problems* 55, no.4 (2008): 573–89.

Zengin, Aslı. "What is Queer about Gezi." *Cultural Anthropology* 31 (2013).

Zihnioğlu, Yaprak. *Kadınsız İnkılap Nezihe Muhiddin Kadınlar Halk Fırkası Kadın Birliği*. Istanbul: Metis, 2003.

INDEX

....

abortion, 23, 66, 67, 69,
109–112, 123, 136
Abu-Lughod, Lila, 10, 15, 37
affect studies, 9
affective habits, 17, 20, 35,
81, 148, 150
affective orientations, 24,
29, 148, 166
agency, 4, 5, 9–11, 13– 17,
20, 126
women's agency, 9–11,
13–17, 163
Ağaoğlu, Adalet, 66
Ahmed, Sara, 12–13, 148
Aktaş, Dilşat, 106–107, 135
AKP (Justice and Development
Party), 2–9, 16, 18, 21–22,
24–27, 31, 70–71, 81, 84,
93, 98, 100–111, 113–115,
117, 119–124, 126, 129,
131–142, 145, 147, 149,
152–154, 156–158, 161,
165–170 (See also
Erdoğan, Recep
Tayyip)
AKP's gender politics, 3, 9,
25, 98, 110, 130, 153–154,
157 (See also gender)
AKP's moralist politics, 25,
101, 109–110, 140–141
(See also moralism)
Allami, Lobna, 129–130
alienation, 39–40, 42, 93, 166
alienated body, 39
Ankara University, 26–27
Arat, Yeşim, 6, 67–68
Arınç, Bülent, 22, 111
Aslan, Özgecan, 146–147
Atatürk, Mustafa Kemal, 17
(See also Kemalism)
Atcan, İpek, 1, 144

authoritarianism, 4, 9, 16, 19,
30, 101, 106–107, 127,
160, 163, 165–166
autonomy, 8–10, 17, 31, 45–46,
56, 77, 87, 93, 112, 138,
124, 152, 170
bodily autonomy, 7, 31, 71,
124, 159, 164–165

bacı (sister), 65–66, 86–87
bacı talk, 86
backlash, 5, 7–8, 93, 164–166,
170
bairam, 1, 143, 148
Bartky, Sandra, 38
birth control, 66–67
body, 4, 5, 9, 11–14, 16, 19–21, 23,
28, 30, 36–42, 48, 53, 59,
66, 68, 88–90, 105, 107,
111, 113, 121, 123–124,
126–127, 129, 141, 147–148,
165–166, 168, 170 (See also
embodiment)
alienated body, 39
bodily autonomy, 7, 31, 71,
124, 159, 164–165
body politics, 21, 121
Cartesian body, 12
feminized body, 16, 38, 51,
88–89, 109, 165
forces of body, 35, 40
worker's body, 88
phenomenological body,
9–12
bombings, 28, 140, 149, 155
Bora, Tanıl, 36, 152
Bourdieu, Pierre, 7, 9,
21, 39
breadwinner, 63–64, 102, 105,
112, 154
Buğra, Ayşe, 62–64, 102

bully, 91, 100, 115–116, 135 (See
also kabadayı)
Butler, Judith, 10–11, 20

capitalism, 8, 24, 45–46, 60, 62,
98, 100, 120, 164, 167
capital accumulation, 45, 88
consumer capitalism, (See
consumerism)
global capitalist
restructuring, 18, 20, 29,
31, 43, 84, 123, 141,
163–165
neoliberal global capitalism,
5–6, 18–19, 30, 45, 77, 79,
165 (See also
globalization;
neoliberalism)
caregiver, 63, 102–103
CEDAW, (See Convention on
the Elimination of All
Forms of Discrimination
against Women)
chastity, 7, 22, 50, 52–57, 60–62,
66, 71,, 115,, 117, 123
Certificate of Chastity,
60–61
unchaste behavior, 54,
116, 135
Chomsky, Noam, 131
Civil Code, 3, 51–52, 54–55,
69–71,164
Article, 159, 54, 69
Civil Servants Law No., 657, 44
Coetzee, J.M., 133–134
commodity, 24, 36, 46, 60
commodified, 6, 45
commodity fetishism, 46
Commission for Preventing
Violence against
Women, 137

community surveillance, 112
consent, 22, 71, 110, 114
conservative, 2–3, 22, 36–37, 66, 70, 98, 100, 108, 116–117, 134, 156 (*See also* neoconservative)
consumerism, 45–46, 77, 79, 81
consumer services, 80
consumer capitalism, 6, 46, 77
consumerist culture, 46
consumption sites, 29
consumption venues, 29, 65, 77, 80, 83–84
Convention on the Elimination of All Forms of Discrimination against Women (CEDAW), 70, 97
corporeality, 5, 8–9, 11–13, 16–17, 20, 25, 31, 58, 68, 114, 149
corporeal mode of being, 6, 9, 19, 149, 164
corporeal openness, 20, 121
Council of Europe Convention on Preventing and Combating Violence Against Women and Domestic Violence (Istanbul Convention), 147, 169–171
Çınar, Alev, 124

Democrat Party, 63
demonstration, 4, 23, 26, 51, 66, 106, 115–116, 119–120, 122–125, 128–129, 135, 156, 158, 170 (*See also* Gezi Uprising)
street demonstrations, 9, 23, 68, 99, 147, 156, 158, 170
LGBT demonstrations, 150
"Don't Mess with My Outfit", 155–157
discourse, 2, 6–8, 10, 12, 19, 24, 45, 63, 67, 114–115, 137, 152
shame-honor discourse, (*See* shame-honor discourse)
neoliberal discourse, 6, 17, 46
moralist discourse, 6, 29, 109, 123, 165
justice discourse, 152, 154 (*See also* gender-justice paradigm; justice)

ease, 14, 39, 75, 81, 83, 114, 148, 170

embarrassment, 7–9, 14–17, 20, 22–24, 36–39, 48, 59, 77, 80–81, 101, 115, 164 (*See also* ease; emotions; shame)
absence of embarrassment, 2, 14, 29, 77, 81
affective dictates of embarrassment, 5
cultural politics of embarrassment, 23–24, 37, 51, 67, 164
feminine embarrassment, 40
forces of embarrassment, 35–36, 164
embodiment, 5–11, 13–15, 17–22, 24–26, 29–31, 37–38, 60, 63, 72, 76, 81, 86–87, 89, 101, 104, 114, 117, 127, 130–132, 136, 144, 148–150, 156, 158, 164–165 (*See also* body; feminine embodiment)
embodied capacities, 5–6, 21, 25, 42, 109–110, 121, 123
embodied openness, 21, 25, 42, 107, 116, 124, 131, 167 (*See also* openness)
embodied orientations, 5, 10, 21, 29, 35, 45, 59, 77, 81, 100, 116, 124, 159, 166
embodied presence, 2, 4, 9, 14
embodied response, 14, 126
embodied self, 12
embodied vulnerability, 5, 21–22
embodied practices of femininity, 9, 19, 48
gendered embodiment, 7, 23
emotions, 4, 7–9, 12, 16, 19–21, 23–24, 28–29, 31, 37–39, 45, 77, 80–81, 83, 92, 107, 113, 121, 132, 134, 148–149, 164, 166 (*See also* ease; embarrassment; feelings; honor; humiliation; shame; shyness)
emotional abuse, 167
emotional disciplinary mechanisms, 164
emotional modalities of power, 15
emotional obligations, 15, 48
emotional orientations, 5–6, 81
emotional state, 40, 116, 128
positive emotions, 78
self-conscious emotion, 16, 36–37, 115
sociology of emotions, 9

Erbakan, Necmettin, 152
Erdoğan, Recep Tayyip, 3, 91, 97–98, 100–101, 104–108, 110–117, 123–124, 129, 131–140, 142, 158–159, 166, 169 (*See also* AKP)
Erhart, Itır, 128
Eslen-Ziya, Hande, 128
Esping-Andersen, Gøsta, 102
European Union, 3, 6, 17, 22, 70, 77, 98, 163, 169
ethnography, 4, 8, 20, 29–30, 99
eye contact, 21, 59, 77–82

factory worker, 86, 89–90
failed coup attempt in July 2016, 4, 27, 134, 140, 142, 145, 149–150
familialism, 63, 65–66, 84, 86, 90, 99, 102–103, 124
familialist policies, 103
paternalist-familialist ethos, 103
feelings, 4, 6–14, 19, 22, 24–25, 28–29, 31, 33, 35–43, 54, 80, 86–87, 92, 101, 108, 115, 121, 127, 134, 143, 148, 150, 152, 159, 167, 171 (*See also* ease; embarrassment; emotions; honor; humiliation; shame; shyness)
feminine, 4–5, 13, 16–17, 25, 36, 38, 40, 42, 45–46, 51, 58, 63, 66, 72, 81, 85, 90, 124, 131, 140–141, 144, 149, 159, 163, 165, 170
cultural politics of feminine respectability, 18, 163–164
feminine embodiment, 7–9, 15, 17–18, 30–31, 130, 164–165
feminine modesty, 7–8, 16, 22–23, 36, 51, 58–59, 67, 82, 101, 149, 159, 170
feminine virtue, 5, 7, 9, 17, 117
new modality of femininity, 4, 19–20, 101, 141, 167, 179
norms of feminine, 2, 7, 16, 88
feminisms and feminists, 5–6, 9–11, 13, 16, 22–23, 25, 27, 30–31, 46, 68, 70, 98, 101, 103, 106–107, 110, 113, 115, 117, 128, 146, 156–157, 165–166, 171
feminist campaigns, 16, 50, 97
feminist dream, 25
feminist night walks, 4, 151

feminist thinkers, 8, 10, 26, 50, 59
radical feminist groups, 50, 116, 163
feminist movement in Turkey, 5, 7, 18, 26, 31, 51, 55, 57, 67–69, 111, 132, 157, 169
feminist phenomenology, 12, 24, 35, 164
Feminist (journal), 50
fertility, 73
reduced fertility rates, 99, 164
fictive kinship, 65–66, 87
Free Girl, 45–46, 86, 92–93
Foucault, Michel, 10

Gambetti, Zeynep, 121
Gaslighting, 167
Gatens, Moira, 20
gecekondu, 64, 66, 112
gender, 3, 5, 7–9, 12, 15–24, 29–30, 35–37, 46, 48, 55–56, 58, 62–63, 65, 68–72, 85–86, 90, 100, 102–103, 105, 119, 121, 128, 137, 141, 152, 159, 163–165, 167
gender convergence, 86
gender equality, 3–9, 16–19, 36, 45, 51, 70–72, 77, 85, 93, 97–99, 102, 106, 110, 123, 152–154, 164–165, 169–170
gender hierarchies, 15, 21, 40, 44–45, 65, 76, 141
gender justice, 3, 22, 141, 152–155, 170 (*See also* discourse; gender justice paradigm)
gender norms, 15, 45, 83, 145, 154, 168
gender order, 7, 18, 36, 124, 160, 164–165
gender performances, 56, 83, 110
gender policies, 3, 107, 110
gender politics, 3, 9, 15, 25, 31, 63, 98, 130, 154, 157, 164
gender segregation, 60, 103–104, 156
gendered bodies, 4, 7–8, 15, 17, 163
gendered division of labor, 72, 98
gendered emotions, 15, 37, 164
gendered interaction order, 77, 83, 89

gendered means of violation, 25, 42
gendered social order, 165
mixed-gender interactions, 56, 64–65, 87, 138, 142
nonnormative genders and sexualities, 164
gender justice paradigm, 22, 141, 153, 170
fıtrat, 3, 106, 154
fair treatment, 3, 153–155
General Directorate on the Status and Problems of Women (KSSGM), 69
Gezi Uprising, 25, 119–141, 145, 153, 155, 166
ghosting, 167
girl (*kız*), 13, 22, 36–37, 45–46, 55, 57, 75, 82, 100, 106, 136, 147 (*See also* Free Girl; girl power; virginity)
girl power, 45
globalization, 5, 7–9, 16–20, 22, 31, 45, 70–71, 99, 101–103, 123–124, 163–164, 166, 170
globalization project, 22, 98
neoliberal capitalist globalization, 4, 17, 22, 79, 163 (*See also* capitalism; neoliberalism)
Goffman, Erving, 5, 14–15, 19, 20, 77, 83
golden shadow, 127
gossip, 58, 84–85, 88–89, 112
Gökarıksel, Banu, 121
Gülbahar, Hülya, 99
Gülen Movement, 149

habit, 8, 11, 13, 31, 38, 48, 82, 89 (*See also* embodiment)
affective habit, 17, 20, 35, 81
embodied habit, 12, 19
habit body, 13, 16
habitual ways of being in the world, 5, 9, 13, 31
habitus, 21
headscarf ban, 141
herstory, 121–122
heterosocial, 55, 65, 113
hierarchies, 18, 37, 50–51, 63, 68, 87, 153–154
class hierarchies, 12, 21, 39, 44, 76, 86, 90
fundamental status hierarchies, 3
gender hierarchies, 8, 15, 21, 40, 44–45, 65, 76, 141
structural hierarchies, 12

homophobia, 146
homosocial, 103, 113
honor, 7, 12, 37–38, 41, 53–54, 62, 69, 71 (*See also* shame-honor discourse)
family honor, 53, 61
honor codes, 113, 132
honor killings, 53, 69, 71
honor-based murders, 53
ırz, 53, 71
male honor, 52–54, 58, 63–64, 66, 69, 85–88, 101–102, 104–105, 110, 114, 119
"neighborhood's honor" (mahallenin namusu), 58–59, 84–85, 104–105, 113, 137
housewives, 56, 63–64, 76, 103
humiliation, 42, 57–58, 115 (*See also* embarrassment; emotions; feelings; shame)

Islahat Fermanı, (Royal Edict of Reform), 153
İmam Hatip schools, 57, 67, 113
industrialization, 19, 24, 30, 51, 60, 62–64, 72, 165
industrial workplaces, 76, 86
interaction order, 19, 77, 83, 89 (*See also* gender)
International Day for the Elimination of Violence against Women, 101
International Women's Day (March 8), 4, 98, 101, 171
Istanbul Convention, (*See* Council of Europe Convention on Preventing and Combating Violence Against Women and Domestic Violence)

Jung, Carl Gustav, 127
justice, 105, 120, 137, 139, 152–154 (*See also* discourse; vigilantism)
gender justice, (*See* gender, gender justice paradigm)
Ottoman notion of justice, 3, 153
Justice Party, 152

kabadayı, 104–105, 115–116
Kandiyoti, Deniz, 8, 52, 71, 73, 104
Karaibrahimgil, Nil, 46

Kaymakçı, Canan, 144
Kemalism, 17, 105, 108, 116,
    120, 163 (See also
    Atatürk, Mustafa Kemal)
Kemalist elite, 3
Kemalist ideology, 17–18
Kemalist reforms, 71
Keyder, Çağlar, 79, 99, 102,
    122–123, 139
Köse, Çağla, 145
Kurdistan Workers' Party
    (PKK), 69
Kurdish women's movement,
    69, 146

labor, 6–7, 9, 30, 43, 63, 72, 81,
    83, 98, 165
    forces of labor, 35, 44, 48
    immaterial labor, 24
    labor market, 18, 44, 47, 60,
        64, 83, 102
    labor power, 88
    labor process, 24, 77, 88, 90
    service labor, 79
    women's labor force
        participation, 62–63, 79
    women's unpaid labor, 103
Law to Protect the Family and
    Prevent Violence
    Against Women (Law
    Number 6248), 147
LGBTIQ+, 3, 8, 26–27, 43, 54,
    70–71, 107, 117, 120, 128,
    132, 146, 150, 163, 166,
    168–169
liberalism,
    economic liberalism, 22, 141
    political liberalism, 22, 141
love-bombing, 167

mahalle (neighborhood), 58–59,
    84–86, 104, 108–109,
    136–137, 159
    bekçi, 168–170
    mahallenin namusu (honor
        of the neighborhood),
        58, 84, 104–105, 137, 168
    mukhtar, 61
Mahmood, Saba, 10–11, 16, 37
male, 2, 8–10, 15, 24, 34, 38, 45,
    50, 52, 58, 61, 63, 66,
    68–69, 71–72, 87–89,
    100–105, 111, 116, 130,
    133, 136, 138, 142,
    144–145, 152, 154–155,
    157, 150, 165, 168
    male gaze, 14, 40–41, 170
        (See also objectifying
        gaze)
    male honor, (See
        honor)

male hostility, 41, 85
male jealousy, 43
male privilege, 12
male surveillance, 41, 85, 159
male violence, (See
    violence)
manspreading, 38
masculinism, 7–8, 13, 31, 38, 43,
    56, 69, 3, 85, 101, 104–106,
    110–111, 113, 116, 121,
    124, 128, 131–132, 152,
    154, 157, 159, 163, 166,
    170 (See also kabadayı;
    vigilantism)
    masculine enhancement
        effect, 104
    masculine guardianship, 137
    masculinist enforcement of
        morality in public, 101,
        136, 170
    masculinist restoration, 8,
        152
    reactionary masculinist
        state, 9
    loss of masculine authority,
        8, 159, 164
Mediterranean societies, 7, 15,
    147
Merleau-Ponty, Maurice, 11,
    13, 21
Middle East, 73, 137
migrant, 63–66
military, 16, 44, 67, 107–108,
    120, 122, 134, 140, 146,
    160, 171
    military coup, 66–67, 120
        (See also failed coup
        attempt)
    military intervention, 120,
        142
    military operations, 4, 27
    military tutelage, 3, 120, 160
misogynistic practice, 141
modesty, 7, 16, 19, 22, 37–38,
    41, 61–62, 81, 110–111,
    123, 164
    feminine modesty, 2, 7–8,
        16, 22, 36, 51, 58–59, 67,
        82, 101, 149, 159, 170
    sexual modesty, 82
moralism, 2, 21–22, 106–107,
    109, 111–112, 114–117, 135,
    137–139, 141–145, 152,
    154–156, 159–160, 166
    moralist politics, 4, 23–25,
        101, 107, 109–110, 115,
        117, 121, 132, 139–140,
        159–160 (See also AKP)
    moralist discourse, 6, 29,
        109, 123, 165 (See also
        discourse)

moralist vigilantism, 3, 29,
    114, 136, 138, 141 (See
    also vigilantism)
morality, 7, 36, 51, 53–54, 56, 58,
    60–62, 71–72, 77, 83,
    86–90, 107–109, 113, 116,
    133, 135–136, 139, 141,
    143–145, 153, 160, 168, 170
    moral infractions, 2, 7, 56,
        107, 110, 139
    moral transgressions, 2, 7,
        37–38, 41–42, 58, 107,
        110, 114, 117, 134–136,
        141–143–144
    public morality, 52, 54, 56,
        58, 60–61, 71, 117, 168
motherhood, 98, 103, 111, 113
movements, 4, 23, 27, 30, 66–70,
    72, 120, 123, 125, 132,
    149, 157, 171
    feminist movements, 5, 7,
        31, 51, 55, 67, 69, 111, 132,
        169 (See also feminisms
        and feminists)
    grassroots movement, 4,
        66–67, 135
    Kurdish movement, 17, 22,
        69, 76, 149
    Kurdish women's
        movement, 69, 146
    LGBTIQ+ movement, 27, 132,
        163 (See also LGBTIQ+)
    women's movement, 4, 10,
        23, 30, 52, 109
Muslim, 1, 3, 37, 52, 68, 85,
    134–135, 143, 153 (See
    also Sunni)
    Muslim women, 60–61
    non-Muslim women, 60
    non-Muslim, 3, 153
Müller, Jan-Werner, 105

nation, 7, 19, 22, 56, 67, 69, 105,
    119, 125, 132–135, 138
    nation-state, 15, 18, 45, 52–53
    national belonging, 6
    national will, 132, 134–136,
        142
    nationalism, 6, 17–18, 27,
        36–37, 67, 108, 137, 143,
        160, 164
    secularist Turkish
        nationalism, 6
Nazlıaka, Aylin, 111, 155, 157
    (See also CHP)
neoconservative, 164–165
    neoconservative gender
        order, 124, 165
neoliberalism, 4, 17–19, 30, 77,
    79, 165–167 (See also
    capitalism; globalization)

neoliberal, 4, 26, 45–46, 84,
93, 122, 163
neoliberal global era, 5
neoliberal discourses, 6,
17, 46
New Woman, 2, 4–9, 17–21,
23–26, 29, 31, 35, 38–48,
72, 75–77, 81, 83–86, 90,
93, 100–101, 107, 109,
115–117, 120–121,
123–124, 126, 131,
139–141, 145, 149, 155,
158–161, 163–168, 170–171
nuclear family, 63, 99, 164

objectifying gaze, 39 (See also
male gaze)
Offices for Family Religious
Guidance (Aile İrşat ve
Rehberlik Büroları), 113
openness, 14, 20, 29, 42–44, 48,
89, 91, 109, 122, 125–127,
165, 167–168
bodily openness, 126–127,
130, 166
corporeal openness,
20, 121
embodied openness, 21, 25,
42, 107, 116, 124, 131, 167
forces of openness, 35, 42
orientation towards
openness, 21
politics of openness, 124, 130
trade openness, 20, 167
orientations, 5–7, 13, 16, 19, 21,
25, 30–31, 38, 76, 81, 83,
109, 121, 124, 141, 144,
148, 165–166
disorientations, 13, 23, 25,
29, 121, 141, 148–149,
158–159, 166
embodied orientations, 5,
10, 21, 24, 29, 35, 45, 59,
77, 81, 100, 116, 124
failed orientations, 148
Ottoman Empire, 52–53,
59–61, 104, 134, 154
Ottoman imperial notion of
justice, 3, 153
Ovadia, Stella, 50 (See also
Feminist journal)
Ozyegin, Gul, 16, 55, 84
Öcalan, Abdullah, 69
Özçelik, Başak, 130
Özkan, Yalçın, 62–64
Özkazanç, Alev, 8

patriarchy, 13, 52, 69, 99, 137
patriarch, 105, 119, 137, 160
patriarchal control, 93
patriarchal governance, 127

paternalism, 65, 87, 101, 103,
123, 133, 153
patriarchal social
organization, 13, 116
Peace Declaration in January
2016 ("We Will Not Be
Party to This Crime!"), 27
Penal Code, 3, 50–55, 70–71,
102, 164
Article, 419, 54
Article, 426, 54
Article, 434, 53
Article, 438, 50–51, 54,
68–69
Peoples' Democratic Party
(HDP), 168
petit-bourgeoisie, 39
phenomenology, 5, 11–13, 15,
23, 31, 38, 88, 99,
126–127, 168
phenomenology of the body,
9–12
phenomenological method,
11–12, 20, 28, 126, 149
antiracist scholarship,
12–13
feminist phenomenology,
16, 24, 35, 164
Presidency of Religious Affairs
(Diyanet), 113–114
Pride Walk, 101
protection, 53, 57, 63, 147,
153–155
masculinist protection,
154–155 (See also
masculinism)
paternalist protection, 101
populism, 23, 105, 137, 142,
152, 166
masculinist populism, 8, 31
(See also masculinism)
populist moment, 5, 8, 21–22,
140–141, 152, 158, 161
populist politics, 19, 163
right-wing populism, 17,
21–22, 164, 166
populist authoritarianism,
19, 163, 167 (See also
authoritarianism)
purity, 38, 52–53, 55, 59,
61, 109
"Purple Needle" campaign, 68

racism and antiracism, 9, 12–13
Ramadan, 41, 114, 127, 136,
142, 157
Republican People's Party
(CHP), 52, 100, 108–109,
111, 155–157, 168
Roboski (Uludere), 111
Rosaldo, Michelle, 12

Sağlam, Asena Melisa, 41, 157
saleswomen, 10, 29, 35, 40, 43, 77,
80–81, 83–84, 86, 90–93
sales floor, 8, 10, 24, 29, 77–78,
80–83, 86, 90–92, 113
Savcı, Evren, 8, 142
service economy, 5–6, 16–17, 19,
24, 29, 63, 68, 72, 76–77,
80–81, 93, 123, 164–165
consumer services, 80
interactive service work, 19,
83, 77, 165
service jobs, 76, 77, 79
service workers, 26, 29
service sector, 18, 48, 79, 95
secularism, 4, 17, 22, 81, 120–121,
157, 160
authoritarian secularism, 17
(See also authoritarianism)
politics of secularism, 160
self-righteousness, 109, 117,
121, 132
Serdengeçti, Osman Yüksel,
36, 44–45
Sertel, Sabiha, 61
sex worker, 50–51, 54, 69
prostitute, 50–51
prostitution, 36, 56, 60–61,
130, 169
sexism, 12–13, 55, 128, 141, 157
sexual offenses, 52, 54, 59, 71
sexual assault, 23, 61, 130
sexual insults, 130
sexual harassment, 61, 68,
71, 90, 126, 130, 145
sexual violence, 53, 69, 130
(See also violence)
shame, 6–7, 9, 12, 14–17, 22, 24,
30, 36–40, 42, 54, 56–60,
65, 80, 86, 111, 115–116,
157, 164, 166 (See also
embarrassment)
ar, 54, 71
feminine shame, 38, 51, 81
hayâ, 54, 71
shameful offenses, 44
shaming, 7, 9, 16–17, 42, 58,
101, 107, 114, 159, 164, 166
shame-honor discourse, 7–8,
15–17, 19, 22, 24–25,
36–38, 42, 51, 54–55,
58–60, 65, 67–69, 71–72,
81, 83, 101, 107, 109–110,
116–117, 123, 141, 149,
159, 164, 166 (See also
discourse; honor; shame)
shop floor, 86, 88, 92
shyness, 36–38, 77, 80, 82
single, 46, 61, 91–93, 99, 138, 169
Skeggs, Beverley, 59–60
Smith, Patti, 131

Society for the Employment of
  Ottoman Muslim
  Women (*Kadınları
  Çalıştırma Cemiyet-i
  İslâmiyesi*), 60
state of emergency, 4, 27, 140, 145
state of emergency decrees, 27
Sungur, Ceyda, 125, 130
Sullivan, Shannon, 12
Sunni, 52, 64, 67, 87, 105, 114,
  152, 160 (*See also*
  Muslim)
  Sunni bourgeoisie, 22
  Sunni intellectual
    establishment, 85
  Sunni Islam, 65, 67–68, 114,
    134
  Sunni Muslims, 37
  Sunni women, 68, 87, 103–105
supermarket, 10, 29, 35, 77, 79,
  91, 108, 144
  MajorMarket, 47, 77–78,
    81–82, 87, 89, 92, 97,
    99–100, 108, 112–113, 122
symbolic interactionism, 9
Şişman, Nazife, 85

Terzi, Ayşegül, 1–2, 143–144,
  147–148, 152, 157
Tomkins, Silvan, 42, 80
transphobia, 146
transwomen, 141–142
Tsing, Anna L., 30
Turkish Medical Association,
  66, 129
Turkish Society of Gynecology,
  66
Turkish Family Planning
  Association, 66

Uçma, İsmet, 137 (*See also*
  mahallenin namusu)
urban, 6, 8, 10, 13–14, 18–20,
  28–30, 48, 58, 62–66, 68,

76–77, 79, 81, 84, 86–87,
  99, 103, 112, 123, 136,
  138–139, 142, 149,
  163–166, 168, 170
urban sociality, 65, 163
urbanization, 24, 51, 62, 82,
  99, 123

Vaize (Female Preacher), 113–114
vigilantism, 2, 4, 25–26, 29,
  141–142, 145, 156–157, 166
  moral vigilantism, 3, 29,
    114, 141
vigilante men, 2, 7, 24–25,
  58, 139, 141, 144, 152, 156
vigilante attack, 19, 29,
  141–142
vigilante violence, 2, 4–5,
  25–26, 121, 133, 140–142,
  144–145, 148–149,
  156–157, 159–160
  (*See also* violence)
vigilance, 89, 136, 138
  secularist vigilance, 141
democracy vigils, 142
violence, 2, 5, 9, 15, 20–23, 25,
  28, 42, 53, 57–59, 116–117,
  126, 129–131, 135, 139,
  141, 146–150, 152, 154,
  159, 161, 165–167, 170
  domestic violence, 2, 67–69,
    103, 112, 157
  gendered means of violence,
    7, 16, 55, 57, 107, 139, 147
  institutionalized violence, 55
  partner violence, 146, 167
  performative violence, 4–5,
    19, 25,
    140–141, 147
  police violence, 106–107,
    121, 126, 128–132
  sexual violence, 53, 69, 130
  symbolic violence, 132
  state violence, 55

vigilante violence, 4–5,
  25–26, 121, 133, 140–142,
  144–145, 148–149,
  156–157, 159–160
  (*See also* vigilantism)
violence against women, 2,
  4, 7–8, 16, 26, 58, 111,
  128, 130, 137, 140,
  145–147, 169, 171
virginity, 7, 54–57, 71, 106,
  116–117
  virginity tests, 17, 55, 57, 116
  kadın, 55
  kız, 55

Wages for Work, 103
We Will Stop Femicide
  Platform, 146, 160
Welfare Party, 152
welfare state, 97, 102, 112
work, 6, 8, 10, 14, 18, 24, 33,
  35, 80, 83, 86, 89–91,
  98–100, 127
  factory worker, 60, 86, 89–90
  frontline worker, 46
  garment workshop, 47, 76,
    88–89, 8
  workplace culture, 72, 113
  workplace discipline, 165
  sales work, 35, 80, 82, 86,
    90, 100
  service work, 19, 80, 83, 165
  women's work, 19, 62, 64, 165
  industrial homeworker, 30,
    75–76
  working-class women, 6, 14,
    30, 76, 83, 93, 158
Women and Democracy
  Association (KADEM),
  154, 170

Yalçın, Türkân, 52, 55, 57, 69, 110
Yıldırım, Binali, 2
Young, Iris Marion, 11, 13, 3